Introduction

Rapid change and development in business and technology has led us to a new approach when selecting and defining terminology in this dictionary. Part of this approach has been to regard 'purchasing and supply' as an integral part of the total business activity, rather than treat it as a separate function.

We were asked by the Chartered Institute of Purchasing and Supply to develop a European 'flavour'. This we have done, though the dictionary is prepared from a British perspective, and confines itself to terminology used in the English language.

Our earlier dictionaries, the first of which was produced by H.K.C in 1964 as the Glossary of Purchasing and Supplies Management, provided only outline coverage of standards, health and safety, storage and handling. We have expanded our scope to give more attention to (though still not exhaustive) coverage of these.

We hope we have avoided too academic an approach and that the notes, which are largely from our own practical experience, will be helpful. Definitions are deliberately slanted towards the business and technical aspects of buying and selling and the reader should look elsewhere for more general definitions; ours are drawn in many cases from the sources below and are harmonised with them. Readers are requested to study the following notes before using the dictionary.

ORGANISATION AND PRESENTATION OF TERMS

So far as the variety of sources and disciplines permit, we have drafted our text in line with **BS 3669**, *The Selection, Formation and Definition of Technical Terms*. The sequence of words has thus been kept as consistent as possible so that, as with commodity coding and other data organisation, the primary word is used as the head word, followed by any qualifying adjective, phrase etc. We have included at appendix A a checklist based on BS 3669, which we commend to anyone concerned with the development of terminology.

Readers should note that quotations from standards are indicated by quotation marks, ' . . . ' Our own digressions and comments are indicated by square brackets [. . .]. Where the explanation or definition of a term includes another term, itself defined in our dictionary, we have presented that term in capitals thus:

> **contango**. Premium paid by a buyer of FUTURES to the seller for the buyer's postponement of delivery from the date due to a later one. Sometimes referred to as 'FORWARDATION'.

SOURCES

British Standards Institution (BSI), by whose permission material has been reproduced and from whom copies of the relevant standards may be obtained at:

The British Standards Institution,
Linford Wood,
Milton Keynes,
MK14 6LE.

We acknowledge with thanks the assistance of Mr. R. Choda in the Secretary's Department of the British Standards Institution in reviewing the text of this edition.

A message from the British Standards Institution

Quality starts with standards. Standards lay down the criteria for products, processes and systems, to ensure that they will do the job properly. They influence every aspect of production, from design to after-sales service. They apply from the time a product is conceived, through design, development and manufacture, to testing for fitness for purpose and durability.

The benefits of standards include: easier design and manufacture through the provision of standard components; more efficient, cost effective and easily maintained production systems; greater consumer and customer confidence in products and in the companies that manufacture them.

These benefits are strongly endorsed by the British Standards Society, the UK association for standards users which is administered by the BSI, and exists to promote the application of standards throughout industry and the public sector.

The British Standards below are a few of these which are relevant to the text.

Abbreviated title	BS Number
documentation	5408
environmental control	7750
eye protection	6967
fibre ropes and cords	3724
freight containers	3951 (1.4)
load restraint systems	5759
loaders	6685
materials handling equipment	3810
metrology	5233, PD6461
organisation and methods	3138

packaging	3130
pallets	6637
production planning and control	5191
quality	4778
quality systems	5750
statistics	5532
terotechnology	3811

BSI recommend for general reference the following standards:

BS 4778: Part 1: (ISO 8402), *Quality vocabulary* – international terms.

BS 5532: (ISO 3534), *Statistical Terminology* – a glossary of terms relating to probability and general terms relating to statistics.

BS 5750: (ISO 9000/EN29000, ISO90004/EN 29004) *Quality Systems*.

CEN/CENELEC *Internal Regulations*, Part 2, common rules for standard work.

ISO/IEC *Guide 2*: General terms and their definitions concerning standardisation and related activities.

We have omitted the dates of standards referred to in the text. This has been done deliberately because of the frequency of change. Readers should check with the BSI Standards Catalogue that they are working with the latest editions. We have been unable to quote the 'EN' and other numbers; these will be found in the above catalogue.

Chartered Institute of Management Accountants, to which body thanks are expressed for permission to quote from a large part of their terminology. Much is particularly appropriate for those engaged in buying and selling, and those dealing with value and price/cost related problems. A major source book in this connection is their publication *CIMA Management Accounting – Official Terminology*.

International Chamber of Commerce (ICC UK), which asked us to include its 14 *incoterms*: this has been achieved in outline only. The full text and notes will be found in their publication No. 350, *Incoterms*. Readers requiring authentic translations are directed to ICC publication no. 417, *Key Words in International Trade*, which gives French, German, Spanish and Italian.

Chartered Institute of Purchasing and Supply. We are indebted to the CIPS which was instrumental in providing the impetus for this work, which is intended to complement the Institute's new (1995) education scheme.

Simpler Trade Procedures Board (*SITPRO*). We are grateful for their permission and for their kindly checking and aligning our entries which bear the initials SITPRO.

ABBREVIATIONS

Many of the terms used have more than one interpretation or belong to more than one discipline. We have marked such terms by bracketed abbreviations, *viz.: (econ.)* = economics, etc. The key also gives the meanings of abbreviations employed in our definitions.

abb.	abbreviation
adj.	adjective
adm.	administration
BS 1234	British Standard, with reference number
bibl.	bibliography/reference
CBI	Confederation of British Industry
cf.	compare with authority quoted, from which our definition may differ
CIMA	Chartered Institute of Management Accountants
com. mkt.	commodity market
CIPS	Chartered Institute of Purchasing and Supply
def.	definition
der.	derivation
ecol.	ecology/ecological
econ.	economics
e.g.	for example
env.	environment/environmental
esp.	especially
EU/EC	European Union/European Community
fin.	finance
HMG(UK)	Her Majesty's Government (United Kingdom)
HS	health and safety
i.e.	that is
IL	Institute of Logistics
i.t.	information technology
IM	Institute of Management
imp.	imports/importation
ins.	insurance
law	legal/legislation
mar.	marine, shipping, etc.
mat. man	materials management
med.	medical/medicine
mkt.	marketing
n.	noun
n.b.	note well
no.	number

DICTIONARY OF PURCHASING
AND SUPPLY

DICTIONARY OF PURCHASING AND SUPPLY

Terminology for Buying and Selling

H K COMPTON · D A JESSOP

TUDOR

© H. K. Compton and D. A. Jessop 1995

This version first published in Great Britain by Tudor Business Publishing Limited.
Sole distributors worldwide, Hodder and Stoughton (Publishers) Ltd, 338 Euston Road
London NW1 3BH

A CIP catalogue record for this book is available from the British Library

The right of the authors of this work has been asserted by them in accordance with the
Copyright, Designs and Patents Act 1988.

Typeset by Deltatype Ltd, Ellesmere Port, Cheshire
Printed and bound by Athenæum Press Ltd.,
Gateshead, Tyne & Wear.

OECD	Organisation for Economic Cooperation and Development
p.&s.	purchasing and supply
pkg.	packaging
prod.	production
prodt.	product/products
q.	quality/quality control
SITPRO	Simplified Trade Procedures Board
stat.	statistics/statistical
stk.	stock/stock control
subs.	substances/materials
sym.	symbol
syn.	synonym
tec	technology-science
UN	United Nations
v.	verb
w.e.f.	with effect from
wt.	weight
[.......]	Authors' explanatory notes, examples, comments

Acronyms and abbreviations for terms, e.g. 'ECU', will be found in the main body of the dictionary, while those of institutions, public bodies, etc. will be found in the appendix.

DISCLAIMER

Although every effort has been made to authenticate, simplify and harmonise every entry we are sure that there will be gaps and gaffes and we welcome suggestions for the next edition. We apologise to anyone whose favourite term has been omitted, and refer readers to our 'exclusion clause', which we have adopted from the Chartered Institute of Management Accountants:

'No responsibility for loss occasioned to any person acting or refraining from action as a result of any material in this publication can be accepted by the authors or the publisher.'

Preface

Words are coins with which people trade ideas and communicate their needs for goods and services. Unless the words used are clear and correct the ideas, goods and services are also unlikely to be correct. The cynic who has worked in 'purchasing' or 'sales' for many years will doubtless observe that even accurate information will not always secure the correct response.

People throughout industry and trade are continuous communicators and those engaged in purchasing and supply and sales are 'primary communicators'. Those in 'purchasing' must understand and transmit the needs of the people for whom they make purchases to the suppliers. Similarly, those in 'sales' must understand the messages from the purchasing officers of their customers and translate these rapidly and accurately into instructions to their warehouse or production plant.

In preparing this dictionary it has been necessary to renew, update and harmonise definitions in a field which is changing continuously and rapidly. This has led to our spending considerable time rooting out the new jargon which clings to the growing network of communications both at home and internationally. An example of rapid and continuous change in terminology is exemplified in the entry 'Quality, merchantable quality'. At the time of going to press, consideration is being given to a new statutory definition of 'merchantable quality'. Until a new Act is passed the definition we have given must suffice.

It would be foolish to pretend that those engaged in purchasing and supply use a range of language peculiar to their own area. Purchasing and supply is a wide-ranging field which touches business at many points and it therefore shares a terminology with sales and other areas. This in itself is a common cause of misunderstanding. The terminology included in this volume is much wider in scope than the title would suggest, and we hope it will contribute to the total communication network of those involved in industry and trade. We have, moreover, made a start at international trade and the harmonisation of terminology, with particular reference to the '1992 Single European Act'. We must admit, however, that our work in this field is by no means complete.
H K Compton
D A Jessop
1995

A

ABC. A common abbreviation for ACTIVITY BASED COSTING.

ABC analysis. The application of PARETO'S PRINCIPLE to the analysis of supply data. If items in a store are arranged in descending order of usage-value and the cumulative number of items are plotted against the cumulative usage-value the result would be (expected to) show a curve of the general form associated with Pareto's Principle. In practice, typical observations are as follows: 'A'. 10% of items account for 70% total usage value; 'B'. 20% of items account for 20% total usage value; 'C'. 70% of items account for 10% total usage value. Other proportions also are given and the rule is often abbreviated to the '80:20' Rule.

activity based costing. An accounting method in which variable and all overhead related expenses are specifically assigned to a business activity, rather than a section or department.

A.G.V. Automatically Guided Vehicle.

absolute advantage. (econ). The situation in which an enterprise (or State) can produce a product or substance at lower cost than others for the identical item.

absorption costing. CIMA. Method of costing designed to ensure that total costs, fixed and variable, (direct and overhead) are recovered in the price of goods, etc.

accelerator. (econ). A change in demand for consumer goods which results in a comparatively large change in demand for capital plant supplying the goods.

acceptable quality level. *See* QUALITY, ACCEPTABLE LEVEL.

acceptance. SITPRO. The signing by a drawee of a usance (time or term) of a BILL OF EXCHANGE [DRAFT], which then binds him to pay the bill when due (at maturity).

acceptance of goods. The buyer is deemed to have accepted goods when he intimates to the seller that he has accepted them, or when the goods have been delivered to him and he does any act in relation to them which is inconsistent with the ownership of the seller, or when after the lapse of a *reasonable* time he retains the goods without intimating to the seller that he has rejected them. (Sale of Goods Act 1979, s. 35 (1).

acceptance limits. *See* QUALITY CONTROL, ACCEPTANCE LIMITS.

acceptance of offer. *See* CONTRACT, ACCEPTANCE OF OFFER.

acceptance sampling. *See* QUALITY CONTROL, ACCEPTANCE SAMPLING.

1

accepting bank. SITPRO. A bank specifically nominated in a letter of credit as that on which a bill of exchange is to be drawn at a specified time.

access. physical access. Physical access in the sense of 'free and open entry' into a place etc., has in the context of purchasing and supply several implications: 1. its prevention at stores while they are unmanned and to unauthorised persons. 2. free and unimpeded access for fire and rescue purposes. 3. safety provisions for safe access to tanks, hoppers, silos and similar plant. bibl: HSE. GS5 Entry into confined spaces. HSE G26 Access to road tankers. 4. roadway (and other) access for vehicles to loading bays, etc.

access time. The time taken to obtain information from a computer memory store and its presentation to the user in legible and intelligible form. The term was devised for INFORMATION TECHNOLOGY but has implications for manually operated clerical memory/record systems.

accommodation bill. A bill of exchange signed by one person to 'accommodate' another. The person signing becomes the guarantor.

accommodation stock. *See* STOCK, ACCOMMODATION.

account. (n) cf. CIMA. A structured record of monetary transactions such as purchasing transactions with suppliers, and internal transactions such as stores accounts of stock values, receipts, issues, returns, etc.

accounting. 1. the classification and recording of actual transactions in monetary terms. 2. the presentation and interpretation of the results of those transactions in order to assess performance over a period and the financial position at a given date. 3. the projection in monetary terms of future activities arising from alternative planned courses of action.

account, unit of in EU. *See* EUROPEAN CURRENCY UNIT.

accounting, replacement cost accounting. *See* COST, REPLACEMENT COST, ACCOUNTING.

accounting stock. *See* STOCK, ACCOUNTING STOCK.

accreditation, test laboratories, certification of inspection bodies. (EU). The accreditation formally recognises the competence of the above by a process of expert technical assessment against agreed criteria. This involves regular surveillance and periodic assessment.

accretion. Increase in value of goods, with the passage of time, e.g. wines, timber, cheeses; as opposed to DEPRECIATION.

accuracy. *See* QUALITY CONTROL, ACCURACY.

acid test ratio. Current liabilities divided by current assets (less stock).

2

acknowledgement* of contract/ order. (*Note 'acknowledgment' alternative spelling). See CON- TRACT, ACKNOWLEDGEMENT OF CONTRACT.

acquisition costs. See COSTS, ACQUI- SITION COSTS.

active stock. See STOCK, CYCLE STOCK.

activity chart. One which presents in diagrammatic format the operational activities of opera- tives/machines, plant, etc. It may display working times, outputs, flow of supplies, etc. The chart or diagram, resulting from data obtained by ACTIVITY SAMPLING, can be used to indicate the degree of achievement of a plan that has been subjected to such ACTIVITY SAMPLING. Or, the chart, or layout diagram can indicate the activities, frequency and distance of movements of staff, mobile plant such as lift trucks, etc. with the loads carried.

activity sampling. A technique used in work measurement on such activities as fork lift truck operation, order picking, store- keeping, and so on; by taking random samples of activity and analysing the result to ascertain the working pattern of the total activity ratio-delay study; obser- vation ratio study; snap-reading method; random observation method; work sampling.

act of God. Any event in nature which could not have been prevented and is beyond the con- trol of human foresight. See also FORCE MAJEURE.

adaptive system (it). An adaptive 'self-regulating/self-organising' system is one in which a computer, directed by the program to which it is operating, will react to FEED- BACK generated by (for exam- ple) EXCEPTION REPORT- ING. Thus, changes in demand for supply through stock-control can be sensed and instantly repor- ted and responded to thus avoid- ing a STOCK-OUT or EXCESS- STOCK situation.

added value. See VALUE ADDED.

adjustment money. Sums paid to a supplier (or credit from him) by a purchaser in respect of a change in contract costs because of a VAR- IATION ORDER or ESCALA- TION CLAUSE, etc.

administration. The control and supervision of operations, prac- tices and policies dictated by MANAGEMENT.

ad valorem. According to value, i.e. not according to weight or other measure. A method commonly ap- plied for computing freight and customs duty, etc.

advance freight. See FREIGHT.

adversarial relationship. A rela- tionship between buyer and seller in which it is felt that there is a fixed pool of benefits to be com- peted for. Any gain by one party is seen as a loss to the other. Each

3

party seeks benefit at the expense of the other.

advertising directive. (EU). This Directive (adopted by HMG, UK 9/1984) aims to protect businesses and public from effects of misleading advertising. *See also* TRADES DESCRIPTION ACT.

advice note. BS 5191 (43001). A document sent to a customer advising him of impending delivery of supplies called for on his purchase order.

advising bank. SITPRO. A bank, usually in a beneficiary's country, through which advice of a LETTER OF CREDIT is sent by the ISSUING BANK.

affiliated company. One of a group of two or more enterprises, one of which exercises control or influence over the other(s) by share ownership or other legitimate means.

affreightment. The contract for carriage of goods for a price which is called the freight.

against all risks. Term used in marine insurance meaning insured against all generally accepted risks.

agency bills. Bills of exchange drawn on and accepted by the UK branches of foreign banks, usually in London.

agent. A person, e.g. a buyer or salesman, appointed to represent a firm (his or her principals) and who is 'held out as doing so' by them *or* who without contradiction claims to be an agent and commits the firm accordingly. Hence the importance of properly appointing someone to act as agent for a company's purchasing. *See also* CAVEAT SUBSCRIPTOR.

agent, commission agent. One who buys and sells goods for which a commission is usually paid on each transaction.

agent, *del credere* agent. An agent who, in return for extra commission, guarantees payment for what is sold.

agent, factoring agent. A mercantile agent who handles specific kinds of goods. He sells goods which come into his possession. He may do this with, or without, the consent of the principal for whom he sells on a commission basis.

agent, forwarding agent. (also freight forwarder). A firm specialising in making arrangements for goods to be collected from a CONSIGNOR and passing them to a CARRIER for transport to their destination. The freight forwarder administers the documentation, etc. It is important to establish whether he accepts liability for the actual transit.

agent, manufacturers' agent. Differs from a SELLING AGENT in that he is usually restricted to a limited geographical area, may have sole agency and/or handle several manufacturers' lines;

usually he has little freedom to negotiate or control product design or be involved in credit collection and risk.

agent, mercantile agent. One having in the customary course of his business (as such an agent) authority to: 1. sell 2. consign for the purpose of sale, or, 3. buy goods for such sale or 4. raise money on the security of goods, Sale of Goods Act 1979.

agent, selling agent. Agent who takes on the marketing responsibilities for (usually) small firms, leaving the enterprise free to concentrate on production. Some agents carry the risks of credit loss and may negotiate or fix prices. *See also* AGENT, MANUFACTURERS'.

agent, shipping agent. One specialising in imports and exports of goods by sea and who deals with documentation, insurance, customs, cargo space, etc. May be connected with a shipping company.

agio. 1. the difference between nominal and actual values of a currency, and also the charge payable for conversion of the less valuable currency to the more valuable one. 2. an amount added to the sales price by whichever party accepts a COUNTER-PURCHASE to cover additional costs of disposing of the counter-purchase. 3. charge for changing one currency for another.

agreement. A manifestation of mutual consent between two or more enterprises or persons. An 'agreement' is binding if it is legally enforceable. This will depend upon the provisions of the applicable law in the matter. An agreement may be either explicit or implicit, depending upon whether it is communicated in words spoken or written by the parties or by their actions. 'Agreement' is an essential component of a valid contract and may be made by any means whatever provided the parties communicate.

agreement, service level. An agreement between a SERVICE provider and a CUSTOMER quantifying the minimum acceptable service to the customer.

Agrément Board, The. *See* BRITISH BOARD OF AGRÉMENT. *See* Appendix.

'air rights'. The effective use of otherwise vacant storage space, by the employment of elevated storage facilities such as high stacks, high racking, etc, handled by suitable equipment. The latter may be automated or semi-automated.

air waybill. *See* WAYBILL.

allocation store. *See* STORE, ALLOCATION STORE.

alligation. A method of ascertaining the proportions of substances in a mixture that will produce either a specified price per unit volume (or weight, etc.), or a required specific gravity.

all-in contract. *See* ORDERS & CONTRACTS A–Z.

aligned documentation. *See* DO-CUMENTATION, ALIGNED DO-CUMENTATION (SITPRO).

allocated purchases. An item or items purchased and held for a specific task or project and which must not be issued for normal consumption.

allocated stock. *See* STOCK CONTROL, 'PRE-ALLOCATED' STOCK *and* STOCK, RESERVED STOCK.

allocation. 1. the sharing out between enterprises of available or potential production, products, services, sales, purchases, suppliers, customers, territories or markets, (illegal in many free-enterprise economies). 2. the reservation of material for a specific purpose.

allocation of oncost. The appointment of indirect expenses (on-costs) to the departments, jobs or contracts in which they occur.

all-round price. *See* PRICE.

all-in price. *See* PRICE.

alpha-numeric codes. *See* CODES, ALPHA-NUMERIC CODES.

alpha test. (it). A preliminary test of an experimental PRODUCT or PROTOTYPE, etc. particularly computer software. Such a test is usually done in the enterprise which developed it before applying the BETA TEST. Organisations should be particularly careful to ensure that all information technology programs (e.g. for stock control and provisioning) be subject to rigorous Alpha and BETA TEST.

amendment order. *See* ORDERS *and* CONTRACTS.

analysis, cost benefit. *See* COST BENEFIT ANALYSIS.

analyst. *See* PURCHASING ANALYST.

appraisal chart. One designed to display the acceptability (or not) of the results of a QUALITY CONTROL, inspection/test, etc., or the performance of suppliers.

appraise. (v). To judge the quality of something, or to give an expert opinion on the value or cost. e.g. carry out a value ANALYSIS. Appraisal (n). The result of such action. *See also* ENQUIRY *and* INQUIRY.

appreciation. (econ). The increase in value of an asset. *See* ACCRETION.

approved list. 1. list of approved suppliers. *See also* VENDOR RATING. 2. list of approved supplies (may be recommended or mandatory). 3. may incorporate or be supplemented by a BLACK LIST of non-approved supplies/ suppliers.

apron. *See* HARD STANDING.

arbitrage. (com mkt). Buying commodities in one market, e.g. London, and selling in another, e.g. New York, in order to profit from the price anomalies between the markets.

arbitrage. An expert operation, usually carried out by banks, etc., for taking advantage of different rates at different centres at a given moment. Operation in two centres is known as 'simple arbitrage', and in more than two centres as 'compound' or 'indirect arbitrage'.

arbitration. The referral of a dispute to one or more impartial persons with formal or informal agreement to accept the decisions arrived at. (refer also to International Chamber of Commerce and CIPS).

arbitration clause. A clause introduced into contract setting out CONDITIONS which shall be resolved by ARBITRATION.

arisings. A general term for SCRAP or WASTE resulting from a manufacturing process.

'arm's length' relationship. *See* TRANSACTIONAL RELATIONSHIP.

arrangement. (n). An understanding or agreement in less formal and specific terms than those involved in a firm contract, e.g. in a 'Forward Supply Arrangement'. *See* ORDERS & CONTRACTS. *Note*: Arrangements can become binding contracts if the parties 'communicate in some way so that each has intentionally aroused in the other an expectation that he will act in a certain manner' [Justice Cross, 1962].

arrest. The detention of a vessel temporarily, by Port Authorities.

ascertained goods. *See* GOODS, ASCERTAINED GOODS.

as is. A sales agreement where the buyer takes the goods without warranty, etc.

assay. The accurate examination, weighing, chemical (or other) analysis of a thing, particularly ores and precious metals.

assembly. BS 5191 (12006). A combination of parts and possibly raw materials put together to make up a composite article.

assets. CIMA. Anything of value, owned by an enterprise and which could be used to raise cash to pay debts. *See also* BOOK VALUE, CURRENT ASSETS *and* FIXED ASSETS.

assets, current assets. Cash or other assets (as listed below or short term investments) held for conversion into cash in the normal course of trading, e.g. STOCK, RAW MATERIALS, BOUGHT OUT STOCKS, WORK IN PROGRESS, FINISHED GOODS.

assets, fixed assets. Any asset acquired for retention as an entity for the purpose of providing goods or services, and not for resale in the normal course of trading.

assets, fungible assets. Those which are moveable, may be perishable goods, and which can be measured by quantity, weight, volume, etc. e.g. grains, wines etc., cf. CIMA.

7

assets, intangible assets. Those which are not physical and usually difficult to evaluate, e.g. patents, copyright, designs.

assets, real assets. Assets in the form of buildings and fixed plant.

assignment of contract. The transfer of property or a right; the passing of a contract to a third party.

assigned/assignment of stock. *See* STOCK, PRE-ALLOCATED *and* RESERVED STOCK.

assignment. (law). Something that has been assigned, a mission or task, the transfer to another of a right, interest or title to property.

at sight (also **on sight**). A term sometimes written on Bills of Exchange. The amount must be paid immediately it is asked for, without any such allowance as that known as DAYS OF GRACE.

atmosphere, explosive atmosphere. (HS). An ambient condition in which volatile substances with low FLASH POINTS may easily ignite or even explode. [Apart from segregation and other precautions in stores attention is needed to localised electrical equipment. See **BS 5345** Code of Practice for electrical apparatus for use in potentially explosive atmospheres.]

attestation. (EU) Procedure to show that the essential requirements for Health and Safety, etc. have been satisfied in respect of MACHINERY * supplied. The manufacturer or his authorised representative established in the European Union must draw up and keep available a 'technical construction file' as Annex D of the 'Machinery Directive'. (*See annex to EU Directive for exceptions.)

attractive goods. Goods which although not necessarily of high INTRINSIC VALUE may be subject to petty theft and/or pilferage if not housed in a SECURE STORE.

attribute, an attribute. (BS 4778 (21.23). A characteristic that is appraised in terms of whether it meets or does not meet a given requirement (e.g. 'go' or 'no go' as determined by the use of a 'go: no-go' gauge).

auction. A sale of goods or property in which prospective buyers bid for the goods, the bidder of the highest price securing them. *See also* MARKET, COMMODITY MARKET, AUCTION AT.

auction, Dutch. An auction sale where the AUCTIONEER begins by offering the lot for sale at a price selected by the auctioneer. If no bids are received successively lower prices are offered until a BID is made. The first bidder is the buyer of the lot.

auctioneer, one who conducts an AUCTION.

audit. CIMA. A systematic examination of books, accounts, activities, records, etc. by a qualified person to check they are accurate and properly kept. Also can be applied to examination of procedures to ascertain they have been carried out correctly. *See* STOCK AUDIT.

audit, management audit. A systematic, objective, independent appraisal of the standards, efficiency and techniques of management. cf. BS 5750. It aims to identify existing and potential weaknesses within an organisation and to recommend ways to rectify the weaknesses.

authority. The right to use power. This should be clearly defined, understood and accepted by all those over whom it is exercised. [Excessive use of this power tends to lead to authoritarianism, block lines of communication upwards as well as downwards, inhibit initiative by subordinates and their job satisfaction.] *See also* RESPONSIBILITY *and* 'DEPARTMENTALISM'.

automated purchasing. Orders prepared and communicated direct by on-line computers linked between purchasers and suppliers. Applicable in highly stable, large user, enterprises, e.g. mass production, continuous process industries, supermarkets and large service industries, etc). Also known as 'paperless purchasing'.

automation. Intensive mechanisation with or without the use of robots comprising the co-ordinated automatic control of processes and machine systems, and the automatic transport, testing and treatment of materials and products throughout a sequence of operations depending upon FEEDBACK without human intervention.

avco. Abb. for 'average cost'. Term used for average valuation of stock.

average. 1. a term commonly used as a synonym for the mathematical term MEAN. 2. as used in the context of marine insurance the term 'mean' refers to the loss or damage to a vessel or its cargo, or to both cargo and vessel. (der. from Spanish 'averia' meaning damage/break down, etc. old Italian 'avaria' and ultimately from Arabic 'awar' meaning damage/blemish.) *See also* AVERAGE, GENERAL AVERAGE *and* AVERAGE, PARTICULAR AVERAGE.

average adjuster (or average stater). A person who makes adjustments in marine insurance claims, etc.

average bond. Bond given to the owner or captain of a ship by a consignee pledging to pay their share of average of any loss.

average clause. The clause in a marine insurance policy which deals with several liabilities connected with the AVERAGE.

average cost. *See* COST, AVERAGE COST.

average, Customs average. Average TARE taken by Customs for a number of containers all containing the same kind of goods, for duty purposes.

average, general average. A term in marine insurance signifying that loss or damage to a ship or cargo will be borne proportionally by all parties to the venture and their underwriters.

average, particular average. A marine insurance term meaning the loss of a particular thing which must be borne by its owner alone, or his insurers, i,e. it is not shared amongst the other participants in the venture, for which *see* GENERAL AVERAGE.

average price. *See* PRICE, AVERAGE PRICE.

B

BACAT. Transport by barges carried on catamarans.

backfreight. *See* FREIGHT.

backhaul. The return journey of a truck or other vehicle. Attempts will often be made to find a load to defray the total cost of the round trip.

back order (production order). BS 5191 (31006). An order against stock which cannot be met until a replenishment quantity is received.

back order (purchasing). That portion of an order which a supplier cannot deliver on schedule and which he enters for shipment at a later date. A former practice which has now been largely abandoned.

back order (stores). The order document prepared by stores for an item currently out of stock which will be supplied when new supplies are available.

backwardation. The difference between the spot price and futures price at a particular date for the same commodity.

bad debt. A debt owed by a person or organisation which has gone out of business or is unable to pay for some reason.

bad faith. A deliberate attempt to deceive and avoid the honouring of an agreement, e.g. the offer of a delivery which the supplier knows to be beyond his capability. *See also* GOOD FAITH.

bailee. The person, such as a warehouseman, a carrier, to whom goods are temporarily entrusted. He is fully responsible for their safe custody while in his possession.

bailment. The temporary handing over of goods to another for custody.

bailor. The person who hands over goods temporarily into the custody of another, without transfer of ownership.

balance, credit/debit balance. A credit balance is where positive values exceed negative ones, i.e. gains exceed losses, credits exceed debits. A debit balance is the converse of a 'credit balance', i.e. a loss.

balanced ordering. Ordering for assembled products in which all materials and parts are ordered in product sets modified only as necessary for spares supply and for addition of a scrap allowance.

bale. A parcel (usually large) of goods compressed and bound securely with (cordage, plastics or steel) bands. **BS 6874:** Specification for dimensions and density of cotton bales: dimensions for optimum stacking and container utilization. *See* TRUSS.

bankruptcy. CIMA. Bankruptcy occurs when a 'bankrupt' not only makes it clear he is INSOLVENT but also that he does not expect to pay his debts in full, and an adjudication order has been made by a court for this reason.

bar coding. *See* CODES AND CODIFICATION, BAR CODING.

bar diagram, bar chart. BS ISO 3534–1 (2.18). A graphical representation of the FREQUENCY DISTRIBUTION of a DISCRETE VARIATE. Straight line bars, proportional to the absolute (or relative) frequencies of the variates, are drawn perpendicular to an axis on which the values of the variate are represented on a linear scale.

bargain. (n). 1. a contract or agreement concerning sale. 2. any agreement or stipulation. 3. a purchase on favourable terms. (v) 4. to seek an advantageous outcome to negotiations.

barratry. (mar). The desertion or wilful damage to a ship and/or its cargo.

barter. *See* ORDERS AND CONTRACTS, A–Z.

base stock-control. *See* STOCK-CONTROL, BASE STOCK-CONTROL.

basing point price. *See* PRICE, BASING POINT PRICE.

basis price. *See* PRICE, BASIS PRICE.

batch. BS 5191 (31002). A definite quantity of some product manufactured or produced under conditions which are presumed uniform, and for production control purposes passing as a unit through the same series of operations. *See* LOT.

batch costing. *See* COSTING, BATCH COSTING.

batch frequency. The number of batches of an item produced, planned for production or delivery in a given period of time, e.g. per week, month or PRODUCTION PERIOD, etc.

batch life. The length of time a given batch of supplies can be expected to last at a given rate of production output. *See* STOCK LIFE *and* SHELF-LIFE.

batch production. A type of production in which the batch quantities used are greater than one and in which material flow is of the functional type.

batch quantity. *See* QUANTITY, BATCH QUANTITY.

bay. Name sometimes used for a group of bins or shelves.

bear. (com & fin mkts). A speculator who trades in the expectation of a falling market.

beneficiary. SITPRO. The party in whose favour a LETTER OF CREDIT is issued.

benchmarking. A technique used by firms to help them to become successful. The technique involves: (a) establishing what makes the difference in the eyes of their customers between an ordinary supplier and an excellent supplier, (b) setting standards in each of the above things according to the best practice they can find, (c) finding out how the best compromises meet those challenging standards, (d) applying both the experience of others and their own ideas to meet the new standards – and, if possible, exceed them. The goal is to build on the success of others and to improve future performance.

berth, LO-LO berth. A berth (usually for short sea transits) designed for lift-on lift-off of containers. *See also* BERTH, RO-RO BERTH.

berth, RO-RO berth. A berth designed so that vehicles may roll-on and roll-off ships.

berth, side-loading berth. A berth designed to facilitate loading and unloading vessels with side opening doors in place of the more conventional hatches and rear opening doors. Fork-lifts in place of cranes are needed for this traffic.

beta test. (it). A test upon an experimental or newly developed (or developing) product – such as, for example, a computer program for stock control, provisioning, etc. The beta test should be carried out

by an external and independent organisation after ALPHA TESTS have been carried out.

bid. An offer to buy, as at an auction. Also, an offer made by a seller to a buyer in response to an enquiry, particularly an invitation to TENDER.

bid. (fin mkt). The rate at which a dealer will buy currency or borrow funds.

bid. An offer to buy or sell at a stated price.

bid bond. *See* BOND, BID BOND.

bill. A seller's statement of money owed, usually for immediate payment, e.g. in a shop or cafe as distinct from a credit sale when an INVOICE is appropriate.

bill of entry. A certified statement by an importer to Customs giving the nature, amount and value of goods.

bill of exchange (draft). CIMA. An unconditional order in writing addressed by one person to another and signed by the person giving it and requiring the person to whom it is given to pay on demand or at a certain fixed time or date a certain sum of money to the person named on the bill (or to the bearer).

bill of lading. An acknowledgement for the receipt of goods for shipment. It contains terms and conditions of carriage. It is not a negotiable instrument as it gives no special title to the possession of the goods. *See also* WAYBILL, SEA.

bill of lading, clean. A bill of lading is said to be 'clean' if it bears no declaration (usually by the master of the ship) that the goods or their packaging, etc. are defective, in which case it is termed a 'foul' or 'dirty' bill.

bill of lading, combined. One where several consignments are covered on the same bill.

bill of lading. (short form SIT-PRO). A bill of lading where the carrier's normal detailed conditions shown on the reverse of a 'long form bill of lading' are written into a brief incorporation clause on the front of the form. This form is recognised by the International Chamber of Commerce and supported by the United Nations. It is acceptable for DOCUMENTARY CREDITS, unless the letter of credit specifies otherwise.

bill of lading, house bill of lading. A certificate issued to the exporter of a small shipment which has been consolidated into a larger load (e.g. a container) which has its own bill of lading for the entire consignment. The certificate does not have the status of a bill of lading but confirms shipment to the small shipment exporter.

bill of materials. *See* PARTS LIST *and* BILL OF QUANTITIES.

bill of quantities. A list of numbered items, each of which describes the work to be done in a civil, engineering or building contract. When the procedure of TENDERING for such projects is used the bill of quantities is submitted to the tenderers who return it endorsed with the costs of each item. These are usually arranged (abstracted) in 'trades' facilitating comparison of the tenders and the work of the QUANTITY SURVEYOR, and the CLERK OF WORKS when the project is in progress.

bill of sale. A way of raising cash by means of a written agreement to transfer ownership of goods to a purchaser while possession (and therefore use) remains with the seller.

bill of sight. If an importer has not received the shipping documents when the ship arrives he may not have sufficient details to pass the required customs entry. Customs will provide him with a 'bill of sight' enabling him to examine the goods in the presence of a Customs officer. He must then complete the entry as soon as possible (known as 'perfecting the sight') and may take delivery after payment of any duties, if dutiable.

bill of store. 1. an import licence giving permission for the re-import (within a statutory time) of dutiable goods which had been previously exported. 2. a document exempting from duty those goods which had only been imported and stored in transit for early re-shipment.

14

bi-modal transport: The utilisation of more than one means of transport for shipments, e.g. use of ISO containers or swap from road and rail for a transit.

bin card. BS 5191 (33022). 'A local stock record, normally simplified and kept close to the parts', e.g. at the bin where the stock is held.

bin, storage bin. Colloquialism for adjustable steel shelving used in stores and generally to BS 826.

biodegradable. (env. ecol. pkg). The property of a substance which enables it to be broken down by the action of bacteria upon it. e.g. packaging, the disposal of which can be facilitated by degradation resulting from exposure to the elements.

black list. *See* APPROVED LIST.

blank-cheque ordering system. *See* ORDERS & CONTRACTS, CHEQUE ORDERS.

blanket buying. *See* ORDERS, CONTRACTS, BLANKET ORDERS.

blanket orders. *See* ORDERS *and* CONTRACTS, BLANKET ORDERS.

blanket rate. A shipping charge that does not vary according to the distance the cargo is shipped.

blending. The mixing of various grades or qualities in such a way as to produce a new desired or specified standard uniform variety or quality.

Blue Book, the. *See* INTERNATIONAL MARITIME DANGEROUS GOODS CODE.

bond, a bond. A document binding one party to pay a sum to another party, or to perform – or not to perform – some action or deed.

bond (in contracts for supply). In general, a bond is a deed by which a person binds himself to pay a sum of money at a certain time, or under certain conditions. In contracts, *see* CBI TERMINOLOGY.

bond, advance, progress or repayment. CBI. These guarantee that any monies advanced will not be lost through default or poor performance by the seller.

bond, bid/tender. CBI (abb.). These assure the buyer that the bid is a reasonable one and that the bid is guaranteed by a bank and also that the bidder will not withdraw his bid, or depart from the conditions set out in his tender.

bond, contract/performance/supply. CBI (abb.). These guarantee that a seller will satisfactorily perform the contract in accordance with all its terms and conditions.

bond, maintenance bond. CBI. These guarantee that once the construction has been completed the contractor will fulfill his obligations throughout the maintenance period.

bond note (a bond note). A note countersigned by a Customs officer authorising the transfer of goods from one warehouse to another or for export.

bond, performance bond. CBI. 'Performance bonds' place the onus (generally on the buyer) to prove default by the seller and generally indemnify the principal for any loss he may have incurred, but only up to the value of the bond.

bond, retention bond. CBI. These are used by contractors as a means of financing contracts rather than as a guarantee of performance and in lieu of RETENTION MONEY or against early release of retention money, or of monthly progress payments.

bonded goods. *See* GOODS BONDED.

bonded store warehouse. *See* WAREHOUSE/STORE BONDED. *See also* STORE, SECURE STORE.

book value. cf. CIMA. The recorded value of an asset in a company's books. May be: 1. 'historical cost' = original cost of asset (goods or services). 2. 'net book value' = historical cost or valuation less depreciation, etc.

bought-in (supplies). Term sometimes used for supplies purchased from an outside source. *See* BOUGHT OUT. Both terms have double and ambiguous meanings and the words 'purchased' or 'bought' should be used. *See also* IN-HOUSE.

bought-out (supplies). A term

sometimes used for supplies obtained from outside the firm requiring them. The preferred term is 'purchased, goods or supplies'. *See also* IN-HOUSE.

Box, Jenkins and supply control. A statistical supply routine based on works done by Professor Box and Dr Jenkins. 'One of a number of advanced statistical procedures. Generally these procedures call for a large amount of *consistent historical data*, such as four years of history. Growth and seasonality are taken into account, and forecasting is possible using available computer packages. However, the large amounts of data, the costs, and extensive knowledge of statistical theory may prohibit their use for stock control of individual items'. (abb. from former **BS 5729 Part 2. (6.4.2.)**) A summary of the package for supply routine is given below: 1. stock profile analysis = a review of the total inventory in the light of its contribution to its turnover, stock-holding and profitability. 2. demand analysis = a statistical examination of demand characteristics. 3. optimised prediction parameter analysis – with a further analysis of selected items needing attention. 4. performance analysis = a routine to assist in deciding policy. 5. normal stock up-dating routine. 6. stock forecasting and systems monitoring – leading to re-calculating optimum re-order points and re-order quantities.

brain storming. (adm). A technique whereby group members throw in ideas and suggestions for later analysis and discussion. e.g. may be employed in VALUE ANALYSIS or (particularly) in VALUE ENGINEERING.

brand loyalty. The (often subjective) wish of users of supplies to restrict their usage to a particular brand in preference to others.

brand name or trade mark. The name (or mark) used by a manfacturer or supplier for a particular make (or commodity) to distinguish his product from others and to promote its sale. A brand name or mark gives no warranty as to *suitability for purpose*, maker, or other features unless these are incorporated into the name or mark e.g. 'instant cold cure'. *See also* QUALITY, MERCHANTABLE QUALITY.

breach of contract. *See* CONTRACT, BREACH OF CONTRACT.

breach of duty. *See* CONTRACT, BREACH OF DUTY IN.

break-bulk. (n). Break-bulk cargo is general or conventional cargo as distinct from UNITISED, CONTAINERISED etc. cargo.

break bulk. (v). To break down a bulk or unitised cargo (or material in bulk) into its component parts or smaller lots.

break clause. A clause in a contract enabling the purchaser to foreclose on the contract without redress should he wish to do so. [A condition in some government contracts].

break-even analysis. The technique to establish the point (or points) at which two (or more) functions give the lowest total value – known as the 'break even point'. For straight line functions this point will be where the lines cross. But this will not necessarily apply where one or both the lines are curved – as is often assumed in the analysis. *See* CIMA. *See also* BREAK-EVEN CHART.

break-even chart. A statistical chart developed from DATA derived from BREAK-EVEN ANALYSIS. A curve is the developed for each of the functions being considered. A further curve may be developed for the sum of the two curves. This curve displays the total of the others and also the combined effects of the functions. Where the curves are rectilinear or symmetrical the break-even point occurs at their intersection. Where one is curved and the other straight (as in the formula for ECONOMIC ORDER QUANTITY) this may not be the case. In such circumstances care must be had to ensure the correct decisions are taken. *See also* BREAK-EVEN ANALYSIS.

break-even point. The point at which the sum of two (or more) functions – e.g. costs for alternative courses of action (purchases etc.) – are at their lowest total. *See also* BREAK-EVEN CHART.

bribe. A secret and corrupt gift. Can be money or money's worth offered to a person in a position of trust and influence in order to persuade him (or her) to use their power to the advantage of the person (or firm) offering the bribe. *See* 'IPS Ethical Code', IM 'Code of Best Practice for Professional Managers', and ICC Code 'Extortion and Bribery in Business Transactions' also the various 'Corruption Acts' of the UK.

Brisch coding. *See* CODING, BRISCH CODING.

British Board of Agrément. A national authority for the testing and assessment of new building methods and materials. The organisation was set up by the Minister of Public Works and Buildings in 1966.

British Institute of Management. *See* INSTITUTE OF MANAGEMENT at Appendix.

broker. A firm (or person) who buys and sells for a client on commission called 'brokerage'.

brought on charge. Stock is said to be brought on charge when it is accepted and accounted for in the supply system.

Brussels Nomenclature. An internationally agreed system of classification of goods with notes defining tariff headings now adopted by most states.

***BSI News* (monthly from BSI).** News of new and amended Standards and other information.

budget. cf. CIMA. Financial and/or quantitative statement prepared prior to a defined period of time of the policy to be pursued during that period for the purpose of attaining a given object.

budgetary control. CIMA. The establishment of budgets relating the responsibilities of executives to the requirements of a policy, and the *continuous* comparison of actual with budgeted results, either to secure by individual action the objective of that policy or to provide basis for its revision.

budgetary period: The period for which a budget is prepared and used. It may be sub-divided into control periods. (CIMA) In purchasing and supply it can have important implications for control of stocks and intake of supplies.

buffer stock. *See* STOCK, BUFFER STOCK.

bulk buying. The concentration of total demand for a commodity into one purchase; also, buying in large quantities to achieve economies of scale. *See also* ORDERS AND CONTRACTS, BULK ORDERS.

bulk cargo. A cargo not in separate bags, bales or other containers, such a cargo is usually all of one commodity such as oil or wheat, etc.

bulking. (v). Turning out the contents of numerous containers of the same commodity and mixing them to achieve a uniform quality/variety for the whole.

bull, (a 'bull') (com. & fin. mkts.). A

speculator who trades in expectation of a rising market.

business sale (business contract). 'Sale to a person who buys or holds himself out as buying in a course of business', Paraphrase of Supply of Goods (Implied Terms) Act 1973 now embodied into other Acts.

buy. To acquire by paying money. *See also* PURCHASING *and* PROCUREMENT.

buy-back. A transaction in which the seller agrees to purchase goods or services from the buyer up to an agreed percentage of his deliveries to the buyer.

buy out/bought out. 'Buy-in', 'buying-in', 'buy-out', 'buying out' are terms frequently used (indiscriminately) for SUPPLIES (goods, materials and services) obtained from a source outside the enterprise which requires them. The terms are all tautologisms, and lack the precision required for purchasing and supply. One at least has a double meaning*. Recommended terms are 'purchased' or 'bought'. [*The term 'buy out' has increasingly become associated with the acquisition of the equity of an enterprise by its staff and operatives and their subsequent management and control of it, by for example a 'management buy-out'.]

buy, sell and lease back. *See* ORDERS & CONTRACTS, BUY, SELL & LEASE BACK.

buyer. An official appointed to buy supplies and services sometimes styled as a purchasing officer. *Notes:* 1. legal definition: 'A person who buys or agrees to buy goods'. 2. under the Supply of Goods and Services Act 1983 the legal terms for the parties to contracts are: for the 'seller' read 'transferor' and for the buyer read 'transferee'.

buyer's market. *See* MARKET, BUYER'S MARKET.

by-product. CIMA. A product which is recovered incidentally from the material used in the manufacture of recognised main products. Such by-product may have either a net realisable value or a usable value. A value may be relatively low in comparison with the saleable value of the main products. In the contexts of ENVIRONMENTAL CONTROL and HEALTH AND SAFETY, etc. it is not unknown for pollutants, waste and scrap to be converted into viable and sometimes valuable by-products.

C

C.A.D. Computer Aided Design.

C.I.M. Computer Integrated Manufacturing.

CALS. Computer Aided Acquisition and Logistics Support System; EDI system for transmitting technical information, including drawings.

cabotage. 1. restriction of the use of coastal waters and air space by a country for its own domestic use. 2. agreement between airlines that where passengers or goods are loaded and discharged within the territories of one State, including colonies and protectorates, they shall be carried by the airline of that State. Cabotage Community rules. Adopted by HMG.UK 1.1.1993

call-off. BS 5191 (42006). Specific request for delivery(ies) from time to time. *See* ORDERS & CONTRACTS, CALL OFF ORDERS.

cancellation order. *See* ORDERS & CONTRACTS, CANCELLATION ORDER.

capability study. A study in which machines and processes are measured and analysed to show whether they are capable of the full required output.

capacity per ton-mile (tonne-kilometre). The capacity of a vehicle multiplied by the distance travelled. Used for costing a transport operation.

$$Ctm = Cv \times Dt$$
Where:
Ctm is Capacity per ton/mile[1]
Cv is capacity of vehicle[2]
Dt is total distances travelled
[1] units of capacity appropriate to those applicable to the operation; metric or other.
[2] May require adjustment for less than FULL LOAD, RETURNS, etc.

capital commitment. cf. CIMA. Future capital expenditure in respect of which contracts have been made. Important in the financial management of purchasing and supply in relation to CASH FLOW.

capital goods. *See* GOODS, CAPITAL GOODS.

capital intensive. UN. A method of production which uses relatively more capital investment and capital goods, e.g. machinery, than labour, per unit produced.

capital sanction (financial sanction). cf. CIMA. A procedure usually in documentary form whereby expenditure on major projects and other large commitments are subject to scrutiny and approval by top and principal functional managers.

capitalised, -over-under capitalised. CIMA. Terms used to describe a surplus or deficiency of capital in relation to the current level of activity of a business. [Important to financial management in purchasing].

carbon/energy -combine tax. (EU) A tax proposed by the Commission of the European Union. The purpose is to reduce carbon-dioxide emissions by encouraging the efficient use of energy and by switching to low carbon fuels.

carcinogens. Substances liable to cause cancer.

care; 'duty of care'. This term, which has many applications to business contracts, is best defined by the following example. 'You must take REASONABLE care to avoid acts or omissions which you can reasonably foresee would be likely to injure your neighbour . . . i.e. the person or persons closely and directly affected by any act that ought reasonably have been in contemplation . . . when directing the mind to the acts or omissions which are called in question'. Judge Lord Atkin in Donaghue v Stevenson 1932

cargo. Goods and materials loaded for transport.

cargo manifest. A document listing all the cargo on a ship, truck or aircraft. Gives identification marks, names of CONSIGNEE and CONSIGNOR of each item.

carnet. A customs document providing certain limited facilities for movement of goods, etc., temporarily waiving certain formalities.

carnet. (ATA). Simplified Customs document issued by the International Chamber of Commerce enabling businessmen to take valuable goods across frontiers temporarily avoiding duty and formality at Customs.

carnets. (TIR). International shipping documents of simple form used by Customs at frontier points for international through traffic to certify that the traffic has passed through their control in good order. Carnets must travel with the goods.

carousel. Storage equipment which brings its material to the picker; may turn on a vertical or horizontal axis.

carriage. 1. a vehicle which carries goods. 2. the act of conveying goods. 3. cost of conveying goods, more accurately the 'freightage'.

carriage forward. An arrangement whereby carriage is paid by recipient.

carriage (or freight paid to). *See* FREIGHT, CARRIAGE PAID.

carrier. (ICC). Any person by whom or in whose name a contract has been made for carriage by road, rail, sea or air – or a combination of these. *See also* CARRIER, COMMON CARRIER.

carrier, common carrier. A person who for hire or reward undertakes as his particular business to carry goods for anyone who hires him.

carrier's lien. *See* LIEN, CARRIER'S LIEN.

carrier's risk. *See* RISK, CARRIER'S.

21

cartel. (OECD). Any agreement between enterprises, or concerted decisions of associations of enterprises; practices between enterprises which have the purpose or effect of preventing, restraining or distorting competition. Applies to all aspects of business including sales, production and purchasing. Usually in breach of national or European Community laws.

case. BS 1133 Packaging Code (pkg). A close boarded timber container to completely protect goods from the elements. *See also* CRATE.

case marks. Markings on cases which enable them to be identified during transit to their destination. *See also* SHIPPING MARKS.

case numbers. Numbers which are unique to each case in a consignment. Usually the number of each case is followed by the total in the consignment, thus 3/24 is the third case in a consignment of 24 cases.

case register book. *See* PACKAGE REGISTER.

cash against documents. Terms in a contract under which the captain of a ship will not (on arrival in port), hand over the BILL OF LADING and DOCUMENTS OF TITLE, or the goods, until the covering draft from the consignor has been paid. *See* PAYMENTS AGAINST DOCUMENTS.

cash and carry. *See* ORDERS & CONTRACTS A–Z.

cash on delivery (COD). *See* ORDERS & CONTRACTS A–Z.

cash flow. The movement of cash into ('positive flow') and out of ('negative flow') in an enterprise. The difference is 'net-cash flow'.

cash flow, discounted cash flow. CIMA. The estimation of cash flow which will be generated in the future from a capital investment made in the present. The method involves DISCOUNTING BACK the estimated flows from the investment in each future year (or other period). Methods include: 1. internal rate of return (IRR). 2. net present value (NPV). *See* VALUE.

cash, prompt. *See* PRICE, TIME RELATED PRICE.

cash, spot. *See* PAYMENT, SPOT CASH PAYMENT.

cash with order (CWO). *See* ORDERS & CONTRACTS A–Z.

catalogue, commodity catalogue. A list of all the commodities normally used in an enterprise. It usually incorporates, or is integrated with a STORES CATALOGUE but may well include non-stock items such as infrequently used but vital plant spares, etc. It should as far as practicable be based upon the firm's vocabulary of supplies. (*Note:* Many organisations adopt their own title for this record.)

catalogue library. The filing place for suppliers' catalogues and price lists, etc. Usually it is (or should be) situated in the purchasing department with full availability to all other departments.

catalogue number. *See* CODE, COMMODITY CODE.

catalogue, sales catalogue. A classified list of goods or services for marketing with brief or detailed specifications, illustrations, identifying code or list numbers *See also* PRICE LIST.

catalogue (stores commodity catalogue). A classified list of supplies which are normally carried in stock – may also include some 'exceptional' and 'difficult' items. Gives COMMODITY CODE for each item, may give: specification reference, location, user department, FORWARD SUPPLY ARRANGEMENTS, UNITS OF ISSUE, and so on.

caveat emptor. 'Let the buyer look after himself' or 'let the buyer be on his guard'. It reflects the tendency of the law to protect the possessor of property against more powerful parties.

caveat subscriptor. Let the person who signs be on his guard. A warning to all who sign purchase orders or other supplies documents.

caveat venditor. 'Let the seller look after himself' or 'let the seller be on his guard'.

CD-Rom. Compact Disc(k) Read Only Memory. Optical high capacity data storage device, used by some organisations to store parts coding information.

CEN/CENELEC, Central Secretariat. (BSI). The administrative headquarters of the Joint European Standards Institution formed by CEN and CENELEC, located in Brussels. [CEN = Comité Européen de Normalisation] [CENELEC =Comité Européen de Normalisation Electro-technique] *See also* EUROPEAN COMMITTEE FOR STANDARDISATION, etc.

census of production. *See* PRODUCTION, CENSUS OF PRODUCTION.

centralisation, administration. (adm). The control and exercise of administration of operations, such as purchasing and supply, from a central point as distinct from decentralisation of the function to a number of points. e.g. a central office controlling or serving a number of operational units which may be dispersed over a wide area. *See* MANAGEMENT.

centrally planned economy. *See* ECONOMY, CENTRALLY PLANNED ECONOMY.

certificate of adequacy, application for. (EU). An application for a 'certificate of adequacy' must be accompanied by the design and manufacturing schedule. A United Kingdom 'approved body' must, if satisfied that the schedule contains all the required information and that the subject of the certificate manufactured in accordance with the schedule would conform with the relevant na-

23

tional standard, issue the CERTI-FICATE OF ADEQUACY.

certificate of adequacy, the certificate. (EU). A statement by an impartial CERTIFICATION BODY that a product, process or service conforms with a specified standard or similar document. Certification bodies certify either companies' QUALITY SYSTEMS or their products [and services]. This generally involves ASSESSMENT and regular surveillance and often draws on results of testing and inspection.

certificate of conformity. *See* QUALITY CONTROL-CERTIFICATE OF CONFORMITY.

certificate of damage. (mar). An inspection document prepared by a dock survey officer concerning goods found damaged on receipt at the dock. The document is needed by the importer to recover insurance.

certificate of inspection. *See* QUALITY CONTROL, INSPECTION, CERTIFICATE OF *also* RELEASE NOTE.

certificate of origin. A statement required by customs to indicate to their officers the country of origin of goods.

certificate of survey. *See* CERTIFICATE OF DAMAGE.

certification. characteristic. BS 5532 pt.1 (2.3) (stat). A property which helps to differentiate between ITEMS in a given PO-PULATION of DATA. The differentiation may be: 1. quantitative-'variables' e.g. varying quantities of supplies. 2. qualitative e.g. 'attributes', e.g. properties of various supplies.

charge. A sum demanded for (principally) a service or supply (e.g. energy, water, etc.) as distinct from that demanded for goods, also, for an additional facility, or a premium above the price of goods (or service) e.g. a 'charge' or 'surchage' for 'express delivery'.

charges forward. A term used when the purchaser is to pay freightage and any other charges on receipt of the consignment. *See also* CARRIAGE FORWARD AT EX WORKS.

charter. An arrangement by which a shipowner hires out a ship to a consignor on a single written agreement known as a CHARTER PARTY. The charter may be either 1. a voyage charter or 2. a time charter.

charterparty. The contract by which a ship or aircraft is hired or rented (chartered).

Chartered Institute of Management Accountants (CIMA). *See* APPENDIX.

Chartered Institute of Purchasing and Supply (CIPS). *See* APPENDIX.

chattel. Moveable property such as furniture, stocks of materials, machinery.

check digit. *See* CODES AND CODING.

check lists. Questions in list form to remind, enquire or act upon matters which require attention.

check, internal check. CIMA. Procedures designed to provide assurance that all transactions and other accounting information which should be recorded, have in fact been recorded. *See also* STOCK CHECK.

checking. 1. comparisons of figures or words between a copy and an original or other document. 2. count of actual quantities received with supplier's *advice note*. 3. to check the condition of something (e.g. packages received at GOODS INTAKE to see if undamaged). *See also* EXAMINATION and INSPECTION.

chronic effects. (med) (HS). Health conditions which develop slowly, or are of long duration, or in an H&S context are PRO-ACTIVE i.e. effect may appear long after exposure to the agent(s) which caused it, e.g. asbestosis. May also result from prolonged or frequent exposure.

claim. CIMA. An assertion of a right; a demand for something due; a right or just title to something; the basis for a demand.

class, supplies; class of supplies. A range of similar items forming a section within a group.

class (statistical class) BS ISO 3534–1 (2.7). In the case of quantitative characteristics, 'class' is each of the consecutive intervals into which the total of all the intervals (e.g. the RANGE) is divided.

classification. CIMA. The arrangement of items (e.g. items of supplies, stock, etc) into logical groups having regard to their nature (subjective classification) or the purpose to be fulfilled.

clearance. An indication that goods have been passed as in compliance with some regulation, duty or other condition.

clearance inwards. A certificate known as a clearing bill or jerque note given by the customs house officials after searching a ship on its arrival at port and satisfying themselves that all duties have been paid or that all goods on which duties can be levied are under seal awaiting payment.

clearance, negative clearance (EU). An individual examination granted by the Commission in respect of an article of Community enactments. [May be needed for some special purchasing contract which otherwise may be in breach of e.g. Community requirements on competition].

clearance outwards. Before a ship proceeds to sea a list must be handed in to the Customs authorities of the goods making up the cargo, and permission must be granted before she can leave port.

25

Note: with the adoption of Community Rules, those for import and export clearance are waived in respect of intra-community traffic.

clearing and switch buying. A bilateral trade agreement whereby two governments agree to exchange a given value of specified goods over a specified period.

Clerk of Works. A client's representative at site on construction, civil engineering works, etc, under instructions of the architect or engineer. He is responsible for execution of the contract in quantity and quality, also to keep records of work done, particularly work which is later hidden, such as foundations.

closed height. The height of a fork lift truck with the mast fully lowered.

clothing, personal protective. *See* PROTECTIVE EQUIPMENT.

cocooning. The practice of heavily coating or wrapping items for long-term storage.

codes and codification. A system of symbols for identification of items, e.g. for supplies, commodities, equipment, spares, cost-centres, accounts and so on; whereby each item is given a complete and unique identification symbol which cannot be confused with another and can be recorded, retrieved and recognised throughout the enterprise, and also by its customers

where appropriate (kinds of code and their characteristics are listed below).

code, accommodation of codes. Indicates the number of items a code is able to define.

code, alphabetic. Those based on a combination or sequence of letters of the alphabet.

code, alpha-numeric. Those in which a combination of letters and numerals are combined to give greater 'hospitality' or provide a mnemonic. *See* CODES, MNEMONIC CODE.

code, bar code. A bar code comprises an array of parallel lines (bars) and spaces between the lines. The bars and spaces of varying widths are arranged in such a manner as to represent a sequence of numerals or other characters. These are read automatically by a bar code reader, or 'scanner' which translates the bars and gaps into data. Bar code Symbologies PrEN769 to PrEN841 are available from BSI.

code, binary. The numerical system of coding used in computers and similar equipment whereby the numerals '0' and '1' denote (or cause) the absence or presence of an electrical impulse in a given time or sequence.

code, Brisch coding. A method of coding adopted by Brisch and partners for identifying and classifying stock. A significant system usually classifying by blocks of digits describing the goods.

code, check digit. BS 5408. A check digit is a symbol which is included within a code and whose value is based mathematically upon other characters in the code. It is used to provide a mathematical check upon the accuracy of reading or transcription of the code.

code, classification by identity. A number of digits (the 'hospitality' of the code) are used to define the article either by kind or by function, e.g. (kind) 'Batteries/6 volts/dry/for bells' or (function) 'Bells/batteries for/6 volts/dry'.

code, colours. Combinations of colours (often bands or dots) providing codified identities for items (particularly those which are too small to accept other forms of coding).

code, commodity code. A code identifying a commodity and unique to that commodity. Usually, such codes are related to the physical or other descriptive attributes of the commodity. [Complications may arise where end-use or function are combined with description].

code of conduct of the Institute of Management (abb). A code of practice which embodies a number of principles which are relevant to purchasing and supply administration and management. These are quoted below, but it is recommended that the full text should be studied. Para. 4: as regards others external to, but in direct relationship, with the organisation, or function:– a. ensure the interests of others are properly identified and responded to in a balanced manner. b. establish and develop a continuing and satisfactory relationship based on mutual confidence. c. avoid entering into arrangements which unlawfully or improperly affect competitive practice. d. neither offer nor accept any gift, favour or hospitality intended as, or having the effect of, bribery or corruption. Also from Clause 1: g. openly declare any personal interest which might be seen to influence managerial decisions'.

code, European country codes. The ISO code adopted to identify goods, transits etc within the European Community: BE – Belgium: DE – Germany: DK – Denmark: ES – Spain: FR – France: GB – United Kingdom: GR – Greece: IE – Ireland: IT – Italy: LU – Luxembourg: NL – Netherlands: PT – Portugal.

code, European Article Numbering System (EAN). A coding system widely adopted by retailers for stock items. The code is compatible with BAR CODING.

code, ideograms (or ideographs). Symbols used to convey ideas or concepts.

code, key. The number of digits or other positions in the hospitality of a code which are taken to define a particular feature, e.g. at least two positions are usually needed to define measurements such as diameter.

code, location code. A code for location of stock in stores or stockyard. The code should define the floor layout and the elevation of the rack or bin into which supplies are to be stowed and retrieved. The location code can be used to program the automated stowage and retrieval of supplies by automated handling equipment.

code, mnemonic code. Codes which are designed to trigger memory recall and/or the recognition of the item.

code, NATO code. The code used by North Atlantic Treaty Organisation based upon USA Federal Classification.

code, pictograms. Representation of a feature or hazard such as *hazard codes* by a picture of the hazard.

code, product block code. A code where blocks of numerals are allocated, e.g. for raw materials and components of an end-product, such as, an electric motor.
e.g. field windings 1000 to 1100
    bearings   1101 to 1199
    shafts   1200 to 1250
    (and so on . . .)

code, random. A code issued without regard to sequence or classification.

code, sequential code. Codes which are allocated to items in sequence as they arise without reference to classification except that codes allocated will relate to time sequence and may therefore indicate batches of product or supplies etc., e.g. wall-papers, etc.

code, significant code. A code where the individual characters have a special meaning, e.g. product block code.

coding, harmonised for commodities. (EU). The system of commodity coding used by the Community and accepted worldwide for trading in place of the (previously used) Brussels nomenclature and codification. The extension in use of the coded data facilitates the transfer of information by Electronic Data Interchange methods.

coemption. Buying up the whole supply of a commodity, 'cornering the market'.

cohesion, social cohesion. (EU). 'Commitment by the Community to help the less well-off regions to achieve the average level of Community development. A cohesion Fund will contribute to this goal.' 'Cohesion' may help to create the 'level playing field' when purchasing and selling from and to the 'less well-off' regions. cf. Article 2 of Maastricht.

collusion. The action in agreement or concert with others either in a clandestine manner or for an illegal end or by illegal means or by some or all of these.

Co-makership. Jargon employed where buyer and seller organisations cooperate closely on the development, manufacture or supply of a product.

combined bill of lading. *See* BILL OF LADING, COMBINED.

combined transport operator (CTO). 'One who undertakes responsibility for an entire (usually) containerised consignment over its entire journey'.

'combo' ships. Vessels, usually a combination of BREAK-BULK – conventional between deck – and container ships. They are particularly used in feeder services between ports.

comfort letter. (EU). A document provided by the Commission upon appeal by a person against an article of the Community. e.g. a letter stating that in the opinion of the Commission an agreement (i.e. a purchase contract) does not infringe article 85 of 'Competition Law'.

commission. Amount paid for services rendered, usually a percentage, e.g. commission on sales paid to a sales representative.

Commission of the European Union. (EU). The Community body which makes 'PROPOSALS' for legislation. The COUNCIL of the EUROPEAN UNION which discusses, adopts or amends. The Commission executes Council decisions and supervises day to day running of policies. (*See* COUNCIL (EU)). (*Note:* Legislative power rests with the Council, but some legislation may be made directly by the Commission in order to implement Council decisions).

commissioning. BS 5643. The advancement of an installation from the stage of static completion to full working order to specified requirements.

commitment, inadvertent commitment. The creation or modification of a contractual commitment through the AGENT of an enterprise making an unguarded verbal or written comment which could be reasonably constructed as an intention to create or modify a binding commitment.

committed stock. *See* STOCK, PRE-ALLOCATED STOCK *and* STOCK. RESERVED STOCK.

commodities. Goods which are the subject of trade and commerce as below: 1. 'consumer goods' – those which have already reached the domestic market. 2. 'economic' commodities; an element of wealth: an economic good; articles of utility which are not in unlimited supply. 3. primary commodities = RAW MATERIALS. 4. 'PRODUCER GOODS'. 5. Secondary commodities = manufactured goods. 6. Sensitive commodities. *See* COMMODITIES, SENSITIVE COMMODITIES.

commodity/commodities, 'hard'. Term referred to on COMMODITY EXCHANGE as applying to metals.

commodity, 'soft' commodity. Term used on the COMMODITY EXCHANGE referring, in general, to agricultural products and their derivatives –

cocoa, fishmeal, sugar for examples.

commodity agreements, multilateral agreements. UN. Multilateral arrangements between consumer and producer nations to stabilize supplies and prices of individual commodities.

commodity catalogue. *See* CATALOGUE COMMODITY CATALOGUE.

commodity code. *See* CODE

commodity exchange. *See* MARKETS.

commodity market. *See* MARKETS.

commodity numbers. (UN). Numbers assigned to commodities for their identification and use in commodity coding, etc. United Nations commodity numbers, for example, must be stated when shipping dangerous goods. The numbers displayed in a label (such as a 'Hazchem' label) alert and inform fire, ambulance and other rescue services the steps needed to prepare for any associated hazards.

commodity, 'sensitive commodity'. A commodity the price of which in the market is sensitive to economic and market conditions such as supply and demand, shortage, the exchange rate and many other international and national factors.

common carrier. *See* CARRIER, COMMON.

common law. *See* LAW, COMMON LAW.

Common Market. UN. Usually refers to the EUROPEAN UNION (EU) but can also mean any Customs union which eliminates all trade barriers within the group and establishes a common external tariff on imports from non-member countries. Common markets similar to the EU exist in Central America, EFTA, etc.

common user items/supplies. Those items of supply, usually stock items, which are used in more than one department or work-centre of an organisation. e.g. furniture, tools, stationery, etc.

communication. The sending and receiving of information, instructions, ideas, intentions and so on by means of language symbols (written* or spoken), electrical or other impulses, between people, and/or (in the case of machines) by FEEDBACK. Communication is particularly important in SUPPLIES administration, and vital in PURCHASING for which absolute accuracy and clarity are essential. Communication is essential for the creation of a valid contract. (*Written communications in contracts can constitute DOCUMENTS OF RECORD).

communication, oral in supplies. This kind of communication, or the conduct of the parties, can bind both seller and buyer in a contract. In all important cases, oral communications should be confirmed in writing. *See* SALE OF GOODS ACT 1979.

communication, written in supplies. Although for creation of a valid contract, communication need not be in writing, written communications can, as DOCUMENTS OF RECORD, provide valuable evidence of the INTENTIONS OF PARTIES to create a contract. Usually the latest communication is the governing document – hence the need for careful scrutiny of ACKNOWLEDGEMENTS from suppliers, of purchase orders.

compensation trading ('buy-back'). A form of COUNTERTRADE in which the exporter may be required not only to supply plant and instal it, provide the technology and training of the work-force but also to purchase the end-product, i.e. the output of the plant.

compensatory financing. UN. A programme of the International Monetary Fund (IMF) which offers loans to countries suffering temporary shortfalls in income due to temporary falls in prices of commodities.

competition. (def). Competition in business can be described as the effort of one trader to secure financial advantage over others who vie for the same business. In economic theory, competition between buyers for each to secure the best price for himself, while sellers equally compete each to secure the

best bargain. This should tend to equalise rates of profit into approximate equality. Competition is also expected to drive suppliers to improve their efficiency so as not to lose business to their rivals. (*Note:* In the domestic field, prices, product and availability may be subject to the somewhat unpredictable 'rules' of MARKET FORCES. However, in the industrial, commercial and business fields Purchasing Officers tend to be working against such rules so as to achieve the best bargain for their enterprise by negotiating on quality, price, availability, service etc.)

competition, business competition. The efforts of each enterprise in the market-place to increase its market share. Competition is a vital component of the 'market economy' in which each enterprise seeks to maximise its profit (or, in a public authority its PROFITABILITY) by improving performance in all fields of its activities including PURCHASING and SUPPLY. Seeking the best bargain for the enterprise in the general community.

competition, market competition. The general 'imperfect' competitive condition encouraged by trade and met with in most environments of purchasing and supply. It requires free market conditions in which a variety of products/services are available to satisfy given needs at competitive quality, prices, deliveries, etc. to numerous buyers – who may themselves be competing for the same supplies and services.

competition, monopolistic competition. A hypothetical condition as by definition it excludes true competition – until an alternative source, product or service becomes available. (*See also in this section* MONOPOLY, DUOPOLY, OLIGOPOLY AND OLIGOPSONY.)

competition, non-price competition. Aspects of competitiveness which, unlike relative prices and costs, are not readily quantified. [May be effective in results of VALUE ENGINEERING and VALUE ANALYSIS.]

competition rules, community rules. (EU). The rules are those set down in the Treaty of Rome and are aimed at ensuring the equality of treatment of organisations throughout the Union. The rules restrict practices which contravene Section 85(1) of the Treaty of Rome dated 1957. This has been strengthened by later DIRECTIVES of the EUROPEAN UNION. The Treaty prohibits all agreements between enterprises which may affect trade between Member States of the Union and which have as their objective or effect the prevention, restriction or distortion of competition within the Union. (*Note:* The 'competition rules will be expected to cover the whole of the European (enlarged) economic area (the EEA) concerning: restrictive trading agreements, monopoly abuse, mergers and takeovers, State aid rules (incl.

European Coal and Steel Community).)

competition, perfect competition. A theoretical condition in the market wherein the following conditions must exist: 1. no single producer, seller or buyer can by his own action affect price. 2. all are free to enter and leave the market. 3. all suppliers offer the same identical product. 4. all products are equally acceptable to the purchasers. 5. there are many buyers and sellers. 6. there is complete freedom from State interference. *See also* MONOPOLY, etc.

complementary demand. *See* DEMAND, COMPLEMENTARY DEMAND.

completion date (of contract). *See* CONTRACT, COMPLETION DATE OF CONTRACT.

compliance. *See* QUALITY CONTROL, COMPLIANCE.

complimentary supply. A service or goods supplied without charge.

compounding. Enables the calculation of the value in future of a sum invested today at an agreed rate of interest over a given period, usually 'years'.

computer, analogue/computer. One which represents numerical quantities by their presentation in graphical/pictorial form, e.g. the face and hands of a clock, a pressure gauge, etc.

computer, digital computer. One which confines its operation to the presentation of data by mathematical symbols (i.e. digits). It can thus store, manipulate or present data such as 'stock levels', 'stock movements', etc. in numerical format.

computer aided design (CAD). The use of computers, usually associated with graphical display units having high definition. CAD enables designs to be modified, updated and appraised during design. Where PURCHASING PARTNERSHIP is in operation, the facilities provided by CAD give opportunities for the purchasing officer and his technical colleagues to appraise the design as it emerges and relate not only cost but factors such as compliance with standards.

computerised ordering systems. Systems which rely upon electronic data interchange (EDI) whereby requirements for supplies are notified to a purchasing department direct by on-line computer from the store or other department requiring them. The system may be enhanced by the program initiating the actual preparation of the purchase order and its electronic transmission to supplier, having first checked specification, preferred supplier, price and delivery required/ offered. *See also* AUTOMATED PURCHASING.

concurrent engineering. Undertaking design, development and other processes in parallel to reduce TIME TO MARKET.

conditions of contract. *See* CONTRACT CONDITIONS OF.

conditions of contract, implied conditions. *See* CONTRACT, IMPLIED CONDITIONS OF CONTRACT.

conditions of purchase. Details usually printed on purchase order forms (and enquiry forms) indicating the standard TERMS and CONDITIONS which the purchaser wishes to apply to his contracts. If conditions of purchase etc. are printed on the reverse of the form for legal reasons it is essential to call attention to them on the face of the form. *See also* CONTRACT, CONDITIONS OF.

conference (or 'Liner Conference'). Two or more shipowners operating on a particular trade route between specified ports and providing regular, scheduled, advertised services at a CONFERENCE FREIGHT RATE.

conference freight-rate. IM. Uniform rates of freight based upon published tariffs charged by Member Lines of a CONFERENCE.

conformity. *See* QUALITY CONTROL, CONFORMITY.

conformity, assessment of conformity (EU). The procedures to ensure that products and services purchased and supplied within the Union conform with established STANDARDS, DIRECTIVES, etc. This includes: testing, inspecting, quality systems, CERTIFICATION OF

CONFORMITY and other certification functions with which the purchaser and supplier must comply. Community Council Resolution 21.12.'89. 'Conformity assessment includes testing, inspection, quality systems certification and otherwise certified to be saleable'.

consensus ad idem. A meeting of minds in one and the same intention. An essential component along with others for a valid contract.

consequential loss. *See* LOSS CONSEQUENTIAL.

conservation, monitoring and target setting ('MIT'). The procedure under the acronym 'MIT' for target setting and monitoring the results of targets for economies, for example in fuel and energy consumption. It is also applied to programmes for new plant and modifications to plant and processes to check on estimated savings. Such modifications, etc. may be financed from savings already achieved in previous periods on other schemes.

consideration. Some 'advantage' (money, or money's worth) which under the terms of a contract moves from one party to the other. The giving of mutual advantages by the parties is the essence of the bargain, and is known as 'consideration'. In any transaction where there is no consideration there is no contract. Strictly speaking therefore PROCUREMENT (in UK usage) does not necessarily constitute a contract.

consign. To forward goods from one place or one person to another.

consignee. SITPRO. Person to whom goods are sent.

consignment. BS 4778 (10.9). Goods or products issued or received as one delivery (and intake) and covered by one set of documents. A consignment may consist of one or more LOTS or BATCHES.

consignment (on-consignment) imports. Goods which instead of being imported against definite orders are brought in and transferred to an agent for sale on commission.

consignment note. CIMA. A haulier's own form of freight contract. It is his receipt for the goods he transports and, by the signature of the purchaser's representative at goods intake, his evidence of delivery in good order. *See* EXTERNAL GOOD ORDER.

consignment stock. *See* STOCK, CONSIGNMENT STOCK.

consignor. A person who sends goods to another.

consolidation (distribution, freight). IM. The grouping together of a number of small consignments into a bulk shipment, for the purpose of qualifying for lower freight tariffs.

consortium. CIMA. An association of contractors or other bodies to carry out a large project. They may issue tenders separately or a single tender, e.g. for a TURN KEY CONTRACT. *See* ORDERS & CONTRACTS.

consortium buying. The use of a consortium may be made by a group of local (or similar) authorities. Such an arrangement may improve price, delivery, etc. from suppliers, but, in doing so such authorities need to be aware of, and avoid conflict with, EU rules on competition.

constructive total loss. *See* LOSS, CONSTRUCTIVE TOTAL LOSS.

consular invoice. *See* INVOICE CONSULAR.

consumables. *See* SUPPLIES, CONSUMABLE SUPPLIES.

consumable stock. *See* STOCK, CONSUMABLE STOCK.

consumer. *See* CONSUMER SALE.

consumer durables. Consumer goods which have a relatively long life, e.g. cars, or a very long life, e.g. houses. cf. non-durables which include consumables such as food, and factory SUPPORTING GOODS e.g. lubricants.

consumer liability. *See* CONSUMER PROTECTION.

consumer protection. The principle enshrined in various enactments for the protection of domestic consumers against the supply of goods and services which are not of *merchantable quality* or *suitable*

for purpose. Such enactments in UK do not usually protect business sales. However, a business purchaser needs to have regard to any supplies he may purchase which pass into a domestic end-product and sale.

consumer sale (contract). A contract (not being one of sale by AUCTION or by competitive TENDER) in which one party to the contract deals, and the other party to the contract (the consumer) does not deal or hold himself out as dealing, in the course of business (abb. Unfair Contract Terms Act 1977 .25(1)a).

consumption (economic). The destruction of value by use. If consumed during a manufacturing process it is known as 'productive consumption'; if there is no direct or indirect end-product it is known as 'unproductive consumption'.

consumption, history. The recorded recurring and/or non-recurring consumption of stock supplies detailed on stock records.

consumption, -, in stores. The usage of stock supplied over a given period. Can be classified into 'recurring' and 'non-recurring' consumption.

containers, freight 'ISO' type. BS 3951. Containers of the ISO type are of modular size 8ft x8ft and of lengths 10, 20, 30 and 40 feet. There are numerous types to suit special cargoes, and all are equipped for lifting by the provision of

35

lifting points at each corner. Some relevant British Standards are:

BS 4654: lifting, hooks for.
BS 5237: lifting, twistlocks for.
BS 5073: packing of containers.
BS 2629: pallets for containers.
BSEN: 284 swap bodies class C.
BSEN: 283 swap bodies, testing of.

container-shipping terms. 1. HOUSE TO HOUSE OR (FCL/ FCL): The container is 'STUF-FED' by the CONSIG-NOR-EXPORTER and 'DE-STUFFED' by the CON-SIGNEE. Containers are presented to the carrier's berth with cargo already packed for ultimate delivery as a full load. 2. HOUSE TO PIER (FCL/LCL): The container is packed by consignor and delivered to carrier's berth or terminal as a full load. At destination, cargo is unpacked by the carrier at his depot for consignee to collect. 3. PIER TO HOUSE (LCL/FCL): Consignor delivers shipment to carrier's depot as BREAK-BULK. Carrier packs container. Unpacking of full load at destination arranged by consignee. 4. FULL CONTAINER LOAD: Acronym 'FCL' indicates that the container is to travel fully laden. *See also* LCL LESS THAN CONTAINER LOAD: Acronym 'LCL' indicates that the container is partially loaded only, see SERVICE CHARGE. 5. SER-VICE CHARGE for LCL: A charge which may be made by a carrier for packing an LCL shipment. (Sometimes called a 'packing charge'. Also applies to inbound container with mixed LCL cargoes.) 6. ZONE CHARGES:

Charges for haulage from the consignor to the carrier's depot for shipment. Also termed 'carrier's haulage'. 7. MERCHANT HAULAGE: The consignor attends to haulage of LCL or FCL cargo to or from carrier's depot. 8. DELIVERED IN CHARGE (DIC): Carrier's charge for transfer of cargo from container freight station to loading port. 9. LIFT ON/LIFT OFF: Charge for CRANAGE when carrier handles a container from consignor's transport onto his own vehicle or ship, etc.

containers, intermediate bulk (IBC). Containers between approximately $0.5m^3$ and $3.0m^3$ (usually) of flexible material, suitable for handling by fork truck or crane and for use in process by direct discharge.

containerisation. The transfer of goods for shipment from the former BREAK BULK methods to their packaging in unit containers thus making possible safer, cheaper transit. IM 'Management Guide No. 6. Distribution'.

contango. (com. mkt.). Premium paid by a buyer of FUTURES to the seller for the buyer's postponement of delivery from the due date to a later one. Sometimes referred to as FORWARDATION.

contents note. A document attached to a container (crate, case, etc.) listing the number of packages within that container. *See also* PACKING NOTE.

contingency cover (ins.). Insurance taken out by a shipper to cover transit where the customer has arranged his own insurance. The policy covers the shipper (exporter) until the property in the goods has transferred to the customer.

contingent liabilities. CIMA. Obligations which may arise in respect of past or future events (e.g. the purchaser or supplier has infringed a patent).

continuation clause (mar. ins.). One covering situations where a ship is still at sea when insurance cover runs out. The insurer agrees to cover risks at *PRO RATA* rate of premium.

continuous inventory. *See* STOCK CONTROL CONTINUOUS *and* INVENTORY.

continuous stock control. *See* STOCK CONTROL CONTINUOUS.

continuous stock-taking. *See* STOCK-TAKING.

contracts and orders: administration of.

Definitions in this section refer mainly, only to the formation and administration of contracts (and purchase orders). For the varieties of 'orders' and 'contracts' *see* the section headed ORDERS AND CONTRACTS: VARIETIES OF.

contract. (def). A 'business contract' implies the entry into an unambiguous legal agreement with a company, another party, person (other supplier) to deliver supplies (goods or services) or to do something (e.g. construct a building) on mutually agreed terms. A business contract generally involves: 1. an offer and an unqualified ACCEPTANCE 2. a *CONSENSUS AD IDEM*. 3. an intention of the parties to contract. 4. a genuine consent of the parties to the agreement. 5. the capacity of the parties to contract. 6. legality of the objectives of the contract. 7. the possibility of its performance. 8. certainty of the TERMS and CONDITIONS applied. 9. the passing of CONSIDERATION.

contract, acceptance of offer in a contract. The agreement of a party that he accepts an offer submitted to him and is prepared to enter into a contract. For a contract to be valid the acceptance must be unqualified. A qualified acceptance is equivalent to a counter-offer or an offer, and is not an acceptance.

contract/order, acknowledgement of order (written). The acknowledgement between parties that a contract exists. A supplier's written acknowledgement of a purchase order establishes the existence of the contract and will (usually) bind the purchaser – unless he responds and signifies he is not making an unqualified acceptance of the acknowledgement, in which event full and unqualified acceptance must be established by further negotiations before a valid contract can be established.

contract/order, acknowledgement of (unwritten). The acceptance and acknowledgement of the existence of a valid contract may be established by non-written means, thus: 1. oral communication e.g. telephone, face to face, etc. 2. evidence of intention to contract e.g. starting work. 3. by 'performance' – actual despatch of the goods. 4. by 'acceptance' of goods, e.g. purchaser does something consistent with his ownership of them. 5. instructions by on-line computers, if a course of dealing exists between the parties, e.g. the computer programs trigger ordering instructions automatically when re-order level is reached.

contract for supply (law). A contract is made where parties have reached an agreement or when they are deemed to have done so, and the law recognises the rights and obligations arising. Almost all industrial contracts are simple contracts, as distinct from speciality contracts i.e. those made under seal. Three of the essential elements are: 1. AGREEMENT (*CONSENSUS AD IDEM*) 2. INTENTION 3. CONSIDERATION. *See also* ORDERS AND CONTRACTS. (*Note:* In purchasing and supply usage the term 'contract' is usually applied to major purchase orders or for future supplies of major value to distinguish such orders from orders of a more routine nature for which the term 'purchase order' is applicable.)

contract bonds and guarantees. *See* BONDS.

contract, breach of (duty in). Breach of (duty in) a contract results from breach of: 1. any obligation arising out of the express or implied terms of a contract, to take reasonable care or exercise reasonable skill in performance of the contract. 2. any common law duty to take reasonable care or exercise reasonable skill.

contract, cancellation of contract. The act of nullifying or invalidating a purchase order, i.e. a CONTRACT. The action may constitute a breach of contract on the part of the buyer, unless the agreement to cancel has been negotiated with the other party.

contract, completion date of contract. The date agreed in a contract for 1. the delivery of supplies. 2. date of arrival of plant on site. 3. its test. 4. its commissioning and certificate of approval by the purchaser. 5. some other date which must be agreed by the parties to the contract. *See* PLANNING *and* PROGRESSING.

contract, conditions, of contract. TERMS which go to the heart of a contract. Traditionally, if a promiser breaks a 'condition' in any respect however slight, the other party may treat himself as discharged from the contract and sue for damages immediately. *See also* WARRANTY.

contract, conditions, legal conditions, (terminology of). 1. Concurrent condition: one depending upon the performance by the other party to the contract. 2. Precedent condition: one where the contract shall not bind the party until it is fulfilled. 3. Subsequent condition: one which shall bind the party or release them upon the happening of another event, e.g. suspension of contracts on the outbreak of war. 4. implied condition: one which although not explicit in a contract have been implied by words or actions and seen to be understood and accepted by both parties to the contract. *See also* DEALING, A COURSE OF DEALING.

contract costing. CIMA. Form of specific order-costing where work is undertaken to purchaser's special requirements and each order is of long duration (compared with those to which JOB COSTING applies), e.g. constructional work.

contract date. (order date for most purposes). The date when a contract or order enters into effect according to the INTENTIONS OF THE PARTIES.

contracts, discharge of contract. The completion of a contract and liquidation. PERFORMANCE must be complete in accordance with the terms and conditions of the contract.

contract, dishonoured contract. One which has suffered breach. [This may be a suitable term to apply when a failure by a supplier to comply with CONDITIONS of a contract such as failure to meet delivery date or quality, etc. appears imminent.]

contract, 'escalation clause'. A clause which allows price to be

adjusted to a predetermined formula which relying on some mutually agreed index or indices published by a third party. Known as a price adjustment clause (cf).

contracts, 'escape clause'. A clause inserted into a contract by the parties to the agreement. The objectives may be various and may involve a BREAK CLAUSE or the cancellation or renegotiation of the contract under certain defined eventualities agreed in advance between the parties.

contract, 'exclusion clause'. A clause which one party to a contract [usually the supplier] endeavours to embody into a contract whereby he can escape liabilities or commitments he wishes to avoid. (*Note*: 'A statement on a purchase order excluding a seller's conditions is no protection to the buyer and does not legally affect the "counter offer" situation').

contract, fixed time-cycle review ordering. Contracts/orders placed at *regular time intervals*, after taking account of DUES IN, stock available (i.e. allowing for any ALLOCATED etc. stock) at the time of review. Quantity is ordered sufficient to bring stock to STOCK LEVEL MAXIMUM, or other quantity to meet expected demand for production, process or sales.

contract, fixed quantity ordering. Orders for fixed quantity may be based upon ECONOMIC ORDER QUANTITY, production or process batch requirements, etc.

39

Frequency of ordering usually varies with rate at which withdrawals from stock depress stock levels to the RE-ORDER LEVEL. *See* **BS5729**.

contract, forward purchase. Buying in advance of need. May, or may not, involve delivery and inflation of stocks and incur increased STOCK-HOLDING COSTS.

contract, frustration of contract. Any situation where the PERFORMANCE of a contract is prevented from being carried out. Under the 'doctrine of frustration' courts provide for the 'discharge of a contract' if certain types of contingency intervene, such as: 1. the basis or subject of the contract is destroyed, 2. an essential event did not occur, 3. government intervenes, 4. method of performance is impossible, (and others).

contract, implied conditions in contract. Conditions in contract. Conditions which although not explicit in a contract have been implied by words or actions and seen to be understood and accepted by both parties to the contract. *See also* DEALING, A COURSE OF DEALING.

contract, inadvertent contract. Apart from one made 'inadvertently' this definition can also apply to a contract made by mistake, made prematurely or by a person who is unauthorised but is HOLDING OUT and may commit the enterprise to a binding contract. [Rules of contract are not at the time of writing uniform throughout the European Union. It is important to check that a contractual commitment will not result from the 'innocent exchange of quotations and letters with a continental supplier.]

contract, 'loyalty contract'. (mar). A contract offered by LINER CONFERENCES to shippers who are willing to guarantee to send their cargoes (in a particular trade or area) exclusively by the ships of that particular conference; 'may involve pooling arrangements'.

contract management. Activities of a buyer during a contract period to ensure that the seller fulfils *all* his obligations under the contract.

contracts, 'model' engineering contract. A 'model' contract developed by the Institution of Civil Engineers with the support of the Chartered Institute of Purchasing and Supply. It is designed to meet the need for a more flexible form of contract, written in clear and simple language with procedures designed to stimulate good management and to promote co-operation between employers, designers, contractors and project managers. It is intended to reduce the risk, cost and time over-runs and to offer contractors, sub-contractors and suppliers the possibility of improved profits. It can be used by all engineering and construction disciplines and almost any type of contract. 'Model forms' are intended to provide the purchaser with the basics for valid contracts in the area in which contracts are being made. The Chartered Institute of Purchasing and Supply publishes 'model forms' covering a wide range of supply, for example: engineering plant and materials, carriage of goods, liquid fuels, etc. Note should also be taken of the standard terms and conditions available from the various other specialist institutions such as the engineering institutes. *See also* MODEL ORDERS.

contract note. Written particulars for a sale made in a central exchange, such as a COMMODITY MARKET – particularly on FUTURES.

contracts, overseas contracts. Those contracts made between businesses in States of differing sovereignties, financial systems, and commercial and industrial laws. Integration of States (*See* COMMON MARKET and EUROPEAN COMMUNITY) involve applications of varying techniques of purchasing and supply. Some examples are: premium and discount currencies, use of 'futures' market. 'traded options' control of payments made in Sterling against foreign exchange commitments: option spreads; rollovers and reconversions; ECUs and Euro-currencies; currency credits, etc.

contract period. The period from the agreed date of the start of a contract to the agreed due date for its completion.

contract price adjustment (CPA). *See* PRICE, CONTRACT PRICE ADJUSTMENT, CONTRACT, ESCALATION CLAUSE.

contract, **price re-opener clause**. *See* PRICE: RE-OPENER CLAUSE.

contract procedures (negotiated) (EU). Negotiating procedures whereby contracting authorities consult suppliers of their choice and negotiate the terms of the contract with one or several of them . [Source P&SM 5/89 p.37] *See also* TENDERS/TENDERING.

contracts, prototype format. An original model or pattern of contract (or purchase order) from which subsequent copies are made. The prototype order procedure lends itself to the use of EDP. The 'model' order may be retained in the computer file and quantity, price, delivery, etc. completed as required and issued to the supplier. *See also* AUTOMATED PURCHASING.

contract, quasi-contract. A contract which does not embody all the conditions needed for a valid contract. A quasi-contract may become a firm legal contract by the words and actions of the parties.

contract record. A record of progress of a contract, e.g. of DRAW-OFF, ORDERS, schedules, etc. from FORWARD SUPPLY CONTRACTS or FORWARD SUPPLY ARRANGEMENTS. See ORDERS & CONTRACTS A–Z.

contract, re-determination clause. A clause in a contract where costs cannot be pre-determined, e.g. after production has started the 'unknowns' become 'known' and a final price may then be agreed. In some instances further 'pre-determinations' may be needed. Such a clause may also be an essential CONDITION in a LONG TERM CONTRACT. This will then enable the purchaser to re-negotiate if market, usage, price or quality vary. *See also* BREAK CLAUSE.

contract, retention of ownership clause. *See* TITLE, RETENTION OF TITLE.

contract of sale. 'A contract for the sale of goods is a contract in which the contract seller transfers or agrees to transfer the property in goods to a purchaser for a money CONSIDERATION called the PRICE'. Sale of Goods Act 1979 Sect. 2 – (1).

contract scheduling. A system of ordering and production control associated with the control of large scale projects where the release of orders is based upon schedules related to the progress of the contract. May be controlled by NETWORK ANALYSIS.

contract, severable. *See* ORDERS & CONTRACTS A–Z.

contract, terms of contract. The language and form of words used in a contract. Traditionally, each TERM of a contract whether express or implied is either a CONDITION or TERM or a WARRANTY.

contract, time the essence. *See* TIME THE ESSENCE.

contract, unenforceable contract. A contract which, though valid in itself, may not be enforceable at law for a valid reason, e.g. an ACT OF GOD or *FORCE MAJEURE* or STATE LEGISLATION.

contract, contracting out. The equivalent of BUYING IN but in this case to place a contract with an outside supplier or service contractor for an operation or supply which the purchaser could otherwise provide from his own facilities IN HOUSE.

contractor. A party who agrees to provide supplies or services in accordance with a valid and legal agreed CONTRACT.

contra-flow. A situation wherein supplies or traffic flow in opposite directions. May result in congestion, wasted movements, etc. Should always be examined in regard to operational efficiency, safety and costs in stores, handling, transportation, etc.

control of substances hazardous to health (COSHH). *See* SUBSTANCES.

contribution. CIMA. The difference between sales and VARIABLE COSTS is expressed as 'contribution' and represents the amounts available to meet overhead costs. It is a useful method for measuring the effectiveness of a single product among all the products produced by an enterprise. 1. 'contribution per unit' is the difference between the selling price of a product or service and its marginal cost. 2. contribution in total is the difference between the sales value and variable cost. Contribution is a very important aspect of supply economics. CIMA.

Convention Internationale de Merchandies (CIM). An international agreement on goods transport by rail.

Convention Merchandise per Route (CMR). An international agreement relating to the carriage of goods by road, incorporated into the Carriage of Goods by Road Act 1965.

convertible (currency). UN. 'Hard currency' that which may be exchanged for gold or other currencies without restriction. Convertible currencies are based on sound, usually developed and industrialised, economies as well as substantial holdings of international reserve assets (gold, US dollars, pounds sterling and SDRs). Unconvertible or 'soft currencies' are usually only used locally in the countries of issue.

copyright. (law). 'The exclusive right to do, and to authorise (or forbid) other persons to do certain acts in relation to that 'work which is copyright' (Copyright Act 1956.) [Such rights include the copying of manufacturer's and supplier's INTELLECTUAL PROPERTY, such as drawings, designs, specifications, schedules and other similar materials which often arise in the course of enquiries, negotiations, etc.]

'cornering the market'. The concentration (usually rapid and temporary) of the major part of supply of a commodity into single ownership, e.g. 'cornering the market in cotton'.

corporate appraisal. ('SWOT analysis'). A critical appraisal of the Strengths, Weaknesses, Opportunities, and Threats in relation to internal and external factors affecting an enterprise so as to consider its condition prior to setting up a long term plan. See PLANNING, STRATEGIC LONG TERM.

corporate planning. See PLANNING, CORPORATE PLANNING.

correlation. (stats). The degree to which (two) variables vary in relation to one another. Correlation is: a. 'positive' when the increase in one is associated with an increase in the other, e.g. throughput of supplies increases with increase in production, b. 'negative' when as one increases the other decreases, e.g. price (should) decrease as order quantities increase, c. 'perfect' when each change in the one is matched by an equal change in the other.

cost. The total sum involved including price plus all sums associated with ownership and use. *Note*: 'cost' should not be used as a synonym for PRICE or VALUE.

cost accounting. The application of accounting and costing principles, methods and techniques in the ascertainment of costs and the analysis of savings and/or excesses as compared with previous experience or with standards.

cost, accrued costs (charges). Costs or charges which should be known at the inception of a project or contract, but which will not be due until some pre-determined date – such as completion or COMMISSIONING of a project or plant.

cost, acquisition costs (total). The total of all costs in acquiring supplies of goods or services by purchase or by other means, eg *hire,* loan, procurement, etc, from the inception of the demand for them until their safe and satisfactory delivery at the point required. They include all administrative and physical costs from the time of determination of the need until and including final settlement with the supplier. In the case of some contracts they may also include such costs as: preliminary enquiries, feasibility studies, design and prototypes, and in the case of major plant the setting down at site, tests and commissioning of such plant. *See also* COST, ORDER PREPARATION COST AND CONTRACT MANAGEMENT,

cost, actual cost ascertainment. CIMA. A principle whereby costs at COST CENTRES and of COST UNITS are ascertained, which, subject to certain approximations are deemed to represent actual costs. The use of the term 'historical costs' is not recommended in this concept.

cost, administrative, cost general. The sum of those costs of general management and of secretarial, accounting and administrative services which cannot be directly related to production, marketing, research or development functions of an enterprise. For purposes of economic order quantity (EOQ) it is important that supplies costs in administration be taken into account.

cost, allocation of cost. CIMA. Distribution of costs to various COST CENTRES, process, services or products in the proportion in which they have been incurred.

cost analysis. A technique used to determine a fair and reasonable selling price of a product. Having carried out the cost estimate, cost analysis studies continue beyond the manufacturing costs and examine administrative costs, MARKETING, selling, distribution, etc, and endeavour to determine the profit the supplier is applying to that particular product. *See also* VALUE ANALYSIS.

cost, anticipated cost. A cost expected to arise through some contingency which may, or may not, be easily estimated. cf. ESTIMATED COST.

cost, applied cost. A cost (actual or percentage) added to costs for ESTIMATE (or sometimes for a QUOTATION) to cover a supplier's contingencies, such as uncertainty as to the purchaser's continued demand for the product, or some special non-standard feature which has been specified by the purchaser. [This emphasises the need to use STANDARDS wherever they are applicable.]

cost, appraisal cost. *See* COSTS, QUALITY RELATED COSTS.

costs, average (or mean) costs. The figure which represents the average (mean) of a number of different costs and may be derived from the 'simple' or 'weighted' mean of all the costs involved. For 'weighted mean' *see* BS 5233 (3·4·4)

cost, batch costing. cf. **BS 5191 (B1001) (prod).** Costing of similar items where these are manufactured in batches.

cost-benefit analysis. The evaluation of the social and economic worths of a proposed project, or a purchase. *See also* VALUE ANALYSIS.

cost, budgeted cost. One which has been provided for in a budgetary controlled system. [May affect the purchasing and supply policy in regard to orders and contract control, and also of INVENTORY.]

cost centre. CIMA. A location, person or item of equipment (or groups of these) in respect of which costs may be ascertained and related to COST UNITS.

cost, contract costing. *See* CONTRACT COSTING.

cost control. The practice of comparing the actual cost of an operation (e.g. total cost of, for example, a 'service contract') with the original cost estimate (or budget) in order to ascertain if the cost is as originally planned or budgeted for.

cost, controllable (or 'managed cost'). *See* COST, MANAGED COST.

cost, conversion cost. cf. CIMA. The sum of the production (process) costs of converting materials (including components for assembly or finishing) into finished products, e.g. direct wages, direct expenses and absorbed PRODUCTION OVERHEADS.

cost, development cost. cf. CIMA. The cost of the process which begins with the implementation of the decision to produce a new or improved product or to employ a new or improved method, and ends with the commencement of formal production of that product or production by that method.

cost, delivered at frontier. *See* DELIVERED AT FRONTIER.

cost, design for cost. To design a product within cost constraints to ensure that it will be competitive in the market place, or as a unit of plant will fulfil its proposed objectives.

costs, direct. *See* COSTS, MATERIAL COSTS.

costs, disposal costs. The total costs to the owner of material in disposing of an item of material when it has failed or is no longer required for any reason.

cost, distribution costs. CIMA. That portion of marketing cost which is incurred in warehousing saleable products and in delivering products to customers.

cost, distribution costs, optimum total distribution costs. The costs resulting from optimum efficiency in distribution costs by selection of storage, handling and transportation of goods from the point of production to the point of consumption at the least 'total expense' (i.e. summation of all expenses rather than dealing with each operation as an isolated and individual expense).

cost effectiveness. The relationship between cost measured in monetary units and effectiveness measured in terms of actual performance. A cost effective supply is one where the effectiveness is equal to or exceeds the BREAK-EVEN POINT of the related costs.

cost, establishment cost. The cost of running a department such as purchasing and supply. [In the context of large contracts consideration may be needed to check the validity of the normal method of calculating ACQUSITION COST used in the ECONOMIC ORDER QUANTITY formulae.]

cost, estimated cost. CIMA. The pre-determination of the probable cost of a job, article, or process.

cost, estimation of costs. A technique used to determine the manufacturing cost of a product, embracing raw materials methods, manufacturing times, labour costs and factory overheads.

cost, 'external failure costs'. See COSTS, QUALITY RELATED COSTS.

cost, factory cost. The total of PRIME COSTS (i.e. 'variable costs' – which depend upon output plus costs of administration) PLUS 'oncosts' (= 'fixed costs') which do not change with every change in output. 'Factory cost' includes production costs of a product up to despatch, excludes all marketing expenses and overheads except those directly attributable to production.

cost, failure cost(s). Cost(s) which are, as a rule, difficult to predict but which need to be estimated when settling the sums to be allowed for in contracts which contain clauses for LIQUIDATED DAMAGES.

cost, fixed. CIMA. That which accrues in relation to the passage of time and which, within certain output or turnover limits, tends to be unaffected by fluctuations in volume of output or turnover. e.g. rent, rates, insurance and executive salaries.

cost (and) freight (C & F), named port of destination. INCOTERM. Seller's obligations end when goods reach their destination. Buyer bears all risks from the moment the goods pass over the ship's rail at the port of destination.

cost, handling costs. IM. A significant factor in supplies costs, usually concealed in purchase price, occurs at numerous points throughout the Supply Cycle. Includes: supplier packing, and loading onto transport; carrier transit and trans-shipment; purchaser off-loading, unpacking, checking, etc. Costs are assessed per unit weight, weight per unit distance, unit volume per unit distance, or other measures.

cost, handling cost rule. Every time supplies are handled, something is added to their cost but nothing to their value. (The value may be reduced if damage occurs in handling through inefficient packaging or handling.)

costs, historical costs. CIMA. Costs based upon the original cost of acquiring an asset, or of purchasing goods (stocks) and services. *See also* PRICE, FIRST-IN, FIRST-OUT PRICE, REPLACEMENT PRICE and CURRENT COST ACCOUNTING.

cost, holding cost. *See* STOCK, COSTS OF HOLDING COSTS.

cost, incremental cost. The cost resulting from raising the rate of production by one unit. *See also* MARGINAL COSTING.

cost, indirect cost. BS 4335. Costs associated with a project that cannot be directly allocated to an activity or group of activities.

cost, insurance and freight (CIF). Named port of destination.

INCOTERM. As COST AND FREIGHT but seller insures goods to their destination.

cost, internal failure cost. *See* COSTS, QUALITY RELATED COSTS.

cost, life-cycle cost. BS 3811(2113). Total costs of an item throughout its life including: acquisition, maintenance and support costs.

cost, managed cost. CIMA. abb. One which can be influenced by the person responsible for the COST CENTRE in which the cost occurs, e.g. cost may arise from excess stock due to bad stock control or excessive scrap through the procurement of faulty material.

costs, material costs (direct), cf. **BS 5191 (B3001).** Costs of those materials (and services) which are embodied in the manufacture of an end-product.

cost, marginal cost. CIMA. The variable cost of one unit of product or service; i.e. a cost which would be avoided if the unit was not produced (purchased) or provided. *Note*: in this context a unit is usually either a single article or a standard measure such as the litre or kilogram, etc., but may in certain circumstances be an operation, process or part of an organisation. *See also* MARGINAL COSTING *and* BREAKEVEN POINT.

cost, marketing (and selling) costs. CIMA. abb. Marketing costs include publicising and presentation of products to customers in attractive forms and prices with all research, securing orders and (usually) delivery and in some cases after-sales service. Selling costs (to industry) include salesmen (and other staff) engaged in securing orders by visits, quotations and associated promotional activities. These are areas where purchasing may assist in cost reduction and earn a reduced price to the company.

cost, normal cost. A cost which is normally incurred at a given level of output in the conditions in which that level of output is normally obtained.

cost, operation cost. Basic costing methods applicable where standardised products or services result from a sequence of repetitive and more or less continuous operations or processes to which costs can be charged before being averaged over the total units or service produced during the period.

cost, opportunity cost. CIMA. The value of a benefit sacrificed in favour of an alternative course of action, e.g. increasing stock investment to ensure continuous production may deprive the firm of the cash (and the opportunity) to buy a more efficient production unit.

costs, order preparation costs. Costs of preparing an actual purchase order. Such costs include: 1. fixed costs which are unaffected by the number of orders placed during any given period, viz. accommodation, plant (computers, VDUs, office machinery, etc.), maintenance of same and salaries of senior staff. 2. variable costs which are largely proportional to the number of orders placed in a given period, viz. typing, checking, filing, stationery, postage, records, statistical work and wages of routine staff. These costs are a major factor in acquisition costs which in turn influence the calculations of economic order quantities.

costs, ordering costs total. *See* COSTS, ACQUISITION COSTS, TOTAL.

costs, overhead costs. CIMA. Costs incurred in manufacturing which are INDIRECT COSTS (indirect materials, indirect labour and indirect expenses) and include items such as ADMINISTRATION COSTS, MARKETING COSTS, SERVICING COSTS and so on.

cost, over-spend costs. BS 4335. The amount by which the incurred cost is greater than the budgeted or planned cost.

cost plus. A pricing method whereby the purchaser agrees to pay the vendor an amount determined by the costs incurred by the vendor to produce the goods or services purchased, and to which oncosts and profit are added at an agreed percentage, or fixed sum, or according to another agreed formula.

cost, premium cost. A method of

remuneration which tends to effect economy in labour costs and materials by the payment of a bonus based on the reduction in total cost compared with standard cost.

cost, prevention cost. *See* COST, QUALITY RELATED COST.

cost, prime cost. CIMA. **BS 5191 (B 3004).** The total cost of direct materials (supplies), wages and expenses. The term is commonly restricted to direct production costs only and so does not customarily include costs of marketing or research and development.

cost, production costs. CIMA. Comprise PRIME COST plus absorbed PRODUCTION OVERHEAD. See also ABSORPTION COSTING.

costs, quality related cost. BS 4778 Pt. 2 (5.5.2). The expenditure incurred in defect prevention and quality appraisal activities plus the losses due to internal and external failure. 12.4 The cost of any action taken to investigate, prevent or reduce defects and failures. 12.5 The cost of assessing the quality achieved 12.6 The costs arising within the manufacturing organisation from the failure to achieve quality specified. 12.7 The costs arising outside the manufacturing organisation by the failure to achieve quality specified (can include costs of claims against warranty, replacement and consequential losses of custom and good will). 12.8 The economic level of quality is that at

which the cost of securing higher quality would exceed the benefits of the improved quality.

cost, replacement cost accounting. A form of CURRENT COST ACCOUNTING in which assets are valued at the current cost of replacing them at the time of a review. Of particular application to INVENTORY by which stock is continuously (or at review) revalued at the current replacement price. *See* PRICE, REPLACEMENT PRICE.

cost, research cost. The cost of seeking new or improved materials, methods of manufacture or process, etc. or sources of supply.

costs, running costs. The total costs to the PLANT owner of the operation, MAINTENANCE and modification of an ITEM of plant. *See also* COSTS USE IN.

costs, salvage costs. Costs of salvaging SCRAP and WASTE; may involve costs of segregation, sorting, handling, storage, baling, compacting, weighing, etc. *See also* COSTS, DISPOSAL COSTS.

costs, semi-variable costs. Costs containing both fixed and variable elements, which are therefore partly affected by fluctuations in the volume of output or turnover (or purchases. An area where purchasing NEGOTIATIONS should look for savings). *See also* COSTS VARIABLE COSTS *and* COSTS, FIXED COSTS.

cost(s), set up cost(s). The

component of production/process or other costs which result from preparation work, e.g. setting machines, robots, process controllers, etc. ready for operation. The costs will be proportional to the labour, robotics, setting up of jigs, tools, gauges, etc. and the SET-UP TIME BS 5191 (26004). 'The time required to prepare a WORK STATION from a standard condition to readiness to commence a specified operation'. In the case of purchasing and supply administration the cost of enquiries and value analysis of them, meetings, preparation of the contract documentation, etc. are 'setting up costs'. [In major contracts these costs may need to be taken into account if applying an ECONOMIC ORDER QUANTITY formula.]

costs, shortage costs. BS 5191 (B 5005). The costs associated with having a shortage of supply or service. (*Note:* These can include: 1. a measure of loss of customer goodwill. 2. the costs of expediting. 3. the costs of holding associated parts until shortage is cleared, e.g. incomplete kits of parts, sub-assemblies, etc.)

cost, standard cost. CIMA. A predetermined cost calculated in relation to a prescribed set of working conditions, correlating technical specifications and scientific measurement of materials and labour to the prices and wages expected to apply during the period to which the standard cost is intended to relate, with an addition of appropriate share of budgeted overhead. Its main purposes are to provide bases for control through VARIANCE ACCOUNTING, for valuation of stocks and work-in-progress, and, in exceptional cases, fixing selling prices.

cost, stock handling cost. BS 5191 (B 5004). The total cost involved in handling and moving stock (including for example order picking and transporting EXCESS STOCKS to other locations).

cost, stock holding costs. BS 5191 (B 5003). The costs of maintaining stock in stores. *Note:* this can include: 1. OPPORTUNITY COST on capital value of stock held. 2. insurance costs and provision for deterioration and obsolescence. 3. cost of storage space, warehouse, stockyard, etc. 4. cost of administration and manning the store.

costs, storage costs. Part of stock-holding cost includes: buildings and equipment mobile (handling) and static (storage); security; first aid, fire and safety protection; preservation (e.g. humidity, pest control, etc); administration; labour; energy; rates; hire; insurance; interest on capital outlay; depreciation of buildings, plant and equipment; deterioration, obsolescence and maintenance of buildings and plant. Costs are best expressed as costs per unit volume of space available for storage, etc. (Excluding actual stock held for which *see* 'COSTS, STOCK-HOLDING COSTS'.)

cost, underspend cost. BS 4335.

The amount by which the incurred cost is less than the budgeted or planned costs.

cost unit, a 'cost unit'. CIMA. A quantitative unit of product, i.e. supply or service in relation to which costs are ascertained, e.g. paper, per ream; sand and gravel, per cubic metre, etc.

cost, unit cost. CIMA. A quantitative unit of product or service in relation to which costs are ascertained. Cost units are basic for VALUE ANALYSIS and VALUE ENGINEERING, and the comparison of QUOTATIONS, ESTIMATES, TENDERS and PRICES.

cost, use in (more generally 'cost in use'). The cost of ownership of an asset such as a building or unit of plant including interest on capital outlay, costs of operation including repairs, maintenance, depreciation, etc.

cost, variable cost. CIMA. A cost which, in the aggregate, tends to vary in direct proportion to changes in volume of output or TURNOVER. Supplies attract VARIABLE or FIXED COSTS according to whether they are embodied in the actual END-PRODUCT or are SUPPORTING GOODS or equipment used for production, handling, transport and so on.

Council of The European Union (EU). The decision-making body of the Community. It legislates on the basis of COMMISSION proposals, subject to amendment. It comprises ministers and working groups of officials. *Note:* Legislative power rests with the Council, but some legislation may be made directly by the Commission in order to implement Council decisions.

counter-offer. *See* OFFER, COUNTER OFFER.

counter-purchase. An aspect of COUNTER-TRADE in which an exporter is requested to purchase goods from the country to which his exports are sold. (*Note:* The 'counter-purchase' purchase from the customer-country may or may not be products used by the purchaser.)

counter-trade. Methods of trading involving exchange of goods rather than money payment. The methods include: BARTER; BUY-BACK; COMPENSATION TRADING; co-operation (production, development, joint marketing of natural resources); COUNTER-PURCHASE; joint ventures.

counting scales. Weighing scales designed so that a read-out of the quantity of items in the balance is given.

course of dealing. *See* DEALING, COURSE OF DEALING.

coverage analysis. A means of establishing optimum stock-holding levels in relation to capital available by making a quantitative analysis of likely demand over a given period of various stock lines and adjusting stock levels to meet demand and at the same time to optimise capital investment.

covering letter. One which accompanies and explains or amplifies the details or data on the principal document – such as a purchase order. If the covering letter is to form part of the contract, attention must be called to it on the face of the purchase order.

cradle to grave. The full lifetime of a product or substance. Of relevance to LIFE CYCLE COSTING and the ENVIRONMENT

cranage. Charge for use of cranes at port facilities. *See also* CONTAINER RELATED TERMS *at* LIFT-ON/LIFT-OFF.

crane. A materials handling device for lifting heavy items by suspending them.

crate. BS **1133 (BS 3810 pt. 4).** A skeleton package or container of open boarded construction. To be clearly differentiated from a CASE.

credit. The opposite of the transfer of cash. This and other meanings briefly as follow: 1. buying and selling without immediate payment. 2. a period of time allowed by a seller for payment. 3. the right-hand column of accounts, or payments received, etc. 4. a document issued by a seller to a buyer entitling him to credit his account with the seller by the sum stated.

credit, acceptance credit. Credit given to a large-scale trader of good standing by a bank or accepting house. The trader draws from this within time and finance limits. If the bill matures within the time limit set and is replaced by another, the arrangement is known as a 'revolving credit'. The provision of an acceptance credit usually involves the trader providing a 'letter of hypothecation' pledging the goods to the bank as security.

credit, documentary letter of credit. (International trade). A facility arranged by an importer (purchaser) for his bank, by means of a LETTER OF CREDIT to the ADVISING BANK of the exporter, to provide credit to pay the exporter (the supplier) on completion of the contract. *See* BELOW.

credit, documentary letter of credit, assignable credit. This arrangement provides for the payment to be made to the supplier's assigns in the event of liquidation.

credit, documentary letter of credit, confirmed credit. SITPRO. IRREVOCABLE letter of credit to which another bank (usually the ADVISING BANK) has added its undertaking on the instructions of the ISSUING BANK. This is in addition to the irrevocable undertaking of the letter.

credit, documentary letter of credit, divisible credit. A credit in favour of a middleman such as an export agent who may transfer the purchaser's money to a number of suppliers in the overseas country, e.g. who may have provided the goods making division according to what they have supplied.

credit, documentary letter of credit, irrevocable credit. SIT-PRO. abb. A letter of credit under which the issuing bank gives its irrevocable undertaking that payment will be made if all the terms of the letter of credit are met and the specified documents provided. This type of credit cannot be amended or cancelled without the beneficiary's consent. The date on which payment is due is crucial.

credit, documentary letter of credit, negotiable credit. In the case of a LETTER OF CREDIT, one in which a NEGOTIATING BANK can purchase the BILL OF EXCHANGE from the ADVISING BANK of the supplier.

credit, documentary letter of credit, revocable credit. SITPRO. One that can be cancelled or amended without prior notice to the beneficiary and is thus of little value to him.

credit, documentary letter of credit, transferable. SITPRO. One under which the original beneficiary has the right to instruct his bank (with which the letter of credit is available) to transfer it in whole or in part to a third party who is termed the 'second beneficiary'.

credit, documentary letter of credit, uniform customs, rules and practice. Standard rules for documentary credit issued by the INTERNATIONAL CHAMBER OF COMMERCE and adopted worldwide. Virtually all letters of credit issued nowadays are subject to these rules.

credit, factoring of credit. The provision of a financial facility by a supplier through a FACTOR who takes charge of the collection of debts from his customers.

credit note. The converse of an INVOICE and a means whereby one party to a transaction (such as a supplier) may make a settlement with another such (such a buyer) to liquidate an overcharge, pay a rebate, meet the value of goods which have been returned to the supplier, etc.

credit, roll-over credit. Extension of a loan by its renegotiation when the sum credited has been exhausted.

credit sale. One in which the purchaser either defers payment or may pay by instalments.

credit transfer. A method of payment by which a purchaser (for example) may transfer to the bank account of a supplier the money he owes without the use of a cheque.

creditors. CIMA. A person or entity to whom money is owed. *See also* DEBTOR.

critical path analysis. cf. CIMA. A

53

form of NETWORK ANALYSIS in which a sequence of operations and their interlinking or subsidiary or conditional operations are set out diagrammatically with times, sequence of operations and target dates leading to the final completion of the project, problem or process. Has wide application for construction and plant projects.

cryogenic. A term applied to low-temperature substances, apparatus, and processes.

cumulative delivery diagram. BS 4335. A curve or block diagram which shows the cumulative number of final products required for delivery in each time period of a manufacturing programme.

current assets. cf. CIMA. *See* ASSETS, CURRENT ASSETS.

current cost accounting (CCA). CIMA. A method of accounting requiring that assets (such as stock) shall be shown in terms of what they are worth to the enterprise at the time of review. Usually expressed in equivalent REPLACEMENT COST at that time.

current liabilities. Those liabilities which must be met within (usually) twelve months of the accounting year ahead.

current purchasing power. abb. CIMA. A method of accounting by which assets are valued at the current purchasing power of the 'present value' of what was originally spent on the asset.

current ratio. CIMA. An important accountancy ratio indicating to (for example) a purchasing officer the solvency (or otherwise) of a supplier.
Formula:
$$Cr = \frac{Ac}{Lc}$$
Where: Cr is current ratio
Ac is current assets
Lc is current liabilities
As a general rule a sound supplier has a ratio of at least 2:1 i.e. assets, twice liabilities. *See also* ACID TEST. *Also* CONTRACT, CONDITIONS OF CONTRACT *and* CONTRACT, TERMS OF CONTRACT.

curvilinear. The line of a graph which is curved. It may be random or display regular CHARACTERISTICS, such as for example an OGIVE, a FREQUENCY CURVE or HISTOGRAM, curve of acquisition costs in the formula for ECONOMIC ORDER QUANTITY. *See also* RECTILINEAR (STAT).

custom of a trade. A term in contracts implied by usage and custom, and/or in writing implying various meanings, practices or restrictions appropriate to that particular trade. *See also* DEALING, A COURSE OF DEALING.

customer. (n). One who is a purchaser (usually) in the domestic market, also one who buys regularly from a shop or other source.

customs. A general term for the DUTIES and TARIFFS imposed by an importing country. Also used for the officials and the office from which the Customs officers work.

customs, integrated tariff system ('taric') (EU). An integrated tariff system of the Union based upon the 'harmonised system of COMMODITY CODING'.

customs, single administrative document ('sad'). A single form introduced within the EU to contain no more than one type of Customs declaration on a single form and reduction of data requirements resulting in harmonisation of trade data. *See also* CLEARANCE, INWARDS and CLEARANCE, OUTWARDS.

cybernetics. The science of communication and control. Applied cybernetics is relevant to ERGONOMICS and especially to automation, such as computer programs for the control of automated storage handling equipment.

cycle, planning cycle. *See* PLANNING CYCLE.

cycle stock. *See* STOCK, CYCLE STOCK.

cycle time. BS 3138 (33004). The total time taken to complete the elements of a work cycle.

cyclical fluctuations. Periodic fluctuations in data which may vary at random, variable or fixed intervals on a time base. Can lead to loss in stock-control where over-ordering can lead to the build up of stock beyond needs, or stock can become OUT OF PHASE with production.

cyclical stock check. *See* STOCK CHECK, CYCLICAL.

D

D.R.P. Distribution Resource Planning.

damages. Money to be paid in compensation for injury, loss, or failure in respect of for example contract.

damages, liquidated damages. Monetary amounts agreed upon by the parties at the outset of a contract and calculated as recompense if the contract is not fulfilled. *See also* DAMAGES, UNLIQUIDATED *and* PENALTY CLAUSES.

damages, remote damages. Damages which are too remote from the execution of the contract and which might have been (and should have been) expected to be contemplated by the parties themselves when entering into the contract.

damages, unliquidated damages. Damages which were not assessed and agreed at the outset of a contract but were claimed by the plaintiff on breach by the other party (e.g. the supplier). A court will award what it considers REASONABLE compensation for 'actual loss' provided damages are not too REMOTE. (*Note:* A court will only award damages for loss which arises out of the breach of the contract itself and/or which could have been expected to have been contemplated by the parties themselves at the outset of the contract).

Dangerous Goods by Road Agreement (ADR). The European agreement for international carriage of goods by road in the EU. It provides for unhindered transits subject to: technical inspection, certification, packing and labelling, vehicle specification and plating, etc.

danger warning level. *See* STOCK CONTROL – LEVELS.

danger zone. (HS). Any zone within and/or around MACHINERY in which an EXPOSED PERSON is subject to a RISK to his health or safety.

data (stat.). A collection of observations, measurements, facts or other information. May be classified and statistically analysed in further stages. *See* **BS ISO 3534** 'STATISTICS, VOCABULARY AND SYMBOLS' for the full range of terminology covering this area. 'Data' is a plural noun.

data bank, data base. (IT). A collection of structured data which supports the operations of the whole, or of a major area of business such as purchasing and supply. The terms are also used to define a centrally located data file which provides the foundations for a computer-based management information system.

days of grace. *See* GRACE, DAYS OF.

dead carriage. *See* FREIGHT, DEAD FREIGHT.

dead freight. *See* FREIGHT, DEAD FREIGHT.

deadline. A definite date by which an action must be completed. TARGETS may be missed but a deadline, if quoted in a contract, is 'of the essence of the contract'. The contract can be deemed to be 'dead' if the deadline is missed.

dead stock. *See* STOCK, DEAD.

dead weight. Heavy goods paying freight by weight and not by volume of space occupied and frequently deployed as bottom cargo in a ship to maintain stability.

deal (n). A term normally reserved for financial transactions, or the result of 'hard bargaining' in a purchase contract situation.

dealer. A person who deals on his own account, and takes the risks of the market in buying and selling to other people.

dealing, 'a course of dealing'. A contractual situation in which a court may find that because of the long association of a buyer and seller both should by now be fully aware of the terms and conditions of contract and trading applied by each to the other.

debenture. A certificate given by Customs to an exporter or importer of goods liable to duty, and entitling him to receive drawback.

debit. 1. to charge for goods or services, etc. showing what is owed. 2. the bookkeeping entry which records a sum due.

debit note. The written document showing the amount by which the recipient's account shall be adjusted. e.g. a purchaser returning goods to a supplier seeking to offset a previous undercharge to his customer.

debtor. CIMA. A person or entity who owes money.

decentralisation. The organisation of smaller, usually specialised, management/administrative units to which are DELEGATED AUTHORITY. These may be manned by specialist staff who have functional responsibility. *See also* CENTRALISATION and SYNERGY

Decision, Community Decision. (EU) A ruling issued by the Community. 'Community 'decisions' are binding in their entirety on those to whom they are addressed, whether member States, companies or individuals. Decisions imposing financial obligations are enforceable in national courts.'

decision theory. (stat). The use of mathematical techniques to study alternative courses of action such as those of purchasing policies, stock control levels, etc. The techniques use the statistical characteristics of NORMAL DISTRIBUTION, STANDARD DEVIATION, etc.

decision tree. CIMA. A means of

clarifying and analysing management and practical choices, risks, objectives, gains and information. It can be used with or without monetary or other valuation, and is suitable for computerisation. At each stage a 'yes' or 'no' decision leads to a branch from a 'decision point' leading to either an 'outcome' or a 'stop'.

decision making unit. A 'unit' comprising a group or persons recognised as, and authorised to make and contribute to the making of decisions, e.g. a Supply Management Team.

deck cargo. Cargo not placed below deck. Special regulations apply to its transport.

de die in diem (law). From day to day.

deed (law). A written signed document under seal in a special form that is used to pass legal title of 'real' property from one person to another, so that the public may know who holds the title to the property.

de facto. As a matter of fact.

defect. *See also* QUALITY CONTROL-DEFECT.

defect, latent defect. A hidden defect which could not be revealed by reasonable inspection. The purchaser is protected by the law if the latent defect is revealed later.

de jure (law). As a matter of right.

del credere agent. See AGENT, DEL CREDERE.

delegation. (adm). The process of entrusting AUTHORITY and RESPONSIBILITY to others in a way which enables them to make the decisions their superior would otherwise make, as opposed to merely carrying out the superior's detailed instructions. The subordinate is RESPONSIBLE to the superior for the results achieved while the superior in turn is ACCOUNTABLE to his own boss for what the subordinate does. [abb. IM]

delimitation. The share of a market (based on previous sales) allocated to the member of a cartel or trade association.

deliverable state. Goods are in a deliverable state statutorily when they are in such a state that the buyer would, under the contract, be bound to take delivery of them.

delivered (at) frontier, named place of delivery at frontier. INCOTERM. Seller's obligations end when he has, at his own risk and cost, delivered the goods at the intake side of the frontier post.

delivered, duty paid, named destination in country of importation. INCOTERM. Seller bears all risks and costs including duties through to destination in country of importation.

delivery 1. The voluntary transfer of possession from one person to another. 2. The act of delivering.

3. The time taken, or required, for the shipment of goods. *Note:* Recommendation by National Economic Development Council: 'Delivery' should be interpreted by suppliers and purchasers as the date when RECEIPT is required at the location of the purchaser. 'Despatch' should always be interpreted as the date when the goods LEAVE a specified location.

delivery note. A document used when a supplier delivers by his own vehicle. Like a CONSIGNMENT NOTE, its endorsement with the CONSIGNEE'S signature is evidence that the goods have been safely delivered. For local deliveries, the delivery note only may be used without a posted ADVICE NOTE.

delivery order. Instructions given by the owner of goods lodged in a warehouse, dock or wharf, etc, and instructing the person acting as bailee and the person holding the documents of title to hand over the goods defined to a person named on the order.

delivery terms, **warehousing.** The following terms are used in warehousing and similar trades: 'forward goods', delivery of future goods; 'near goods', those which will be ready in the near future; 'to arrive', goods are in transit and will be delivered as soon as they arrive; 'prompt', goods will be shipped in a few days; 'ready', goods are in stock at the time of receipt of customer's order.

Delphi technique. (adm). A procedure for arriving at a consensus of opinions among a group of experts who are given a detailed questionnaire about a problem. Each member of the group produces written answers. Everyone reads the answers of the other participants. In the light of the other responses ideas may be revised. Eventually a consensus should emerge. The consensus may be used to formulate development or change.

demand. The requirements called for by production or a process. *Note:* This may not be the same as actual issues or usage.

demand, aggregate demand. (econ). The total demand within a national economy for all goods and services. In purchasing and supply, total demand includes the same economic area within the ambit of the particular purchasing and supply organisation under review.

demand, complementary. A feature of most industries where commodities are interdependent with the production processes, e.g. welding rods needed to complete the fabrication of steel tanks.

demand, composite. (econ). Where a commodity can be used for more than one purpose in an enterprise, e.g. lubricants used in a machine shop, transport vehicles, handling equipment, lifts, air conditioning, etc, equivalent to 'common user' demand.

demand, contingency. Allowances

in provisioning where usage may be dependent upon contingencies which are predictable (e.g. seasonal) or unpredictable, (e.g. storm or tempest, etc.)

demand, forecast. A forecast of future orders for a product.

demand, inelastic demand. (econ). The situation where a large change in price only induces a small change in demand. See also SUPPLY: INELASTIC SUPPLY.

demand pattern. BS 5191 (21006). A time-based representation of past demands, which may be from a number of sources, and may be analysed into the following elements: 1. trend, the general direction in which demand is changing over a period of time; 2. cyclic, the oscillations about a trend of demand. The period of these cycles may be related to the calendar seasons; 3. random variation, the unpredictable element in the demand pattern.

demand, statistical demand characteristics. Trends (rising, falling, level), predictable, unpredictable, regular, irregular, exceptional, secular, long term, short term, discrete, etc.

demand, supplementary demand. Where commodities are required in addition to actual production of final product. Viz. spares for customers; samples for marketing; allowance for rejects, scrap and wastage, pilferage, etc.

demand, supplies demand, characteristics of. A vital aspect of supplies management the analysis of which is essential for the establishment of purchasing and stock-control policies and their administration.

demurrage. A charge made for detaining a vehicle, ship or container beyond a specified time.

denomination of quantity. *See* UNIT OF ISSUE.

de novo. Anew, from the beginning.

departmentalism. (adm). A flaw in ADMINISTRATION or MANAGEMENT in which a department is found to freeze into an isolated unit. It may build up mutual suspicion and hostility with other parts of an enterprise.

deposit. (n). A sum of paid to a supplier: 1. paid (or set aside) as security. 2. as a first instalment of total price. 3. to assist the CASH FLOW of the supplier to set up and/or start work. 4. materials which may be ARISINGS from the processes of production. Frequently referred to in connection with ENVIRONMENTAL CONTROL of POLLUTION, TOXICITY, etc.

depreciation. CIMA. The measure of 'wearing out', consumption or other loss of value of a FIXED ASSET whether from use, passage of time or OBSOLESCENCE through technology and (or) market changes.

depreciation, accelerated depreciation. Depreciation of plant or equipment at a faster rate than planned or normal for that type of plant or equipment. [This is a factor which may need to be taken into account when purchasing plant and equipment which is to be subjected to frequent OVERLOAD or work in exceptionally arduous conditions.]

depreciation, accumulated depreciation. The amount which has been written off the value of plant or equipment at a certain specified date in its useful LIFE CYCLE. [May be a factor for negotiation and investigation when buying or taking over used plant and equipment.]

depreciation, straight line depreciation. An agreed value of an asset which is written off over its life cycle by equal amounts each year against profits from the asset.

deregulation. (EU). The 'reduction of the burden of regulation and the improvement of the business environment'. The Deregulation Unit of the Department of Trade and Industry checks that all United Kingdom legislation, whether 'domestic', 'Community' or 'international' (e.g. UN, NATO etc) in origin is implemented effectively and not officiously.' Contact dti. 'Deregulation Unit'.

design. BS 4778 (Pt.1. (7.1)). The process of task recognition and problem-solving with the object of fulfilling needs by the creation of products and services.

design. BS 7000. Guide to managing product design. **PD 6470** Management of Design for Economic Production. Aims: standardisation to improve performance of electrical and mechanical manufacturing sectors.' *See also* COMPUTER AIDED DESIGN (CAD)

design change. BS 5191 (12012). A change in the specification of a product which generally results in the issue of an amended drawing but does not normally result in a new product, e.g. the introduction of a different thread form in a particular product, or an alteration in tolerances on a machined part.

despatch. *See* DELIVERY.

despatch documents. *See* ADVICE NOTE, DELIVERY NOTE, CONSIGNMENT NOTE, PACKING NOTE, CONTENTS NOTE, INVOICE.

despatch money. *See* DISPATCH MONEY.

despatch note. BS 5191 (43005). A document recording that products are available for despatch and authorising arrangements for delivery.

despatch note, Customs despatch note. A Customs document sent with goods that are subject to import duty at the port of destination and issued by Customs at the port of shipment. The 'despatch note' must be presented to Customs at the port of arrival.

deterministic systems. *See* under PROBABILISTIC SYSTEMS.

61

detinue. Action at law to make the possessor of goods deliver them up to the rightful owner.

development (OECD). 'Use of scientific or technical knowledge in order to produce new or substantially improved materials, devices or products, to install new processes, systems or services prior to the commencement of commercial production or commercial applications, or to improve substantially those already produced or installed'.

development cost. *See* COST, DEVELOPMENT COST.

developed market economy countries. UN. The affluent, highly industrialised countries operating under an economic system in which the private sector plays the major role.

deviation. Statistical deviation refers to the difference between a point (event, etc.) and a fixed value. Usually it relates to deviation of an observed figure from a common MEAN. *See also* STANDARD DEVIATION.

dies non. A day upon which for some reason no business is transacted.

differential cost analysis (DCA). A system under which the probable costs of alternative schemes are prepared and compared. BREAK-EVEN ANALYSIS may be used for this.

diminishing returns, rule of, in supplies. An economic rule whereby progressively smaller reductions in price are available as larger quantities are purchased, after a certain level is reached. The rule may be upset in industrial purchasing owing to a number of factors such as: change in production method, or plant, standardisations, etc. *See also* LEARNING CURVE.

dip rod, measurement by dip rod. A means of measuring quantities of fluid in storage vessels. A dip rod is a 'measuring instrument' and NOT a measure. *See Eric Gnapp v the Petroleum Board (1949).*

directives. (EU). An instruction from the EU to member states to change their laws through the normal processes of parliament. *See also* REGULATION – EU.

direct materials costs. CIMA. *See* COSTS, DIRECT MATERIALS COSTS *and* MATERIALS, DIRECT MATERIALS.

direct materials usage variance. cf. CIMA. That portion of direct materials costs variance which is the difference between the standard quantity specified for the production achieved, whether completed or not, and the actual quantity used, both valued at STANDARD PRICES.

dirty bill. *See* BILL OF LADING.

discharge of contract. *See* CONTRACT, DISCHARGE OF CONTRACT'.

discount. An allowance (usually a percentage) on an amount, (usually) a purchase price, sale price, etc.

discount, at a discount. Something bought below the nominal value, or depreciated.

discounted cash flow. Evaluates the future net cash flows generated by a project or plant during its expected LIFE-CYCLE by DIS-COUNTING THEM BACK to their present-day value. The two common methods are: 1. calculation of the YIELD determining the internal rate of return (IRR) as a percentage. 2. calculation of net present value (NP). In this case a suitable discount rate is chosen and a monetary result is obtained.

discounting back (and gross present value) (GPV). Discounting back (as distinct from COM-POUNDING) gives the sum of the total gross expected income from the investment in a project, or plant, etc. It estimates the 'time value' of money. That is to say, the investment today which involves expenditure of capital which is sacrificed from other purposes in the hope of future profit. Dis-counting back is calculated over the expected LIFE-CYCLE of the plant. The sum obtained is the amount accruing in the future expressed in present-day terms at the time of the investment. When all expected net CASH-FLOWS have been discounted (discount tables may be used) and summed, the gross present value (GPV) results from these calculations.

discount, banker's discount. The amount charged on the face value of a bill by a banker for discount-ing it, i.e. for paying money upon it before it is due.

discount, bill of exchange, discounting of. On a BILL OF EXCHANGE the difference between the full amount of the bill and lower amount accepted by a seller – or creditor.

discount, cash (commercial discount). The amount of discount allowed between traders on cash transactions between them. e.g. on CASH AND CARRY. See also DISCOUNT, REBATE, PROMPT CASH, ORDERS AND CONTRACTS.

discount, cumulative discount. MULTIPLE DISCOUNTS which are added together before being applied to a price structure. e.g. two discounts, one for (say) bulk quantity of 10% and also one for special transportation arrange-ments of (say) 5%.
Cumulatively:£100 − 15%=£85
(*But see* DISCOUNTS, SEQUENTIAL DISCOUNTS.)

discount, loyalty discount. A special discount given by a supplier to a purchaser in return for an agree-ment to confine purchases in full (or in an agreed proportion of total intake) to that supplier. *See also* REBATE, LOYALTY REBATE.

discounts, multiple discounts. The allowance of more than one discount on an account. It is important to agree, when nego-tiating, whether discounts are

SEQUENTIAL or CUMULA-TIVE.

discount, prompt cash settlement. Special discount allowed on settlement of accounts promptly. (Usually in 7–14 days).

discount, quantity discount. Discount given by a supplier in consideration of the size of order placed by the purchaser.

discount register. A purchasing department record showing discounts, rebates and settlement terms agreed with suppliers. Usually kept as a confidential record. *See also* RECORDS, PURCHASING.

discount, resale discount ('trade discount'). The discount allowed by one business to another which buys in order to re-sell by way of trade. e.g. the discount given by a wholesaler to a retailer.

discount, retrospective discount. An arrangement whereby the discount allowed in a given period is based on the amount of business done in the previous period. *Note:* This form of discount may result in a 'windfall' profit (or loss) to either party in the year it is given.

discounts, sequential discounts. MULTIPLE DISCOUNTS which are applied one after the other in sequence. e.g. (*See also* CUMULATIVE DISCOUNT) example. £100 − 10% − 5%
  £100 − 10% = £90
  £90 − 5% = £85.50.

discount, settlement discount. A discount given at settlement of accounts, e.g. PROMPT CASH, to encourage prompt payments of accounts by the purchaser.

discount, sliding scale. A discount which increases with the size of order placed allowed by a supplier to a buyer.

discount, trade. The discount on price allowed by one supplier to another in the same trade. *See* DISCOUNT, RESALE DISCOUNT.

discounted cash flow. *See* CASH FLOW: DISCOUNTED CASH FLOW.

discrepancy. Variation or actual difference between a stated fact or claim and the actual. e.g. difference between quantity advised and received, actual price and that quoted, estimated or forecast, etc.

discrimination. A differentiation in which some purchasers are given preference over others.

dispatch money. Payment by way of a bonus for loading or discharging a vessel in less time than that stated on the charter party. Generally based upon a set figure per day.

display screen equipment (VDUs), Directive (90/270EEC). UK Regulations wef 1.1.1993, employers to: assess risks and take appropriate action, ensure that work stations meet requirements in the annex to the Directive, provide information and training, plan work activities with periodic changes and breaks, give workers entitlement to eyesight tests.

disposal instructions. BS 3811 (5102). The document that describes in detail the method and precautions to be observed in discarding or otherwise disposing of material, plant and equipment when it has failed or is no longer required for any reason.

distrainor. Person who brings an action for distraint.

distraint. The seizure of goods for debt.

distress. In law, the act of distraining goods for debt.

distribution cost. *See* COSTS, DISTRIBUTION COST.

distribution, supplies, distribution of. The process of movement of supplies from location to location by any method of transportation, but usually applied to movement by road or rail.

distribution system. An organisation of administrative procedures, transport, handling, storage and user facilities through which supplies move from a point of origin to user(s). *See also* LOGISTICS.

distribution time. The period of time between the despatch date from the manufacturer and the delivery date to the customer.

distributor. A MIDDLEMAN engaged in the distribution of a category of goods, (especially) in a specific territory and of goods made (or supplied by) a particular enterprise. *See also* AGENTS.

dis-utility. A term sometimes used to express the result of intake of defective, sub-standard (etc.) supplies, or the indications from a VALUE ANALYSIS, COST-BENEFIT or other study.

diversification. The converse of SPECIALISATION. The action of an enterprise to vary (products, operations, etc.) in order to spread risk, expand sales, etc.

dock. 1. a space or artificial basin with water (usually) impounded to high tide level for reception of water-born craft. 2. a raised platform of suitable height for the loading and unloading of rail or road vehicles.

docket. Slips, tickets or forms.

dock dues. The tolls levied on vessels entering and leaving port.

dock pass. Certificate given by harbour authorities to the ship-master on payment of all dock dues.

dock warrant. A document of title given to the owner of goods stored in a dock warehouse.

documentary credit. *See* CREDIT, DOCUMENTARY.

documentation, export/import (aligned). SITPRO. International trade documentation based upon United Nations agreed formats and used in the UK and world-wide. Can be produced from a single master document in association with office copiers, duplicators, WORD PROCESSORS and computers, etc.

documents of record. Written documents, such as those concerning a transaction, e.g. purchase orders, and which may be used as legal evidence, in a contract.

document of title. *See* TITLE, DOCUMENT OF TITLE.

down time. BS 5191 (26008). The period of time in which a workstation is not available for production due to a functional failure. *See also* WAITING TIME *and* IDLE TIME.

draft. 1. An order by which money is drawn from a bank. 2. The money thus drawn. 3. Bill of exchange or cheque drawn by one bank on another for the transfer of money.

draught. The depth of water needed to float a vessel.

drawback. 1. Excise drawback; refunds made when excise duties are returned to the owner of goods on which excise duties have already been paid. 2. 'Customs drawback'; import duties returned to the owner of imported goods which are being re-exported, viz. after treatment, processing or repair, etc.

drawee. SITPRO. The party on whom a bill of exchange (draft) is drawn.

drawer. SITPRO. The party who draws a bill of exchange (a draft).

drawings. SITPRO. Separate presentations of documents under a letter of credit.

draw-off order. *See* ORDERS, DRAW OFF ORDERS.

driver of machinery. (EU) (HS). An operator responsible for the movement of MACHINERY. The driver may be transported by the machinery or may be on foot, accompanying the machinery, or may be guiding it by remote control (cables, radio, etc.) (EC directive 'mobile machinery & lifting equipment.') bibl: [DTI MOBILE MCY & LIFTING EQUIPT 2nd ed. 1991].

'drop shipment' (wholesaling). A shipment made direct from supplier to the customer of a wholesaler without passing physically through the hands of the wholesaler.

due care. That standard of conduct exercised by an ordinary reasonable and prudent person.

due date 'maturity'. SITPRO. The date upon which an accepted usance (time or terms) bill of exchange becomes due for payment under letter of credit arrangements.

dues, harbour dues. *See* DOCK DUES.

dues in. Quantities due to be received against a purchase or production order. In the case of stock *see* STOCK, DUES-IN.

dues out. Quantities due to be issued against known future demands such as production schedules, or the balance of requisitions which have not been met in full and for which a BACK ORDER (STORES) has been raised.

dumping. Selling abroad at prices below the normal value. EU Regulations define this value and set out how it is to be determined – usually the price charged for comparable sales in the country of origin.

dunnage. Wood or other material in strips or blocks, etc. used to separate cargo or goods so as to raise it from the ground, provide ventilation, protect it from other goods or from rising damp, and/or to give space for entry of forks of lift trucks, etc.

duopoly. A near-monopoly situation where there are only two suppliers in the market.

dusts-mobile machinery and lifting equipment directive. (EU). Where MACHINERY may emit dust or gases, suitable containment precautions must be taken. *See also* dti MACHINERY SAFETY BOOKLET. *See also* FIRE.

Dutch auction. *See* AUCTION, DUTCH

duty, customs duty. Duty levied on imports either to raise revenue or to protect home industry.

duty, excise duty. Tax on goods manufactured in home country for revenue purposes.

duty of care. *See* CARE, DUTY OF.

duty free. Goods on which customs or excise duties are not levied.

duty, specific duty. Customs duty at a specific rate per unit weight, volume or other measure.

dynamics. The study of forces which produce, or tend to produce, motion.

67

E

E.D.I. Electronic Data Interchange.

earmarked stock. *See* STOCK, ALLO-CATED.

East European Trade Council. A council in London established to facilitate trade with the Eastern bloc. (Refer to Department of Trade and Industry, Europe Division, Kingsgate House, London SW1E 6SW).

'ECO labelling'. (EU). A scheme for Community-wide positive labelling of consumer goods which are 'environmentally friendly'. The scheme is part of general strategy to reduce pollution and waste caused by consumer goods. Basic objectives are to: define the criteria by which to judge a product; encourage manufacturers to develop products which reach those standards; provide consumers with a guide to such products; encourage 'consumer awareness' of 'environmental control, ecological disciplines, etc. The United Kingdom 'ECO Labelling Board' was set up under Statutory Instrument SI 1992:2383. It receives and determines applications for use of the ECO label from manufacturers and importers. It also develops criteria and promotes the scheme in the UK.

ecologistics. A philosophy which attempts to transform manufacturing companies' existing processes to comply with and surpass the values of environmentally conscious consumers. It does this through a set of practical guidelines. [Dr Mattyhew 'An ecological way forward', The MFg Engineer vol. 72 No.3

The 'EC mark' ('CE'). (EU). A mark which, when applied to a product, signifies that 'it is presumed to be such that it may be supplied lawfully unless there are reasonable grounds for suspecting the contrary, or that requirements for affixing the EC mark have not been observed'. The EC mark consists of the symbol CE and is to be accompanied by the last two digits of the year in which the mark is applied, and (where applicable) the distinguishing number assigned by the Commission to the approved body responsible for verification and for Community surveillance. Before the EC mark may be applied, an approved body must issue an EC VERIFICATION CERTIFICATE and has the responsibility for the application of the EC Mark to every article covered by the CERTIFICATE OF CONFORMITY. Where a manufacturer has obtained an EC CERTIFICATE OF CONFORMITY he may apply the EC mark to any article covered by the certificate. BSI offer through their European Information Service, advice on 'CE marking' also on Community Directives, Standards and approval requirements worldwide.

economics. The study of natural resources, how they are obtained, manipulated and distributed along with the wealth that goes with them. 'Macroeconomics' is largely concerned with the total economy of a country, 'microeconomics' with the components of the total economics of specific firms within the economy.

economic order quantity. *See* QUANTITY, ECONOMIC ORDER.

economy, centrally planned economy. The economic systems of such economies (as the former Eastern block) based on a system which requires close control of the system in the absence of normal MARKET FORCES.

economy, mixed economy. One in which the means of production and the provision of services, particularly within the INFRASTRUCTURE, are partly in private hands or in public ownership.

economy, national economy. The means of, and systems for, production and distribution of the needs (material and services) of a society within the area of State boundaries. Involves the infrastructure and financial structure of the area i.e. the 'macro-economy'.

economy, price. *See* PRICE ECONOMIC.

ECU, the ECU. *See* EUROPEAN CURRENCY UNIT.

edifact. The United Nations standard under which much ELECTRONIC DATA INTERCHANGE operates.

elastic demand. Demand is said to be 'elastic' when a small change in price results in a large change in demand. *See also* ELASTIC SUPPLY.

elastic supply. Supply is said to be elastic when a small change in price results in a large change in supply. *See also* ELASTIC DEMAND. *Note:* This and similar rules of 'supply and demand' do not always apply to industrial purchasing and supply because demands are usually pre-determined by other factors, e.g. sales and production needs, and, not solely by market forces.

electronic data interchange, 'EDI'. The electronic transfer of information between linked computer systems. e.g. the direct communication of purchase order instructions between purchaser and seller may be automatically actuated by FEEDBACK from STOCK CONTROL LEVELS or production demands.

electronic transfer of data 'ETD'. The transmission and receipt of information by electronic means.

embodiment materials. Materials which will be incorporated into some product to be manufactured and which the buying organisation will then sell on.

endorse. To sign the back of a bill of exchange, promissory note, cheque, warrant, delivery order, etc. The person signing it is termed the 'endorsee'.

end-product. The final result of a process of manufacture. This may or may not be a finished product but it may become the raw material for further production or process.

energy (E). The capacity for doing work by a body of matter (e.g. a moving object) or a system (e.g. a stretched spring) The energy capacity is expressed in 'joules'. *See also* ENERGY – KINETIC ENERGY *and also* ENERGY, POTENTIAL ENERGY.

energy, kinetic energy (HS). Energy ('T') derived from the motion of an object or quantity of substance. Formula: $T = \frac{1}{2} mv^2$
Where: T is kinetic energy
      m is mass of the moving object
      v is the velocity of the moving object at the instant of calculation
[Speed control is vital on all mobile stores – and other handling equipment. Stored kinetic energy delivered due to collision (or sudden stoppage) is proportional to the square of the velocity at the instant of impact or other violent stoppage.]

energy management. BS 3811 (3504). The management of the storage, conversion, distribution and utilisation of energy directed to the economic provision of required services and the elimination of avoidable losses.

energy, potential energy. Energy from the position of an object (or a substance such as a liquid) due to

its elevated position. [e.g. dangers from objects stacked insecurely at high level, tanks of liquid feeding inadequate pipework at lower levels, etc.]

enquiry. An invitation to a supplier to submit prices for goods or services by estimate, quotation or tender. *See also* INQUIRY.

enterprise, an. A term describing any commercial or industrial business venture including those in the private, public and worker-cooperative sectors of an economy. (This term is preferred by some to the term 'undertaking' as describing a 'venture, especially one calling for determination and initiative' (Larousse)).

entrepot trade. Trade through a trading centre or port which is imported and re-exported without incurring duty.

environment, the environment. 'Surroundings. Particularly the influences which may affect growth, development, existence of living things.' (Dictionary definition). In the context of purchasing and supply the term 'environment' has a number of important implications. 1. compliance with Statutory laws, Directives, Codes of Practice, etc. relating to health and safety of those who may come into contact with supplies and services which have been procured. 2. the ambient conditions in the environment in which goods are stored. 3. the possibilities of pollution arising from processes, handling or storage of supplies.

Relevant British Standards include the following: **BS 7083** Working environment computer equipment. **BS DD202.** ergonomic principles, work systems design. **BS 6751** machine tools, environmental protection. **BS 5967. pt. 1.** Temperature, pressure, humidity conditions. **BS 5967. pt. 4.** corrosive/erosive environments **BS 6069** Workplace atmospheres. [der.: Hippocrates in the 5th century BC enunciated the doctrine which stressed the influence of the environment on man, the reverse of the modern doctrine to which industry is subjected, namely the influence of man upon the environment].

environmental cleanliness, *see also* **Dust collectors**, clean rooms, **BS 5295.**

environmental control code of conduct. Abb. Extracts from Institute of Management publication dated 11/92 ref. Cl.5: as regards UK society and environment. 'a. Have regard to short and long term effects and possible consequences within society of present and proposed actions. d. Seek to conserve resources whenever possible, especially those which are non-renewable. e. Seek to avoid destruction of resources by pollution and have a contingency plan for limiting destruction in the event of disaster.' 6. As regards overseas societies and the environment: 'a. Be aware of management implications of global environmental issues. b. Decline to solve UK problems of pollution and

processes by their export unchanged to the detriment of quality of life of other societies. d. Respect the customs, practices and reasonable ambitions of other peoples.' [*See also* CARE, DUTY OF.]

environmental control standards, BS 7750. This standard specifies the elements of an environmental management system. In effect it extends the principles of **BS 5750** to cover environmental management requirements. *See also* **BS 7527** Classification of Environmental Conditions.

environmental declaration. (EU). **10/74.** A declaration by members of the Community to: a. preserve, protect, improve the quality of the environment; b. protect human health; c. ensure prudent and rational use of natural resources; d. take preventative action to repair damage at source; e. ensure the polluter shall pay.

environmental engineering, *see* NOISE (ENVIRONMENTAL), NOISE CONTROL (ACOUSTIC), OPERATING STATIONS, SANITARY ENGINEERING; WATER SUPPLY.

environment directives. (EU). There are over three hundred and fifty Directives, Regulations, and Decisions in force at the time of preparing these notes. They include *inter alia* assessments, storage of HAZARDOUS SUBSTANCES and public access to information.

environment, 'Environmental Protection Agency' (EPA). An agency operating in the United States to encourage the safeguarding of the environment. The Agency issues certificates of merit to firms which achieve good effective results in environmental control.

Environment Protection Act 1990. (HS). Section 33 of this Act (*inter alia*) makes it illegal to 'treat, keep or dispose of, CONTROLLED WASTES in a manner likely to cause pollution to the environment or harm to human life.' H & S. *See* WASTE.

EOQ. *See* ECONOMIC ORDER QUANTITY.

ergonomics. The study of the physical relationships between operatives and machines. Objectives are: reduction of strain, discomfort, and fatigue to the operative. These objectives are achieved by the application of CYBERNETIC principles to layout of controls, and the ergonomical and physical design and layout for the posture of the operative. Results should include increased productivity, improved job satisfaction and morale. British standards: Design of work systems **DD 202**. Design and selection of office furniture **BS 3044**. Standards & guidelines for designers **PP 7317**. Visual display terminals, design and use in offices **BS 7179**.

escalation clause. A clause in a contract which permits a seller to adjust his price in the event of market changes. *Note:* In normal times care should be taken to ensure that the clause also covers any fall in costs. *See also* CONTRACT PRICE ADJUSTMENT.

estimate. 1. An (approximate) calculation of the charges or cost. 2. Judgement made by calculation, especially from incomplete data, rough or incomplete calculation. *See also* QUOTATION.

estoppel. (law). Implies that owing to an action by one party, another party is prevented or stopped from completing a task, contract, etc.

ETD. *See* ELECTRONIC TRANSFER OF DATA.

ethics. The theory relating to morality of behaviour. Ethical Standards cover conforming with an accepted standard of good behaviour, e.g. in a profession such as purchasing and supply.

ethics in management. CODE OF CONDUCT of the INSTITUTE OF MANAGEMENT (abb.) A code of practice which embodies a number of principles which are relevant to purchasing and supply administration and management. a. to ensure the interests of others are properly identified and responded to in a balanced manner; b. establish and develop a continuing and satisfactory relationship based on mutual confidence; c. avoid entering into arrangements which unlawfully or improperly affect competitive practice; d. neither offer nor accept any gift, favour or hospitality intended as, or having the effect of, bribery or corruption. Also from Clause 1: g. openly declare any personal interest which might be seen to influence managerial decisions'. *See also* ENVIRONMENTAL CONTROL, CODE OF CONDUCT.

ethics, in supplies activities. The code of behaviour considered to be appropriate to the functions of those engaged in obtaining and administration of supplies. *See* the ethical code of the chartered institute of purchasing and supply, currently under review.

'Eurocheque' scheme (EU). An interbank scheme whereby cheque cards and bankers cards may be used by their holders to make withdrawals within certain specified limits from those continental banks which co-operate in the scheme, within the EU.

Europatents. Patents valid throughout the EU granted by the European Patents Office.

European Committee for Electrotechnical Standardisation 'CENELEC'. (BSI). Western European regional standards organisation comprising the International Electrotechnical Commission IEC, and national committees of the EC and EFTA countries. The UK member, the British Electrotechnical Committee is the European Council of the BSI. *See also* CEN.

European Committee for Standardisation (CEN). European regional standards organisation comprising the national standards bodies (members of the *International Organisation for Standardisation ISO*) of the *EC* and *EFTA* countries. *BSI* is the UK member.

European Community (EC).. The 'community' of European States set up under the Treaty of Rome (1957). Prior to 1985 the Community was styled the 'European Economic Community' and the 'Common Market', and subsequently the 'European Community' (The EC). Finally w.e.f. November 1st 1993, under the Treaty of Maastricht the adopted title became The European Union (The EU). At the time of writing the Community has twelve member States which have agreed to share a measure of their sovereignty in order to develop common policies where joint action will benefit all, with the aim of full integration of policy set by the Single European Act in 1992. The Community is controlled by an elected Parliament and Council of Ministers and served by a Commission. There is a court of Justice and a Court of Auditors. Its Economic and Social Committees act in an advisory capacity. (Full details from: The Information Office of the European Parliament, 2 Queen Anne's Gate, London, SW1H 9AA and the Commission of the European Union, 8 Storey's Gate, London SW1P 3AT.) *See also* DIRECTIVES, EC and REGULATIONS, EC.

European Community Competition rules. Rules set down by the

Treaty of Rome aimed at ensuring equality of treatment of organisations throughout the Community.

European Currency Unit (the ECU). 'The ECU is a basket of currencies but can be regarded as money in most respects, since it is a means of payment, a medium of exchange and a store of value. The value of the ECU is calculated as the sum of the set amounts of the Community currencies within it. These amounts are set broadly to reflect each country's relative economic size in terms of gross national product and the importance of its trade within the Community. They also take into account each country's access to short-term finance within the European Monetary System – the 'EMS'. (HM Treasury).

European Economic Area Agreement (EC). An agreement (pending) to strengthen trade and relations between the Community and the European Free Trade Area ('EFTA') – EFTA's members are: Austria, Finland, Iceland, Liechtenstein, Norway, Sweden and Switzerland. Implications for purchasing and supply: 1. Free movement of goods, services, capital, people. 2. Co-operation on: 2.1. Research and development. 2.2. Simplification of trading procedures. 2.3. Common technical and safety regulations. 2.4. Open public purchasing policy. 2.5. Control of behaviour of State monopolies. 2.6. Harmonisation of STANDARDS. 2.7. Customs formalities by random checks and EDT. 2.8. Extension of competition rules over whole area. *Note:* Border controls will remain EC and EFTA. EFTA will not adopt EC common Customs tariff at the time of writing.

European Free Trade Association ('EFTA'). A European free trade association established in 1960 to eliminate trade tariffs between member States. Has close links with the European Community.

European Monetary Fund (EMF). A fund to be set up as a reserve asset and means of settlement of account via the European Currency Unit.

European Monetary System (EMS). A system to create a zone of monetary stability in Europe through the implementation of controlled exchange rates, credit and resource transfer policies. UK is not a member at the time of preparing this edition.

European Journal: 'The Official Journal of the European Communities.' The 'Journal' – available in the UK from the HMSO – contains DECISIONS, DIRECTIVES, OPINIONS, RECOMMENDATIONS, and REGULATIONS. These all become 'official' when published in the 'Journal'.

European Standards (EN) (BSI). CEN or CENELEC standards implemented by CEN/CENELEC members who adopt them as identical national standard and withdrawing any conflicting national standard. *See also*

HARMONISATION DOCUMENT *and* CEN/CENELEC.

European Union, The (EU). The formation of the European Union arose from the Treaty of Maastricht and took effect on the first of November 1993. The Union is a multi-pillar structure which confers European citizenship on all citizens of the Union, and which incorporates the European Community with its supra-national institutions. THE COMMISSION, THE EUROPEAN PARLIAMENT and the EUROPEAN COURT, together with arrangements for intergovernmental co-operation in foreign affairs and matters of justice.

evidence accounts. A formalised system in trading with the Eastern bloc whereby a record is maintained by the 'FTO' (or an appointed bank) through which all the transactions will pass or to whom details will be notified and verified.

examination. To look very carefully and closely (but *see also* INSPECTION) to discover evident facts, mistakes or, for example, evident damage of goods received at intake following an initial check of the condition of the package in which the goods were received. *See also* QUESTIONING TECHNIQUE **BS 3138,** INSPECTION **BS 4778** *and* INQUIRY.

exception principle. cf. CIMA. The analysis of what is wrong, difficult, important or exceptional. *See* MANAGEMENT BY EXCEPTION.

'exception principle' (in 'Information Technology'). The exception principle is important in INFORMATION TECHNOLOGY and INFORMATION PROCESSING. In applications, particularly where associated with FEEDBACK, the volume of recorded data may be reduced by 'exceptions'. For example: 'demand changes', 'quality failure', etc. can be 'reported' (see below). This can eliminate vast volumes of data which are 'unexceptional' and upon which no management or administrative decisions are needed.

exception reporting. An important asset resulting from EDP is the ability of a computer (when given a suitable program) to report exceptional events, trends, demands, [such as demands for supply, production outputs, etc.] also quality data. Such 'reporting' can then act through FEEDBACK to correct any digression/diversion from the plan or programmes which is in operation.

excess stock. BS 5191. *See* STOCK, EXCESS *and* STOCK LEVEL, MAXIMUM.

exchange. A place where merchants and dealers meet to transact business.

exchange, bill of. *See* BILL OF EXCHANGE.

exchange, commodity exchanges. *See* MARKETS.

exchange, futures exchange. *See* MARKET, FUTURES MARKET.

exchange, market. *See* MARKET, FUTURES MARKET.

exemptions, 'negative clearance'. (EC). Negative clearance is an individual exemption granted by the Commission in respect of an article of Community enactments. *See also* COMFORT LETTER.

exhaust bin level. *See* STOCK LEVEL, EXHAUST LEVEL.

exclusion clause. *See* CONTRACT, EXCLUSION CLAUSE IN CONTRACT.

expediting. A term adopted from the USA as a synonym for PROGRESSING or progress chasing. Expediting may be active. 'Chasing' is implicitly reactive.

expeditor. One who expedites.

expendable supplies. *See* SUPPLIES, CONSUMABLE SUPPLIES.

expert systems. (it). A computer program that imitates a human expert.

explosion. The listing of the various component parts of an assembly, including the quantities of each component.

explosives. *See* SUBSTANCES.

exposed person. (HS). Any person wholly or partially in a DANGER ZONE.

exposure limit, maximum, personal. (HS). The maximum concentration of an airborne substance, averaged over a stated period, beyond which may be hazardous by INHALATION. Levels of concentration. See Schedule 3 of COSHH. bibl: HSE. Occupation exposure limits ISBN 0 11 882080.

exponential. A mathematical expression associated with growth (or decay) and the power (e.g. ^{n}) to which a function (e.g. 'Aa'') is raised. Thus $= A(axaxa. \ldots a^{(n)})$ is an instance where 'n' is the 'exponent' to which the function 'Aa'' is raised. *See* EXPONENTIALLY SMOOTHED FORECAST.

exponentially smoothed forecast. Such a forecast is made by using an exponentially weighted moving average (mean) (acronym "EWMA') which can place more emphasis on recent or earlier data by means of a smoothing constant 'a' (see below)

$Fnp = Ftp + a(Atp - Ftp)$
Where :
> Fnp is the forecast for next period
> Ftp was the forecast for this period
> Atp is the actual data for this period.
> a is a 'smoothing constant' between zero and one.

Note: A low value for 'a' will cause forecasts to lag behind any sudden change, whereas a high value (say 0.9) can lead to undue sensitivity to a recent high value of, for example demand for supplies or other function.
An alternative formula:

$$Fnp = (1 - a) (Ftp) + a (Atp)$$

BS5729 Pt.2. (4.2.4 and 4.2.5)

exponential smoothing. (stat). Exponentially weighted moving averages ('EWMA'). This system places more emphasis on recent data, the relative WEIGHT placed on each observation decreases with increasing age, the 'weights' form an exponential series.

ex quay (duty paid ... named port). INCOTERM. Seller's obligations end when he has, at his own cost and risk, made the goods available to the buyer at the quay at the destination.

ex ship (named port of destination). INCOTERM. Seller's obligations end when he makes the goods available to the buyer on the ship at the destination. Seller bears full costs and risks up to that point.

external good order. A term used in the freight business to convey the assumption that goods tendered for carriage are complete and in good order. *See also* GOODS INTAKE.

external resource management. The management of providers of goods or services, and of relationships with them.

ex warehouse. *See* EX WORKS.

ex works (ex factory, mill, plantation, warehouse, etc.). INCOTERM. Seller's obligations end when he makes goods available at his premises. He is not responsible for loading the goods unless the contract says so.

F

face value. *See* VALUE, FACE VALUE.

facilities management. The contracting out of all activities connected with the organisation and control of a facility such as building maintenance, security or catering.

factor, business factor. *See* AGENT, FACTORING AGENT.

factorial. (symbol '!') The number of different ways of arranging objects, from a given number 'n' down to 'one' – i.e. 'to unity'. It is calculated by the product of all whole numbers from the given number 'n' down to 'unity'.
Thus:
$$n! = n(n-1)(n-2)(n-3) \ldots \ldots$$
where:
n! is the factorial resulting from the products of the series.
n is the initial number.
e.g.
If $n = 3$
Then: $n! = 3(3-1)(3-2)(3-3)$
$= 3 \times 2 \times 1 \times 0 = 6$
In purchasing and supply it is an important consideration when examining alternatives for provisioning, value engineering, value analysis, etc. where mathematical factors and variables are introduced as alternatives courses of action, etc. *See also* 'MURPHY'S LAW'.

factor of safety. The factor set, or allowed for, in the design of a structure, or plant – such as a silo, storage equipment, handling equipment, etc. – so as to ensure that the operational working stress is safely below the safe permissible limit.

factory order. *See* ORDER PRODUCTION.

factoring of credit. *See* CREDIT, FACTORING OF CREDIT.

fail safe. BS 4778 (17.6). A designed property of an item that prevents failures of it being critical failures.

failure modes and effects analysis. (HS). An analytical hazard identification exploring the effects of failures of individual components within a system.

fair price. *See* PRICE, FAIR.

fair wear and tear. The deterioration on plant, equipment, vehicles, etc. which has resulted from the normal intended use and with the required maintenance having been carried out.

faith. *See* GOOD FAITH *and* BAD FAITH.

fast moving stock. *See* STOCK, FAST MOVING.

feasibility study. A method for assessing the viability of a scheme, such as extension of a production or process plant.

feedback. 1. The term feedback is commonly used in regulatory systems for comparing 'output' with some standard to be set and usually maintained at a fixed level. e.g. Stock replenishment may be initiated by feedback via computer (or manual) records when the actual physical stock in hand is compared with the 're-order level' set for a particular item of stock. 2. A system whereby information at an 'output' is compared with forecast and the difference (known as the 'error') is fed back to the input (i.e. 'feedback') and adjusted. *See also* 'HOMEOSTASIS'.

feedback (communication). The return flow of information in a COMMUNICATION NETWORK. May be of an electronic, verbal, numerate or physical nature.

feedback, negative feedback. (it). In supply control systems, future action is often based upon deviations from the forecast which had been made for the present (or latest) event. *See* STOCK CONTROL by EXPONENTIAL SMOOTHING.

feedback, positive feedback. (it). This involves amplification of a signal as distinct from differentiation employed in the application of negative feedback. Positive feedback is acted upon when, for example, increased power is needed for a conveyor or other powered (or power assisted) machinery.

feedstock. Material introduced into a plant in order to be processed.

fee simple. Legal statement for absolute ownership of land.

fiduciary. Referring to trust or trusteeship.

fifth freedom (air transport). The right, allowing an airline to set down and pick up passengers, cargo or mail in an intermediate country before flying on to the country of destination.

final assembly. BS 5191 (12008). An assembly to which no further parts need be added. *See also* ASSEMBLY, SUB-ASSEMBLY.

financial sanction. *See* SANCTION, FINANCIAL.

finished goods. CIMA. Manufactured goods, ready for resale or despatch to a purchaser, agent, etc. *See* CURRENT ASSETS *and* END PRODUCTS.

finished goods stock. *See* STOCK, FINISHED GOODS STOCK.

fire-mobile machinery & lifting equipment directive. (EU). Depending upon the hazards anticipated by the manufacturer when in use, machinery must, where its size permits either allow easily accessible fire extinguishers to be fitted, or be provided with built-in extinguisher systems.

firm offer. *See* OFFER, fiRM.

first-in, first-out ('FIFO'). The materials management discipline

79

to ensure that oldest stock is used first so as to avoid STOCK-LIFE exceeding SHELF-LIFE. *See also* STOCK VALUATION, FIRST-IN, FIRST-OUT; PRICE, FIRST IN, FIRST-OUT PRICE.

fixed assets. *See* ASSETS: FIXED.

fixed costs. *See* COST, COST FIXED.

fixed order interval. An inventory control approach where orders are placed at regular fixed intervals, the order quantity being varied. *See also* CONTRACTS: ADMINISTRATION *and* ORDERS & CONTRACTS: VARIETIES OF.

fixed order quantity. An inventory management approach where the same quantity of materials are ordered at varying intervals. *See also* CONTRACTS: ADMINISTRATION *and* ORDERS AND CONTRACTS: VARIETIES OF.

flash point. The temperature at which a substance gives off a gas which at this temperature will then ignite.

flats. A term for flatbed or platform vehicles or containers, and sometimes for timber, cases and similar goods.

flexible manufacturing system (FMS). *See* PRODUCTION.

float. A sum of money provided or set aside for some specific purpose.

flow chart. (stat) (adm). A process chart using appropriate symbols,* setting out the sequence of flow of a product [or of supplies in the context of purchasing and supply], or of procedures, in an administrative context, by charting all events under review from existing records, etc. Some examples are: 1. management – what workers do. 2. materials – what happens to supplies. 3. equipment – how used, performance, etc. *See **BS 3138 (21061)** for process chart symbols – ASME and Gilbreth styles. **BS 3138 (21087)** for more detailed symbols.

force (f). 1. a dynamic influence that changes (or tends to change) an object from a state of rest to a state of motion, or to change the rate of motion of the object. [e.g. the force applied to a truck (or other mobile stores handling equipment) in order to produce motion]; 2. a static influence that produces strain upon an object or system. [e.g. the force producing strain in an overloaded beam or shelf.]

Formula: $F = ma$

where: F is force (e.g. in Newtons.)

m is mass (e.g. in kilogrammes)

a is acceleration (e.g. in metres per second^2)

force majeure. Circumstances beyond the reasonable control of either party to a contract, e.g. government intervention, a strike or lock-out. *See also* ACT OF GOD.

force, tractive force. *See* TRACTIVE FORCE.

forecast. CIMA. A prediction of future events in the light of circumstances expected to prevail. *See* EXPONENTIALLY SMOOTHED FORECAST.

forecasting horizon. The longest future time interval covered by a forecast; this may be divided into forecast periods.

forecast, rolling forecast. CIMA. A statistical method of forecasting whereby at the close of each period actual results are recorded, noted and adjusted forecasts are made for the next period (or periods) ahead.

foreclose. To seize a security in the event of an unpaid mortgage or debt.

foreign bill. Any bill of exchange which is, or purports to be, drawn and payable outside the British Isles, or drawn within the British Isles on a resident outside.

forex. (abb). Foreign exchange.

forfaiting (forfaitieren). A form of credit whereby the forfaiting bank purchases an exporter's 'receivables', discounting them, usually at a fixed rate.

fortrain. Abbreviation for 'formula translation'. A computer language appropriate for mathematical and scientific problems.

forwardation. *See* CONTANGO

forwarding agent. *See* AGENT, FORWARDING.

forward allocation of supply/

stock. Arrangements to allocate deliveries of supplies/or quantities of stock to meet specific needs. *See also* STORE, ALLOCATION STORE.

forward allocation. Arrangements for ALLOCATION STOCK or advance orders for future delivery to ensure availability of supplies when required. *See also* 'FUTURES'.

forward delivery. Goods to be delivered at a later date but in an agreed period.

forward supply arrangement. *See* ORDERS AND CONTRACTS A–Z.

foul bill. *See* BILL OF LADING.

franchise. The licence (i.e. the right) given by a manufacturer to a distributor to market his products – may include certain territorial or other rights and obligations such as after-sales service, standards, etc.

fraud. Criminal deception, dishonest artifice or trick. To succeed in an action on contract it must be shown that it was: 1. a false statement regarding facts; 2. made knowingly or recklessly; 3. intended that the plaintiff should act upon it.

free alongside ship (FAS) ... at named port of shipment. INCOTERM. Seller's obligations end when he has placed the goods alongside the ship on the quay or in a LIGHTER.

free carrier, named point. INCOTERM. Seller's obligations

81

end when he at his own risk and cost delivers the goods to the carrier at the named point.

free-issue materials. *See* FREE ISSUE SUPPLIES.

free-issue system. A system by which stock is held available in store and is issued for use on demand without a stores requisition, or other documentation *See also* STOCK, FREE ISSUE STOCK.

free-issue supplies. *See* SUPPLIES, FREE ISSUE.

free market (economy). One where price is determined by the free play of MARKET-FORCES such as SUPPLY AND DEMAND without intervention or control by governments. *See* CENTRALLY PLANNED ECONOMY.

free of all average. On a marine insurance policy which is so endorsed, only a claim for total loss can be considered and dealt with; partial loss will lie solely with the owner of the goods lost alone. *See* AVERAGE.

free of general average. On a marine insurance policy which is so endorsed underwriters need not make any contributions towards the general average in the event of loss.

free of particular average. The underwriters are not liable for partial loss unless it is the result of accident or some unavoidable cause. *See* AVERAGE.

free on board (FOB), named port of shipment. INCOTERM. Seller's obligations end when he has placed the goods on board. Buyer's obligations start when goods have passed over the ship's rail.

free on board (FOB) airport, named airport of departure. INCOTERM. Seller must deliver the goods into the charge of the air carrier at the airport. FOB in this case may, or may not, mean on board the aircraft unless so specified.

free on rail (FOR), free on truck (FOT) at named departure point. INCOTERM. (rail transit only). Seller's obligations end when he has loaded the goods into the rail vehicle.

free port. 1. A port where goods intended for re-export can enter duty free. 2. A port open equally to all commercial vessels.

freight/freightage. 1. Commercial transport that is slower and cheaper than 'express'. 2. The price charged for freight transport. 3. The goods transported. 4. A cargo or part of it. *See also* HAULAGE.

freight absorption. The arrangement by a supplier to include freight charges in his price.

freight, backfreight. Freight payable by a supplier for goods to be returned to him for any valid reason such as rejection for non-compliance with contract, etc.

freight carriage paid to named destination. INCOTERM. Seller pays carriage of goods to destination but buyer bears risks and costs from the time the goods were delivered to the first carrier. (Applies to all transport modes, multi-modal, roll-on, roll-off, container traffic, etc).

freight/carriage and insurance paid to destination. INCOTERM. As FREIGHT CARRIAGE PAID TO but seller responsible for insurance.

freight charges, on ISO containers, etc. House to house (or FCL/FCL) packed (STUFFED) by forwarder and unpacked (DESTUFFED or STRIPPED) by consignee.

freight, dead freight. Amount charged by a carrier for 'dead carriage', i.e. that portion of his vehicle, ship, etc. which is empty during the transit.

freighter. A ship or aircraft designed for carrying cargo.

freight forwarder. *See* AGENT, FORWARDING.

freight forward or freight collect. Freight payable by consignee on arrival of the goods.

freight, inward paid. Charges for delivery to the purchaser paid for by the seller, or refunded to the purchaser on delivery.

freight note. Bill for freight charges.

freight outward. Freight included in the price and paid by the seller.

freight release. An endorsement on a bill of lading to indicate that freight has been paid.

freight, shortfall freight. Increased charge by a carrier to cover extra costs where freight charged on a *pro-rata* basis fails to achieve the minimum as per his tariff.

freight tonne (FT). Base tonnage upon which freight charges are calculated. The symbols 'W' and 'M' are often added to signify whether the freight has been calculated on the basis of weight or physical measurement, e.g. in cubic metres.

frequency curve. (stat). A frequency curve can be produced where there are many items and small intervals ('classes') developed from a HISTOGRAM. When the top centre of each pipe is joined the lines may form a continuous curve. Such a curve may display the contours of a normal DISTRIBUTION. If so the curve can be a useful tool in forecasting the usage of supplies, trends, values, prices, etc. *See also* FREQUENCY POLYGON, HISTOGRAM. Refer to **BS 4891 (9.5.1(1) and (2).**

frequency distribution BS ISO 3534 (2.15). The relationship between the values of a characteristic and their absolute or relative frequencies. The distribution is often presented as a table with special groupings (classes) if the values are measured on a continuous scale.

frequency polygon. A simple HISTOGRAM in which the number of items (classes) are too few to produce a true FREQUENCY CURVE. Whilst a frequency polygon is seldom adequate for close mathematical and statistical manipulation it can have practical applications to study, for example: supplier's delivery performance; frequency of damage in transit; analysis of loads transported and their frequency, etc.

frustration of contract. *See* CONTRACT, FRUSTRATION OF CONTRACT.

fund, sinking fund. A fund into which sums are paid (usually) at annual intervals to provide for meeting a future commitment such as the repayment of a loan or the replacement of machinery or of some other asset and to cover DEPRECIATION.

functional profile. The profile of administrative functions operating in an enterprise which is organised on a functional administrative basis. For example, the profile may include specialist areas such as 'production', 'marketing', 'accounting', 'purchasing', and 'personnel'.

futures. 1. Commodities which are the subject of a FUTURES CONTRACT. 2. Contracts of a standard nature under the auspices of a FUTURES MARKET to buy or sell commodities for delivery at a future date, e.g. a contract for next season's crop, or copper due to be mined in say 6 months' time. *See also* ORDERS & CONTRACTS A–Z.

futures contract. *See* CONTRACT, FUTURES CONTRACT.

futures exchange. *See* MARKET, FUTURES MARKET.

future goods. *See* GOODS, FUTURE GOODS.

G

Gantt chart. A diagrammatic time-scaled chart. As used for production, PROGRESSING of supplies, etc. It comprises a diagram in which each horizontal line relates to (e.g.) a supply of goods. Vertical date lines divide the chart into periods of time. Horizontal bars inserted at each appropriate line indicate 'targets' set and the achievement (or failure) by suitable signals.

gap analysis. cf. CIMA. A method used to analyse the gap between the final objectives which have been set for the achievement of a task, project or other aim, and the short-fall (or over-achievement!). This assumes existing performance is maintained until the time set for its fulfilment is reached. The analysis then proceeds to identify the extent of the changes needed and the ways by which the gap can be closed.

GATT (General Agreement on Tariffs and Trade). An agreement established in 1948 as a multinational trade treaty embodying reciprocal commercial rights and obligations as a means of expanding and liberalising world trade. Also embodies a code of practice for fair trading in international commerce.

general administration cost. *See* COST, ADMINISTRATION, GENERAL.

general average *See* AVERAGE: GENERAL AVERAGE

general stores. *See* STORE, GENERAL STORE.

gifts and favours. A phrase usually associated with BRIBES and bribery. No valid CONTRACT can arise from gifts and favours but their acceptance becomes a bribe when their intention or effect is seen to affect a contractual situation.

glut. There is said to be a glut in a market when owing to a super-abundance of supply or a diminution of demand the quantity in the market greatly exceeds what is required for the ordinary trading demands.

good faith. 'A thing is deemed to be done in good faith when it is in fact done honestly, whether it is done negligently or not'. Sale of Goods Act 1979. *See also* BAD FAITH.

goods. Commodities that are tangible and usually capable of being moved or transported. In supplies terminology the term is usually used in the plural form whereas economists and others frequently refer to 'a good'.

goods, ascertained goods. Goods identified and agreed upon after the making of a contract. *Note:* Where there is a contract for sale of ascertained goods no property in the goods is transferred to the buyer until the goods have been ascertained. Sale of Goods Act 1979. *See also* GOODS, UNASCERTAINED GOODS.

goods, attractive goods. Those goods which although they may not be valuable or costly are attractive to pilferage or theft from the workplace or store.

goods, bonded goods. Imported goods on which duty has not yet been paid. *See also* WAREHOUSE *and* STORES, BONDED.

goods, capital goods. Goods which involve the expenditure of capital and generally those which are for the purpose of manufacturing and processing to convert materials into saleable products.

goods, dry goods. Collective noun for domestic goods such as clothing, hardware, etc. but excluding groceries.

goods, durable goods. Collective noun for domestic goods which are used but not consumed, e.g. motorcars, TVs, washing machines, etc.

goods, examination of goods. *See* EXAMINATION.

goods, factored goods. CIMA. Goods bought for resale.

goods, finished. Goods ready for use or consumption.

goods, future goods. 'Goods to be manufactured or acquired by the seller after making the contract for sale'. *See also* GOODS, FUTURE GOODS.

goods, hazardous. *See* HAZARDOUS GOODS.

goods intake (also goods inwards, goods receiving). The place where goods are received into an enterprise. Provisions required for vehicular access, security, facilities for off-loading, sorting, checking, etc. *See also* CHECKING, INSPECTION *and* GOODS INTAKE, SIGNING FOR.

goods intake, signing for. An important function when receiving supplies. In addition to signing goods received notes the goods intake staff may be required to sign the haulier's CONSIGNMENT NOTE endorsed either 'unchecked', 'unexamined', 'subject to examination', 'suspected damaged' or other phrase. *See also* EXAMINATION *and* CHECKING.

goods, intermediate goods. A term sometimes used to describe partly finished goods and materials.

goods inwards sheet. A document on which details of incoming deliveries are recorded before the packages are examined.

goods, merchantable quality. *See* QUALITY, MERCHANTABLE QUALITY.

goods received note. (Known colloquially as a 'GRN'.) A form recording all details relating to a receipt of materials (supplies) from an outside source. *Note:* A variety of names is given to this by different organisations.

goods, receiving. *See* GOODS INTAKE.

goods, specific goods (law). 'Goods identified and agreed upon at the time a contract of sale is made'. Sale of Goods Act 1979.

goods, unascertained goods. Goods to be grown, manufactured and/or supplied in the future. Also goods which are (according to a legal judgment) 'an unidentified part of a specific whole'. *See also* GOODS, ASCERTAINED GOODS.

goods, valuable goods. Goods of high intrinsic and/or high financial value which need special security in storage and preservation. *See also* GOODS, ATTRACTIVE GOODS *and* STORE, SECURE STORE.

goodwill. The intangible assets of the reputation of a business. These are difficult to evaluate but include many aspects of vendor analysis in relation to relationships with, and services to purchasers.

grace, days of. The days (usually three) allowed above the actual term of a bill except where this is not drawn 'on sight' or 'on demand', or if the days of grace are specifically excluded. *See* BILL OF EXCHANGE.

gravity racking. Racking where the contents move to the picking face by gravity. Usually based on roller conveyors.

grid technique. A quantitative method which facilitates the discovery of the least cost centre for locating a factory or warehouse.

gross. Total measure of any quantity such as weight (gross tonnage) value (gross value), etc. with no deductions such as packaging in the first example or discounts in the second example.

gross national product (fin.). The total value of all goods and services produced in a country during a year. The figure excludes indirect taxes such as VAT, etc.

gross registered tonnage. *See* DEAD WEIGHT TONNAGE.

gross weight. The total weight of goods and package or a vehicle and contents before making any allowance.

group contracts. *See* ORDERS & CONTRACTS A–Z.

groupage. A system by which an agent (usually a FREIGHT FORWARDER) groups together small consignments to make up a full load. Savings are: cheaper full-load rates and simpler documentation, such as a single BILL OF LADING.

guarantee. (n). A commitment by a supplier that the goods or services he provides will meet the specifications of performance and/or description agreed in the contract. *See also* WARRANTY. (v) TO GUARANTEE, TO MAKE A GUARANTEE COMMITMENT.

guarantee period. *See* WARRANTY PERIOD.

guarantor. One who gives a guarantee.

H

haggle. To cavil, wrangle when negotiating a bargain.

Hague Rules (law). Legislation by international convention covering the transportation of goods by sea. It is embodied in UK law under the Carriage of Goods by Sea Act 1924 re-enacted 1971.

Hamburg Rules (1992). An international shipping code devised so as to attempt the reconciliation of interests of carriers and owners of the cargoes they carry. The Hamburg Rules replace the Brussels Protocol of 1968 which revised the Hague Rules. [But at the time of preparing these notes the Hamburg Rules had not been adopted by (UK)].

handling cost rule. *See* COST, HANDLING COST RULE.

handling, materials handling. (IM). A branch of industrial engineering and MATERIALS MANAGEMENT defined as 'The techniques employed to move, transport, store or distribute materials with or without the aid of mechanical and/or powered equipment'. NOTE below the selection of British Standards relevant to materials handling.
BS 3810 Glossary of terms used in materials handling. **BS 3811** Glossary of maintenance management terms in TEROTECHNOLOGY. **BS 3951** Freight containers **BS 4155** Trucks, pallet trucks, dimensions of. **BS 5337** Trucks, stillage, manual. **BS 4436** Trucks, fork lift, reach and straddle types. **BS 5073** Guide to storage in freight containers. **BS 5639** Trucks, lift, fork arms for. **BS 5667** Specification for continuous mechanical handling equipment, safety requirements for. **BS 5744** Code of practice for safe use of cranes. **BS 5767** Conveyor belts. **BS 5777** Pallet stackers and high lift trucks, stability tests. **BS 5778** Trucks, industrial, in special operating conditions. **BS 5829** Trucks, industrial, powered, control symbols for. **BS 6166** Lifting slings: Pt:1. Methods of rating. Pt.2 Specification for marking Pt.3 Guide to selection and safe use. **BS 6210** Code of practice, safe use of wire rope lifting slings. **BS 6756** Specification for fibre rope cargo nets.

handling, manual handling. The handling of materials, goods, etc. without the aid of power or mechanical equipment. *See* HANDLING, POWERED HANDLING.

handling, mechanical handling. The use of mechanical aids to handling, such as hand trucks, pallet trucks, rollers, the lever, etc. without necessarily the use of power.

handling, powered handling. (mat. man). The application of power to handling operations.

handling: 'straddle handling'. Systems of handling in which the load to be handled (transported, raised, lowered) is carried between the points of support thus providing stability in operation. Examples are: straddle trucks, straddle carriers and cranes of the gantry and goliath types. *See* TRUCKS.

hardening of market. *See* MARKET, HARDENING OF MARKET.

hard sell. Pressure applied to a purchaser by sellers who may be facing poor market conditions or heavy competition. (See also under NEGOTIATION other eventualities in this area.)

hard standing. A place, such as a concrete apron to an unloading, or loading bay, lay-by, or access to a site, of sufficient loadbearing strength to support vehicles and their loads (e.g. plant, cranage, etc). [Needs careful specification in purchase orders for heavy goods shipments].

hardware. General term for 1. metal tools, domestic goods, etc. 2. the components of a computer (but not the program or associated stationery which is referred to as 'software'), 3. military equipment (guns, tanks, etc.) and (sometimes) for heavy mechanical equipment in a large project, e.g. excavators in a quarry. *See also* MATERIEL.

harmonisation documents (sym. HD). (BSI). (EU). A harmonisation document constitutes a CEN/ CENELEC Standard. It (an HD) carries the obligation to withdraw any conflicting national standards. BUT, the public announcement of its number and title is otherwise sufficient. Harmonisation documents are established if transposition into national standards is unnecessary – because, [for example] a CEN or CENELEC standard is already adopted and ISO or IEC endorsed in Europe – or impracticable, and particularly if agreement is subject to the acceptance of national deviations'.

haulage. The charge made for carrying goods. Does not usually include loading and unloading. *See also* FREIGHT.

hazard. (n) (HS). 'The hazard [danger, risk, etc.] presented by a substance is its potential to cause harm.' [To persons or to other matter.]

hazards, measurement in reliability tests. (HS). The ratio of failures during a measured period divided by the size of the sample at the start of the period.

hazard rate. (HS). A measure of the instantaneous failures and hazard per unit time.

hazardous goods. Those which in transit, storage, handling, etc. present a danger to other goods, property or persons. In purchasing and supply due regard must be paid to scientific MATERIALS MANAGEMENT with full documentation, labelling instructions for storage and handling, etc. *See* VICE, INHERENT.

hazardous substances (goods, etc.). *See* SUBSTANCES.

hazard signs. *See* SIGNS, HAZARDS. Health and Safety at Work Act 1974.

health and safety. (HS). The Single European Act introduced into the Treaty of Rome new provisions for Community legislation on Health and Safety. Some provisions are listed below: Safety Framework Directive (6/89): responsibilities of employers *and* employees. Workplace requirements (11/ 89): Structural stability, electric and fire safety, ventilation, lighting, windows and doors. Work Equipment (11/84) Health and Safety requirements for existing and second-hand EQUIPMENT and MACHINERY. Manual handling of LOADS (15/90) PERSONAL PROTECTIVE EQUIPMENT (11/89) Safety signs (67/92)

Health and Safety at Work Act 1974 (HSWA). The Health and Safety at Work Act together with subsequent regulations, codes of practice, etc. lays down stringent conditions for the maintenance of plant and equipment in a safe operational condition. [For handling and stores the chief implications are the regular testing, certification and marking of lifting and handling appliances.]

Health & Safety at Work Regula- **tions general notes.** At first sight the HSWA and REGULATIONS (EU) may appear not to affect purchasing and supply, but, the following should be noted: 1. their effect is to establish a 'level playing field throughout the Community and thus costs for and prices in ESTIMATES and QUOTATIONS. 2. the purchaser must: 2.1. buy/provide suitable PERSONAL PROTECTIVE EQUIPMENT for workers. 2.2. arrange suitable safety labelling for hazardous supplies – incoming and outgoing; and, for safe handling – including MANUAL HANDLING. 2.3. provide PACKAGING subject to the same rules. 2.4. have regard to any STORAGE hazards and precautions for same. 3. comply with Statutes including those arising from DIRECTIVES of the Community.

Health and Safety Audit (EU). A review of the effectiveness of Health and Safety (HS) policy, paying particular attention to: 1. degree of compliance with H and S performance standards including legislation. 2. areas where standards are absent or inadequate. 3. achievement of stated objectives within a stated time scale. 4. data on injury, illness and incidents 5. analysis of immediate and underlying causes, trends and common features.

Health and Safety Codes of Practice. (HS). These Codes provide practical guidance on the requirements of Sections 2 to 7 of the HSWA, or in health and safety regulations, or in any of the existing statutory provisions. Special status of approved codes of practice is provided by Section 17 of the Act. Sections 23(2) and 21, 22 apply to Codes of Practice in respect of prohibition notices, etc. HSC7.

Health and Safety Commission (HSC). A Commission consisting of representatives of both sides of industry and local authorities. It takes over from government departments the responsibilities for developing policies in the health and safety field. (Sections 10 and 11 of HEALTH AND SAFETY AT WORK ACT. bibl. HSC4.)

Health and Safety Executive. (HSE). The statutory body set up by the HEALTH AND SAFETY COMMISSION which works in accordance with the directions and guidance given to it by the Commission. The Executive enforces legal requirements, provides an advisory service to both sides of industry, and embraces all major inspectorates in the health and safety field. (Sections 10 and 11 of the Health and Safety at Work Act apply). bibl. HSC4.

health and safety, hazard studies. Such studies involve safety, health and environmental consideration at each stage. [Purchasing and supply and Standards are likely to be involved at each stage also.]

health and safety: planning and setting standards for Health and safety. 1. Identify HAZARDS, assess RISKS, plan their elimination or control. 2. Comply with all HS laws, codes of practice, and DIRECTIVES and the corresponding UK Regulations. 3. Agree targets with all staff. 4. Take HS into account in purchasing and supply policy. 5. Design tasks, processes, equipment, products, services taking account of HS. 6. Set standards against which performance can be measured. 7. Apply standards to: 7.1. premises, place of work and ENVIRONMENTAL CONTROL. 7.2. Plant and substances, purchase, supply, transport, storage and use. 7.3. Procedures, design of jobs, way work is done. 7.4. People, training and supervision. 7.5. Products, services, design, delivery, transport and storage.

health and safety, related system. A system wherein the functioning, or mal-functioning, of the system may affect safety.

health and safety, Safety-Critical (Control) System. A control system the function of which is to assure safety of the system it controls.

hedge, buying hedge. The buyer covers his risk that uncovered sales will result in a loss if prices rise. In this case he buys FUTURES to mature at the time he requires the supply.

hedging. A manoeuvre to reduce risk by making opposing (i.e. counter-balancing) speculations, e.g. a buyer using a commodity exchange can safeguard the price he must pay at the time he needs the commodity by purchasing equivalent FUTURES (i.e. the 'hedge') which he will sell on the 'exchange' when the due date arrives. He can then set off any gain or loss against the rise or fall in price at the due date. He thus pays the amount he originally expected plus any charges for the use of the market.

heuristic methods. BS 4335. Procedures based on experience to rank activities and/or schedule activities to produce a feasible solution. *Note:* usually time-based information derived from the time analysis of the network(s) is used. [The term can also involve search for a goal (or solution) by steps, or by trial and error, or by a suitable computer program using, e.g. a BINARY CODE. [der. 19c New Latin 'heuristicus' from Greek 'heuriskein', to discover.]

hire. 1. Wages paid for any service. 2. Price paid for temporary use of any item. *See also* ORDERS & CONTRACTS, HIRE PURCHASE.

hiring. A way of achieving the use of an asset whilst another party (the hirer) retains ownership. Items are usually hired from an organisation specialising in the class of goods hired. *See* LEASING.

historical costs. *See* COSTS, HISTORICAL.

holding costs. *See* COSTS, STOCK HOLDING COSTS.

holding out (law). The action of a

person presenting themselves, falsely, as authorised to act officially on behalf of an enterprise. [Can be a serious business risk in purchasing and supply]. Unauthorised persons may deliberately or inadvertently commit the company to an unauthorised and inadvertent CONTRACT.

homeostasis. The process of balancing or holding steady the parameters essential to the effectiveness of a system despite disturbances or 'buffeting' to which the system is subjected. e.g. maintenance of availability of supply/stock despite changes in rate of consumption, demand, delivery lead times, etc.

home use entry. An order for the removal from a bonded warehouse of goods required for consumption in the home country.

honour, to honour (contracts). (v). to respect and carry out in full TERMS and CONDITIONS agreement freely entered into. (e.g. of a purchase contract).

hopper. A storage container which allows bulk loading of loose materials (e.g. grain) from the top, with a controlled discharge from the bottom.

horizons. The periods over which (particularly, long term) supplies, production and/or sales can be forecast and planned.

horizon, planning horizon. BS 5191 (22001). The longest time ahead for which plans are normally made. *Note*: Period varies with subject being planned and the planning organisation. e.g. it may be 10 years for facilities and one year for materials.

housekeeping, industrial housekeeping. A cliché with important implications in storage, handling and distribution. It implies the maintenance of clean, well-lit stores and areas such as loading bays, clearly marked aisles and hazards with correct and well-positioned signs; aisles and walkways clear of obstructions of any kind, etc. Savings from good industrial housekeeping almost invariably far exceed costs of accidents, spillage, and wastage which may otherwise occur.

hub airport. An airport that serves as a destination for long haul flights; dispersing passengers or freight locally by smaller aircraft or carriers.

I

IBC. *See* CONTAINERS, INTERMEDIATE BULK CONTAINERS.

ICC. *See* INTERNATIONAL CHAMBER OF COMMERCE at Appendix.

ILDM. Institute of Logistics and Distribution Management. Now merged with the Institute of Materials Management to form the Institute of Logistics.

identification (of supplies). The process of systematically defining and describing items e.g. stock, of all kinds, supporting goods and all commodities used in a firm. Usually associated with a VOCABULARY and COMMODITY CATALOGUE, leading to CODING, CLASSIFICATION, STANDARDISATION, VARIETY REDUCTION and STOCK CONTROL.

ideogram. *See under* CODES.

idle stock. *See* STOCK, IDLE STOCK.

idle time. BS 5191 (26009). The period of time for which a workstation is available for production but is not utilized due to shortage of tools, materials, or operators. *See also* DOWN TIME *and* WAITING TIME.

igloo. A specially shaped pallet or container for transport in aircraft.

ignition. The action of causing a substance to ignite (or explode) when and if the temperature of the substance(s) is raised to the ignition point (i.e. The FLASH POINT).

illegal. Contrary to law. The legal code draws a distinction between contracts which break a criminal law, and those which are contrary to public policy. The former are wholly void, the latter only in respect of those portions contrary to public policy.

immiscible. *See* SUBSTANCE.

impartiality. A lack of prejudice towards any particular side in a study or debate. An important quality in all who are engaged in interdepartmental services, such as those provided by the staff of purchasing and supply. *See also* OBJECTIVITY, VALUE ENGINEERING, VALUE ANALYSIS, etc.

implied terms (contract law). *See* CONTRACT, CONDITIONS, LEGAL CONDITIONS.

imports. Goods and services which one country buys from another.

import licences. *See* LICENCE, IMPORT LICENCE.

importer. For Customs' purposes this includes the owner or any other person possessed of or beneficially interested in, the goods at any time between their importation and their clearance from Customs' charge.

imposts. Taxes, particularly those on imports.

imprest. cf. CIMA. A method for controlling cash needed for small payments (or stock) of very low value by provision of a fixed sum (or stock) at the beginning of a period and its replenishment at the end of that period equal to the amount spent (or issued). *See* STOCK-CONTROL, IMPREST.

imprest stock control. *See* STOCK CONTROL, IMPREST CONTROL.

improvement curve. *See* LEARNING CURVE.

in ballast. A ship is said to be in ballast when she carries no cargo but only water or heavy material to maintain stability.

in bond. Goods subject to duty stored in a BONDED WARE-HOUSE under the control of the Customs' authorities until the owner pays the duty. When goods in bond are sold the buyer must pay the Customs' duties in addition to the value of the goods.

incentive clause. A contract clause which rewards the contractor for better performance.

incentives. BS 3138 (A5001). A motivating influence or stimulus. In the business context a legitimate offer of a bonus or discount to encourage the establishment of a contract. Illegitimately it may be a bribe for acceptance of which criminal proceedings may follow.

A procedure designed to encourage a desired reponse from people, by, for example, 'payment by results', 'target time/output', 'bonus', 'piece-work', 'measured day-work', 'graded performance', etc. [der: 15C Latin = setting a tune from 'incinere' to sing.]

inclined plane. The description of a surface which is at an angle to the horizontal. The angle may be used to calculate the force required to move (say) handling equipment (e.g. a gravity conveyor), or to examine the safety (or otherwise) of storage or handling on a sloping surface.

INCOTERMS. International rules for the interpretation of terms used in foreign trade contracts and recognised by buyers and sellers world-wide. INCOTERMS are listed below. *See separately:* COST AND FREIGHT (C & F); COST, INSURANCE AND FREIGHT (CIF); DELIVERED AT FRONTIER; DELIVERED, DUTY PAID; EX QUAY; EX SHIP; EX WORKS; FREE ALONGSIDE SHIP (FAS); FREE ON BOARD (FOB); FREE ON BOARD, AIRPORT (FOB); FREE ON RAIL/TRUCK (FOR/ FOT); FREE CARRIER; FREIGHT/ CARRIAGE PAID TO, INSURANCE. *See* INTERNATIONAL CHAMBER OF COMMERCE at Appendix.

increment. An amount added to a previous amount, e.g. a sum added to the value of a contract to cover a contingency such as inflation, the escalating cost of transport, etc.

incremental cost. *See* COST, INCREMENTAL.

indemnity. Security against loss or damage; legal exemption from penalties incurred.

indent. A word sometimes used as a synonym for a REQUISITION or a PURCHASE ORDER. Strictly speaking it refers to the indenting of legal documents and agreements.

indifference curves. These are devices for making choices between alternatives, such as the proportion or mix of two similar sources of supply in which it is desired to select the optimum mix based on price or other considerations.

index numbers. A statistical device to facilitate comparison between DATA at different times obviating the need for repetition of the full data for each period. Thus, for example, in purchasing and supply one may take a typical price at a selected (or seasonal) date or one which has been calculated (say) over twelve months. Using this price (or other data) as basic, then subsequent annual (or other) prices can be expressed as a percentage of this basic figure (price), e.g. a basic price at a basic year is (say) £100. If next year the price is £105. The increase is 5% and this is the index number.

indirect expense. *See* COSTS, INDIRECT.

indirect labour. Those wages which cannot be directly traced to a particular job or contract. One of the items included in works ONCOST.

indirect materials. CIMA. Materials costs other than DIRECT MATERIALS COSTS.

indirect oncost. A term used in connection with departmental oncost, and which represents items of any works oncost which cannot be directly traced to any single department.

indirect stock. *See* STOCK, INDIRECT STOCK.

inductive technique. (adm). The process of drawing general conclusion from a number of known facts by objective and rational reasoning and discussion. *See also* INQUIRY AND INVESTIGATION TECHNIQUES.

industrial classifications. Standard government classification of the 21 main groups (and numerous subgroups) of industry, designed to promote uniformity and comparability in the official statistics of industry in the UK. The classifications follow the general principle of the International Standard Industrial Classification by activity and not by commodity. They can be of considerable assistance in purchasing research. *See also* CENSUS OF PRODUCTION.

inert. *See at* SUBSTANCES.

inertia selling. *See* MARKETING.

inflation (price inflation). An

economic condition where prices are rising generally.

inflation accounting. *See* CURRENT COST ACCOUNTING.

information agreements. Agreements whereby information is circulated between firms party to an agreement in respect of: 'prices charged, terms of supply, costs, quantities or descriptions of goods, processes of manufacture or places and persons supplied.' Such agreements are (in nearly all cases) contrary to the Restrictive Trade Practices Act and conditions for trading within the European Union.

information processing. A specialist activity performed by the administrative organisation of an enterprise. It is concerned with the systematic recording, arranging, collating, processing, filing, retrieval and dissemination of facts relating to the physical/financial events occurring in a business. *See also* DATA PROCESSING *and* MANAGEMENT INFORMATION SYSTEMS.

information technology (IT). The application of technological means for processing and transmitting information. Such means include the use of computers, telecommunication, micro-electronics, etc. Purchasing and supply are areas for increasing applications of information technology and the application of INFORMATION THEORY where the systems are large and complex. [It may be worth noting that the application of information technology relies upon the integrity and accuracy of the basic system to which it is applied].

information theory. The study of information flow. Initially applied to communication systems. More recently applied universally to business systems. It concerns the flow of information, capacity of channels, and many other factors relevant to use of information technology in business. Information theory is therefore important to purchasing and supply organisations where these rely on the use of information technology.

infrastructure. Originally a term coined by French railways, later adopted as a military term for basic military equipment associated with logistics. Latterly its use has become associated with basic needs of a developed economy. These needs include: transport networks, communications, provision of water, power, education, health needs. These are considered determining factors in economic growth, and all can have direct, or indirect, bearing on purchasing and supply activities – or the results of such activities. The term is also used to describe the basic structure of an enterprise.

ingestion. The taking of substances into the digestive tract through the mouth. *See also* INHALATION.

inhalation. The drawing of substances (gases, dusts, etc.) into the lungs. For permissible levels of concentration *see* Schedule 3 of COSHH.

inherent vice. *See* VICE, INHERENT.

in house. A term used for work done within a plant instead of buying from outside source or PRO-CUREMENT from another plant of the same GROUP. *See also* MAKE OR BUY.

injunction. (n) (law). A court order to a person, Company, etc. engaged in litigation, the order may: 1. prohibit something being done, e.g. forbidding details of a contract being passed on to a third party, or 2. be a 'mandatory' instruction, something to be done, e.g. to complete a contract against a purchase order.

inquire (v) **inquiry** (n). To make a search or an investigation in depth. Some examples of techniques which may be appropriate to inquiry are: DELPHI TECHNIQUE, questioning technique, Inductive technique, VALUE ANALYSIS and VALUE ENGINEERING, BRAIN STORMING, etc. *See also* ENQUIRE *and* ENQUIRY. (appropriate terms for an invitation to a supplier for a QUOTATION or ESTI-MATE, etc.)

inquiry technique, inductive technology. A method of collecting many facts (or data) which appear relevant to a problem or investigation and classifying and analysing them, e.g. in VALUE ENGINEERING, COST BENE-FIT ANALYSIS. *See also* BRAIN STORMING.

inquiry technique, questioning technique. BS 3138 (21064) (adm). First stage, primary questions, e.g. the need for each activity (or other matter under investigation), its means, sequence, place and person, etc., justification sought for each reply. Secondary questions: the second stage examines remaining essential activities (or other matters). These are further questioned to determine alternatives and to select those that are practicable and preferable. The techniques are applicable (suitably modified) for purchasing negotiations, materials management problems, work study in stores and handling, etc.

insolvent and insolvency. A person is deemed to be insolvent within the meaning of the Sale of Goods Act 1979 if he either ceases to pay his debts in the ordinary course of business or he cannot pay his debts as they become due, whether he has committed an act of BANKRUPTCY or not.

inspection. BS 4778 (pt.1: 3.14). The process of measuring, examining, testing, gauging, or otherwise comparing the item with the applicable requirements. *See also* CHECKING *and* EXAMINING.

inspection, by attributes inspection (BS 4778 pt.2: 7.1.13). 'Inspection whereby certain characteristics of an item are assessed without measurement and classified as conforming, or not conforming, to specified requirements. An 'attribute' is a characteristic which is appraised in terms of whether it meets or does not meet a given requirement (e.g.

'go' or 'not go'. (*See* **BS.4778** for further notes.)

inspection certificate. *See* QUALITY CONTROL, CERTIFICATE OF CONFORMITY.

inspection clause, in a contract. A clause inserted into a contract for construction or for plant. It gives the purchaser the right to inspect the working of the contract and its progress at all reasonable times and to reject any part which does not comply with the contract. A similar clause may be applied to contracts for products, where appropriate.

inspection, stores inspection. The formal inspection of stores by a qualified person (such as the stores superintendent) to examine the condition of all stock, its effective housing, stacking, security, safety, fire, vermin, contamination, etc. (Sometimes misleadingly referred to as a 'Stores audit'.) *See* STORES INSPECTION.

inspection and test. 'A technical process which uses a specified procedure to measure one or more characteristics of a product [or service]. A major activity undertaken during design, product development, manufacture and product [service, service or use].

inspection, 'hold point'. The stage during a contract beyond which the supplier must not proceed without the operation being oversen by the designated inspector.

inspecting orders. Documents

authorising the official in charge of a bonded warehouse or other storehouse to grant permission to the holder to view the goods.

Institute of Logistics. *See* APPENDIX.

insurance, in contracts The provision of financial protection in the event of certain foreseen contingencies which may arise in the performance of a contract, such as: loss or damage in transit, failure in completion of contract, loss, damage or injury to personnel or members of the public.

insurance stock. *See* STOCK, SAFETY STOCK.

intake. *See* GOODS INTAKE.

intent, letter of. *See* ORDERS AND CONTRACTS, LETTER OF INTENT.

intention (legal). An essential component for a valid contract. The parties must have intended to create legal relations. Intentions in any contract must be clear and unequivocal. In the absence of such conditions the court will seek to discover the intentions of the parties to the contract at the time it was made. The test is 'what would a reasonable man understand to be the intention of the parties, having regard to all the circumstances?'

interest. (fin). 1. Payment by a borrower for the use of a sum of money loaned to him. 2. As payment for risk in making a loan. 3.

As recompense for overdue settlement of an invoice, etc.

interest, legal interest. (fin). A legal or financial stake, right or title to a thing or moneys, capital, etc.

interest, annual percentage rate, APR. (fin). Annual Percentage Rate of charge is a measurement of the *TOTAL* cost for credit expressed as an annual rate. Unlike most other rates in the past, APR includes the interest on the loan itself and any other charges which may be due as a condition of obtaining the loan (for example: documentation fees, maintenance charges for items on hire purchase). (Office of Fair Trading).

interest, financial interest. (fin). The charge for the use of credit, overdue payment for purchases. Usually expressed as a percentage of the sum outstanding per unit of time it is outstanding.

interest, vested interest. The interest of (usually) an individual, with a strong personal concern in some matter, or thing, which it may be expected will influence their judgment or the course of events in which they are involved and over which they have influence. Such an interest may involve a 'declaration of interest' where it is supposed that the 'vested interest' may adversely affect a decision. [For example a purchasing officer in a position to influence the placing of contracts by holding equities in a supplier company.]

Inter-firm Comparisons (IFC). A 'pyramid' or 'tree' of ratios starting at its head with ratio of 'profit: capital employed' and analysing progressively each ratio of 'costs to sales' at each cost and profit centre of the firm. A chief authority (set up by the Institute of Management and the British Productivity Council as the Centre for Interfirm Comparison.

interim certificates. Certificates signed by a person authorised in the contract confirming the progress of a project (plant or building) so that STAGE (or PROGRESS) PAYMENTS may be made by the purchaser.

intermediary. Third parties who provide services in connection with the movement of goods and payment between buyer and seller. Example of intermediaries include banks, shipping companies, freight forwarders.

intermediate bulk containers. *See* CONTAINERS.

intermediate stock. *See* STOCK, INTERMEDIATE STOCK.

intermediate goods. A term sometimes used to describe partly finished goods and materials.

intermodal units (ts). Units and unit loads, e.g. containers, capable of transfer between systems, e.g. sea-borne containers delivered finally on a road vehicle. *See* CONTAINERS.

internal lead-time. *See* LEAD-TIME.

internal rate of return. (fin). A percentage discount rate obtained from discounted CASH FLOW used in the appraisal of capital investment appraisal which should bring the cost of a project, or plant, and its future cash inflows into equality.

International Maritime Dangerous Goods Code. A code published in four loose-leaf volumes by the International Maritime Organisation – United Nations body headquarters in London. This code replaces the 'Blue Book' which is no longer published by the Department of Transport. [Noted from the Marine Safety Agency, an executive agency of the Department of Transport.]

inter-State (trading). Trade between members of the European Union and States outside the Union. *See also* INTRA-UNION.

intra-Union (EU). Trade within the Union between member States. *See also* INTER-STATE and THIRD COUNTRY.

in transitu. On the way, from one place to another, in transit.

intrinsic value. *See* VALUE INSTRINSIC VALUE

inventory. cf. CIMA. Alternative term for STOCK CONTROL, common in the USA and some public authorities for the quantities of stock *and/* or its value held by the Authority. *See also* STOCK *and* note at **BS 3811** regarding use of this term.

invitation to tender. *See* TENDER, INVITATION TO TENDER.

invitation to treat. See TREAT, INVITATION TO TREAT.

invoice. A priced list of goods or services supplied, showing the sums due from a purchaser.

invoice, certified invoice. One issued by a firm and certified as a true copy of the original.

invoice, consular invoice. One certified by the consul of the importing country who is situated in the exporting country to enable correct import duties to be charged.

invoice, pro forma invoice. One prepared by a seller to show the sum due from the purchaser in a transaction, usually before shipment is made or the service is rendered.

inward goods. *See* GOODS RECEIVING, GOODS INTAKE.

irrevocable credit. *See* CREDIT, DOCUMENTARY LETTER OF CREDIT.

issue note. BS 5191 (43003). A document recording the issue of products or raw materials from stores and which authorises the revision of (stock) records in terms of quantity and value.

issue (usage take-off). BS 5729. 1. The actual results of stores activities expressed in terms of quantities issued in a given period. 2. The number of issues made per day, per week, or per production period, etc. *See also* SUPPLIES THROUGHOUT, SUPPLIES TURNOVER OF SUPPLIES *and* STORES SERVICE FACTOR OF STORES, etc.

issue, units of. *See* UNITS OF ISSUE.

issuing bank. SITPRO. A bank which issues a LETTER OF CREDIT on the instructions of the importer (purchaser). Usually the importer's own bank.

item (stats.) BS ISO 3534–1. An 'item' in the context of statistics comprises the following: 1. an actual physical object upon which a set of observations may be made (e.g. item of plant, etc.) 2. a defined quantity of material upon which observations may be made (e.g. issues, or, usage of materials). 3. an observed value. This may be either 'qualitative' (*See* 'QUALITY: ATTRIBUTES) or 'quantitative' – measurements of count (e.g. numbers passed or rejected on quality control. *Note:* The English terms 'individuals' and 'units' are preferred by some and are sometimes used as synonyms for 'items'.

item, an item (in supplies). Any finished or partly finished product or raw material which can be identified as an individual item.

item, an item (of production). An identifiable item, sub-assembly or equipment supported by a manufacturer's part or drawing number.

J

jerque. Examination of a ship's cargo by a Custom's officer known as a 'jerquer' to ensure that it and the captain's list agrees with that of Customs. When he is satisfied the 'jerquer' issues a certificate known as a 'jerque note'.

job. BS 5191 (31001). That work which is undertaken to meet a customer or production order and which, for production control [and purchasing] purposes, has a unique identification.

job analysis. Detailed analysis of a job to agree the best method and qualities needed by the operatives/staff.

job breakdown. An up-to-date, step-by-step account of the operation(s) being, or to be, performed. Often associated with WORK STUDY and associated with a study of effective and/or standard methods.

jobbing, engineering production. The manufacture of customers' orders by the job, usually in small lots or batches, and of different products within the range and capacity of the enterprise.

job costing. cf. CIMA. That form of specific order costing which applies where work is undertaken to purchasers' special requirements. As distinct from CONTRACT COSTING, where each job is of a comparatively short duration. The work is usually carried out in a factory where each job moves through the processes or operations as a continuously identifiable unit. Also applied to work such as property repairs or work for a customer.

job description. A statement of the purpose, scope, organisational relationships, responsibilities, authority and tasks that constitute the job, for which the personnel must satisfy the job specification.

job evaluation. The determination of the relative standing of jobs within an organisation. Four basic systems are: 'Classification/grading' – placing tasks within the appropriate grades where these are established in the organisation. 'Factor comparison' – analysis based on requirement of job, skill, mental ability, physical requirements, responsibility, working conditions. 'Ranking' – placing jobs in order of importance or value. 'Rating, points rating' – analysis of full description of work to be done and full range of factors involved.

job lot. 1. Production. A relatively small number of specific types or products produced at one time. The part or product may be a standard item that has been, and will again be produced, or a special item destined for an individual customer who has not ordered it before and may not do so again. 2. Purchasing. (a) Goods arranged in separate portions or parcels for sale by auction. (b) A collection of odds and ends for sale. (c) A lot offered for sale by a merchant being a special 'once off' line not usually repeatable.

job satisfaction. The extent to which the desires and hopes of a worker are fulfilled as a result *OF* his work and also *IN* his work.

job specification. A specification of the qualities, abilities, character and skills needed by the person being considered for a job so that they may meet the requirements of the JOB DESCRIPTION.

joule ('W'). The SI Unit of work/energy applied when the point of application of a force of one newton is displaced through a distance of one metre.

just in time (JIT). A policy or procedure to produce daily (or as otherwise programmed) materials in the precise quantities required, usually direct from source to production lines – or process plant. The approach relies upon co-ordination of production and purchasing to ensure synchronisation of supplies and manufacture, and also upon ZERO DEFECTS technique and the use of KANBAN procedures. *Note:* Also referred to by the acronym 'WIN' when it's needed, and sometimes (incorrectly) as 'kanban' which is *NOT* a synonym for 'just in time'. The formal procedure is now extending to major retail stores outlets through sophisticated distribution systems, in cases where regular and predictable domestic demand enables the distribution network to replenish stock quickly, often on a 'next day' basis.

K

kaizen. Japanese word translating into English as 'continuous improvement'.

kanban. Japanese term which translates literally as 'card', meaning something like 'sign' or 'flag'. It is the signal which triggers deliveries of specific quantities of supplies in a JUST IN TIME system. The term is often used erroneously for 'just in time'.

kite mark. A symbol by the British Standards Institute authorised to be used by manufacturers on products which comply with British Standard Specifications. *See* appendix C

kitting. *See* PRE-ASSEMBLY.

knocked down. 1. A machine or article supplied unassembled usually to facilitate transport, etc. 2. Term used when an auctioneer or salesman accepts a bid and assigns the lot to the person bidding the lot is said to be knocked.

Kyoryoku kai. Japanese term for SUPPLIER ASSOCIATION.

L

labour, direct labour. Productive wages which can be definitely traced to a particular job, contract or process.

lagan. Goods or wreckage found on the bed of the sea. Provision may be made for its recovery.

landed terms. The price including LIGHTERAGE and DOCK DUES until goods are landed at the port of destination.

landing order. A document given by a Customs authority to the captain of a ship authorising him (after the dues have been paid) to hand over the goods for landing.

landing (or landed) weight. The actual weight of cargo removed from a ship.

lash. Lighter aboard ship, similar to BACAT but lighters instead of barges aboard the vessel.

last in first out. *See* STOCK VALUATION.

lay days (ts). The number of days allowed for the unloading of a ship.

law, case law. The principles of law laid down in cases heard in the higher courts.

law, common law. That part of law based on established customs and usages recognised by the courts

including CASE LAW. (*See also* STATUTE LAW.)

law, equity law. Addenda to Common Law, largely concerned with the equitable interpretation of contracts, agreements, documents, etc.

law, maritime law. That portion of commercial law that deals with ports, harbours, docks, ships, seamen, navigation, pilots, lighthouses, etc.

law, mercantile or commercial law. The term generally used to denote those portions of the law that relate to the rights and obligations arising out of the transactions of mercantile persons.

law, statute law. Laws derived from statutes enacted by parliament. It is 'written law'. In buying and selling and in industry such laws increasingly derive from international agreements, DIRECTIVES from the European Union and other sources.

lead time. BS 4335. The time which elapses between the achievement of an event and the completion of the last activity in the line of balance network, after allowing for all network logic restraints.

lead time, external (supplier's lead time). (P&S). The time taken from the date of an order to the time goods are received from the supplier cf **BS 5191(25004).**

lead time, internal lead time (P&S). The administrative purchasing office time taken from the receipt of the indication of a need by the purchasing department to the placing of the purchase order to meet that need.

lead time (total lead time) BS 5191 (25001). The total time (usually in weeks) between the recognition of a need and the satisfaction of it. For numbering of weeks. *See* BS 4760/ISO/R2015.

leads and lags. An expression to describe the activities of those who hasten or delay payment to take advantage of anticipated changes in the rates of exchange. [Such speculative trading is uncommon in normal purchasing practice where stability of price and cost are preferred.] *See also* PRICE ADJUSTMENT.

leakage or breakage. A mercantile term sometimes included in a Charter Party or Bill of Lading to protect the captain of a ship from claims on these counts where the cargo is particularly subject to these risks. It excludes protection for a captain's own negligence.

lean production. *See* PRODUCTION, LEAN.

lean supply. *See* SUPPLY, LEAN.

learning curve. The rate at which the CYCLE TIME decreases or is expected to decrease with increasing experience. The term, also known as 'improvement technique' and 'cost experience curve', is used to describe by graphical representation the rate at which the cycle-time of a task decreases, or is expected to decrease, with increasing experience of learning a task, or in training. As applied to purchasing and supply it postulates a relationship between quantity purchased or produced and the price per unit, or other appropriate measure. If quantities are specified in geometrical progression the reduction in price for each successive quantity is likely to be related to the 'learning factor'. 'Lc'. This is dependent upon the kind of industry/production involved. For a process plant Lc may be .95, for general engineering a figure of 0.65 may be appropriate.

leasing of plant and equipment. Contracts giving possession of plant and equipment for a specified period for which the lessee makes payments during that period to the lessor. At the end of the lease the lessee usually has the option to purchase at a nominal or other agreed charge. *See also* ORDERS & CONTRACTS A–Z.

leaseback (fin.). A financial arrangement under which the owner of property or plant sells it to a purchaser (usually a finance house) and retains the use of it under a leasing arrangement. *See also* ORDERS/CONTRACTS (kinds of) BUY, SELL & LEASE BACK.

lease (n). An arrangement whereby a lessor puts property, plant, etc. at the disposal of a lessee for an agreed period after which the subject of the lease returns fully to the owner (the lessor). The lease is also the document of contract. *See* ORDERS & CONTRACTS A–Z; *also* LEASING OF PLANT.

lease, residual lease. One in which the full cost of the leased item is not repaid during the primary period of the lease. [Leasing payment may be lower than with a FULL PAY OUT LEASE, but the LESSEE may find additional costs after the end of the primary period.]

lease, full pay out lease. One where the total cost is repaid during the primary period of the lease. At the end of the lease the LESSEE may be able to continue by renting the item for a period to be agreed or indefinitely, for an agreed sum (or a nominal amount to be agreed), there may also be a credit for a portion of the final disposal of the item.

least squares (stat.), method for 'line of best fit'. If a SCATTER DIAGRAM appears to be RECTILINEAR this mathematical technique known as the least squares calculation is suitable for determination of the LINE OF BEST FIT (LOBF). The LOBF is found to be that for which the sum of the squares of the deviations of the SCATTER POINTS from the LOBF are minimised.

least-time track. Flight navigation technique to find the best flight path to avoid head winds and take advantage of tail winds.

ledger, purchase, or bought ledger. CIMA. The record of creditors' individual accounts and transactions.

less than container load ('LCL'). Containerisation term used when there is less than a full container load for a single complete shipment. *See* GROUPAGE.

letter of credit. *See* CREDIT, DOCUMENTARY LETTER OF CREDIT.

letter of indemnity. 1. One containing an undertaking on the part of the writer to be responsible for any loss or damage or other specified claims in the circumstances detailed. 2. One sent by an exporter agreeing to make good any loss due to faulty packing, etc., thus ensuring a 'clean' BILL OF LADING.

letter of intent. *See* ORDERS & CONTRACTS – LETTER OF INTENT.

letters patent. Right granted by the Patent Office to protect an invention or process from being copied.

levels, stock levels. *See* STOCK LEVELS, MAXIMUM, RE-ORDER, PROVISIONING, DANGER/ WARNING, SAFETY, STOCK-OUT, DEFICIENCY, ETC.

leverage. 1. The ratio between the debts of a business and its capital assets. 2. A term to describe the negotiation potential which a purchaser possesses over a supplier to ensure a satisfactory and competitive outcome to negotiations. *See also* FINANCE.

leverage. A state of obligation, such

as liability for breach of contract if a supplier fails to deliver or a purchaser refuses to accept delivery to him.

liability, product. *See* PRODUCT LIABILITY.

licences (import). Licences granted for the import of goods. Such are: 1. open general licence for specified classes of goods which may be freely imported by any trader from any country or from designated countries of origin. 2. open individual licence authorising a trader to import unlimited quantities of specified goods from any country or from a designated country of origin. 3. specific licence authorising the designated trader only to import the stated quantity of specified goods within the time stated on the licence.

lien, carrier's lien. The right of a carrier, road, rail, etc., to detain release of goods to the consignee until e.g. freight has been paid.

lien (general). The right to retain the possession of property or goods until all debts due have been paid.

lien (particular). The right of the possessor of goods, who has not been paid for his services in connection with them to retain those goods (but these only) until he has been paid for the debts relating to them.

life cycle. The expected useful life of plant and equipment. In many instances life cycle of plant has inherent features at different phases of the cycle: initial teething troubles and breakdown, rising output associated with a LEARNING CURVE, later increasing repair costs and down-time costs leading in final phases to rapid increases in such costs, fall in output and loss of competitiveness in relation to new technical developments when available.

life cycle costs. *See* COSTS, LIFE CYCLE COSTS.

life, useful life. BS 4778 3.2 (191–10–06). The period from a stated time, during which, under stated conditions, an item has an acceptable failure rate, or until an unrepairable failure occurs. *Note:* The useful life of an item may also be determined for reasons other than failure. *See also* COSTS, LIFE-CYCLE COSTS.

lift table. Device, usually hydraulic, for lifting heavy loads so they can be placed on trucks, etc. **BS 5323** Scissor Lifts.

lift trucks. (BS 3810). The term is used here to signify a wide range of handling machines referred to in **BS 3810** as 'fork trucks'. However, in modern practice such machines are equipped with many handling attachments besides forks for handling pallets and palletised loads. The ancillary equipment includes attachments such as: crane jibs, clamps for timber and bales, roll clamps, reach forks, and many more to provide the almost infinite variety of handling needs in industry, commerce and services. Many are described in BS 3810.

lift trucks, safety versus hazards in use of. (HS). 'As with other forms of transport and handling, lift-trucks contribute to ease and efficiency in movement of supplies, *BUT* at the expense of introducing potential hazards.' (bibl. 'SAFETY IN WORKING WITH LIFT TRUCKS' HSE: From HMSO. ISBN 0 11 886395 9). This book outlines areas which require attention, operator selection and training, layout and maintenance of areas and the mode of operation of the different type of truck and accessory.

lifting accessories (mobile machinery and lifting equipt. Directive). (EU) (HS). 1. 'Lifting accessories'. means components or equipment not attached to the machine and placed between it and the load in order to attach it. 2. 'Separate lifting accessories' are those which help to make up or use a slinging device e.g. eyebolts, shackles, rings, eyehooks. 3. 'Guided load' is one where total movement is made along rigid or flexible guides whose position is determined by fixed points.

lighter. A vessel, usually a barge, used for conveyance of goods to or from a ship lying off shore.

limits. *See* QUALITY CONTROL LIMITS.

limitations, statute of limitations. Legal enactment which establishes the period in which legal action must be brought in order to enforce a right.

limitation clause. A clause which suppliers, particularly of a service, may seek to insert into a contract, which, while not excluding liability for BREACH OF CONTRACT or negligence, seeks to restrict liability to a specific sum. *See also* EXCLUSION CLAUSE.

linear programming. An operational research technique which can be used to determine an optimum solution within the bounds imposed by constraints upon the decision.

line of best fit. (LOBF). A statistical device which is important when seeking to establish a relationship between points in a SCATTER DIAGRAM (or 'Scattergraph') for two variables. When the 'scatter' points are dense it may be possible to draw in the LOBF by visual inspection. If this is not the case, or it is desired to find a more accurate LOBF, and provided the relationship appears to be RECTILINEAR, can be found mathematically by applying the LEAST SQUARES method of calculation. [The relationship of the variables may however be CURVILINEAR, such as properties of materials (substances) or the results of laboratory tests, etc. In such cases mathematical solutions are extremely complex. For many such applications it is often best to try and obtain a high density of scatter points and apply a visual LOBF – this may also give practical benefits.]

liner. A means of transport proceeding at regular times between specified destinations, particularly of ships.

line organisation (adm). One in which AUTHORITY is DELEGATED from top management to departmental heads of staff who are given full (or stated) authority within their department.

liquid assets. CIMA. Cash and other assets readily convertible into cash. Very little of normal industrial stock falls into this category.

liquidated damages. *See* DAMAGES, LIQUIDATED DAMAGES.

liquidation. cf. CIMA. The WINDING UP of the affairs of a business when it ceases from trading and appoints a liquidator to set its affairs in order, realise its assets, and with the proceeds pay its debts and distribute any surplus to its shareholders.

liquidity ratio. *See* CURRENT RATIO, ACID TEST RATIO.

load board. BS 3810 The collective term for any portable platform with or without a superstructure, for the assembly of goods to form a UNIT LOAD, or for handling and storage by mechanical appliances (powered or manual). *See* BS 3810 FOR TERMINOLOGY OF COMPLETE RANGE OF HANDLING EQUIPMENT.

load line (the Plimsoll Line). The level below which a vessel may not be permitted to sink when fully laden in any waters into which it may sail.

log book (transport, etc.). A book in which are recorded the arrivals and departures of vehicles at an enterprise, giving details such as: vehicle registration number, name of haulier, date and time of arrival and departure, etc., along with other relevant particulars.

logistics. The process of managing both the movement and storage of goods and materials from their source to the point of ultimate consumption, and the associated information flows.

logistics. 'The handling of an operation involving the movement of labour and materials, etc.' (Collins' Dictionary).

long. The position of a trader who owns physical commodities which he has not hedged, or one who has bought 'future'.

Lorenz curve. A graphic method of measuring divergence from an average. Originally devised for measuring the distribution of wealth it also applies to supplies analyses and can be used as an alternative, or supplementary to PARETO'S PRINCIPLE, and ABC ANALYSIS but showing how blocks of stock (or supplies) may vary from the mean.

loss, consequential. A loss due to breach of contract (through accident or similar event) which is in addition to the direct loss such as destruction of stock or property. It may result in loss of profit, losses due to interruption of business. Consequential loss is not normally covered in a contract unless special terms make it so.

111

loss (constructive total loss). This is said to occur where the subject matter of goods insured is justifiably abandoned because its total loss appears inevitable, or where it is so damaged that it is uneconomic to repair it.

loss leaders. Item(s) offered at cost or below cost in order to attract business. *See* PRICE, LOSS LEADER PRICE.

loss, partial loss/total loss. Liability in marine insurance covered by the peril against which insurance has been arranged. 1. Partial loss, is a loss other than total loss. 2. Total loss, 'total actual loss' is where the subject of the claim and the insurance cover is destroyed or so damaged as to be no longer the kind of thing insured. 3. Total loss 'CONSTRUCTIVE TOTAL LOSS' is a situation where the thing insured has been abandoned because 'total actual loss' appears certain.

lot. BS 5191 (31002). 1. A definite quantity of some commodity manufactured or produced under conditions which are presumed uniform, and for production purposes passing as a unit through the same series of operations. In some industries 'lot' and 'batch' are not regarded as synonymous. Where they have distinctly different meanings, these should be defined. Where it is unnecessary to retain the distinction, the word is preferred. In purchasing and supply the term 'lot' may be related to quantity for storage, handling, packaging, inspection, test, transportation, sampling, etc. It also has the commercial connotation of an article, or set of articles, offered for sale at an auction. *See also* BATCH.

loyalty discount. *See* REBATES, LOYALTY REBATE.

loyalty rebate. *See* REBATES, LOYALTY REBATE.

lpg. (LPG) abb. Liquid petroleum gas.

lump sum. *See* PAYMENT, LUMP SUM PAYMENT.

M

MRO Materials. Maintenance, Repair and Operating materials used up in the running of the organisation. Similar to 'consumables'.

MRP. Material(s) Requirement Planning. *See under* MATERIALS REQUIREMENT PLANNING.

MRP2. Manufacturing Resource Planning. *See under* MANUFACTURING RESOURCE PLANNING.

machine down time. *See* DOWN TIME, IDLE TIME *and* WAITING TIME.

machine utilisation index. *See* UTILISATION FACTOR.

machinery (def) (EU) safety directive. An assembly of linked parts or components at least one of which moves with the actuators, control and power circuits, etc., joined together for a specific application, in particular for the processing, treatment, moving or packaging of a material and including 'complex installations'. (There are exclusions but these are covered separately in the Directive.)

machinery: code of safety practice. 89/368 (UK Regulation SI.1992/3073) and amendments. (EU) (HS). In order to comply with the DIRECTIVE all MACHINERY purchased, imported, exported or used must satisfy the essential health and safety requirements set out in annex B of the directive. [Not only must purchasers of machinery comply with the directive but may also need to consider standard **BS 5304** 'Safeguarding of machinery' also later standards on 'safety devices' and 'ERGONOMICS' and any specific machinery class needs.] *See also* **BS EN 349,** Safety of Machinery. Identifies hazards arising from use of machinery. Describes methods for elimination or reduction of these hazards, for the safeguarding of machinery and for the use of safe working practices. Intended for those who design, manufacture, supply, install, use, maintain or modify machinery, machine guarding or safety devices, including those concerned with instruction and training in safe working practices.

macro-economics. *See* ECONOMICS.

maintainability. BS 3811(4304). A function of the rapidity and ease with which maintenance operations can be performed to help prevent malfunctions or to correct them if they occur. *Note:* **BS 3811** Appendix A, notes as below: the following terms should not be used in connection with maintenance: 'routine maintenance' sometimes used in the context of tasks of a minor or repetitive nature for which the terms RUNNING MAINTENANCE and 'shut down maintenance' should be used. Similarly, 'scheduled maintenance should not be used as a synonym for 'running' or 'shutdown maintenance'.

maintenance. BS 4778 (3.2 (191–07–01). *See also* **BS 3811 (4114).** 'The combination of all technical and corresponding administrative actions intended to retain an item in, or restore it to, a state in which it can perform its required function. *Note:* The required function may be defined as a stated condition.'

maintenance, corrective maintenance. BS 3811 (4208). 'The maintenance carried out after a failure has occurred and intended to restore an ITEM to a state where it can perform its required function.'

maintenance, emergency maintenance. BS 3811 (4213). 'Maintenance which it is necessary to put in hand immediately to avoid serious consequences.'

maintenance history. BS 3811. A history record used for the purpose of maintenance planning. May be combined with the PLANT REGISTER and also helpful in PROVISIONING.

maintenance materials (supplies). Those supplies specially PROVISIONED for, or carried in stock for, maintenance. They usually require priority action to ensure continuity of production. They are sometimes referred to as MRO (maintenance, repair and operational) materials.

maintenance period. A period (usually 12 months) during which plant supplied and installed under a CONTRACT WITH ERECTION will be maintained by the contractor. *See also* WARRANTY PERIOD, RETENTION MONEY, *and* ORDERS & CONTRACTS A–Z, 'TURNKEY' CONTRACT.

maintenance, planned maintenance. BS 3811 (4254). 'Maintenance organised and carried out with forethought, control and the use of records to a predetermined plan.'

maintenance, preventive. BS 4778 3.2 (191–07–07). 'Maintenance carried out at predetermined intervals or corresponding to prescribed criteria and intended to reduce the probability of failure or the performance degradation of an item.'

maintenance, remedial, corrective. BS 4778 3.2 (191–07–08). 'Maintenance carried out after a failure has occurred and intended to restore an item to a state where it can perform its required function.'

maintenance, routine. *See* MAINTENANCE, SCHEDULED MAINTENANCE.

maintenance, running maintenance. Maintenance which can be carried out while the item is in service.

maintenance, scheduled maintenance. BS 3811 (4261). 'The PREVENTIVE MAINTENANCE carried out to a predetermined interval of time, number of operations, mileage etc. **BS 3811** deprecates the use of the words "routine maintenance".'

make or buy, decision. A decision to be made whether to manufacture IN HOUSE or to purchase from an outside supplier, or from another plant within a GROUP. Usually based upon BREAK-EVEN ANALYSIS and sometimes also on a FEASIBILITY STUDY. (In the event of procurement from another plant within a group TRANSFER COSTS should be included.)

management (cf. **administration**). The formulation of strategy, policy, and direction of an enterprise in all its vital functions, with effective communication and rapport with those appointed by management to ADMINISTER the execution of such strategies, policies and directives.

management accounting. CIMA. The preparation and presentation of accounting information in such a way as to assist management in the formulation of policies and in the planning and control of the activities of the enterprise.

management by exception (adm.). The application of the 'exception principle' under which managers and staff concentrate time and effort on the 'vital fewer' matters and less upon the 'trivial many'. [For examples *see* ABC ANALYSIS and the PARETO PRINCIPLE. But, note that in purchasing and supply some apparently

'trivial' items (e.g. spares) may be vital to the continued functioning of production or a process].

management/executive development. (adm). The systematic process of developing effective managers and executives at all levels required in an enterprise. It involves the analysis of present and future management/ executive requirements, assessing existing and potential skill of managers/ executives and devising the best means for their development to meet these requirements.

management by objectives. (adm). The technique under which targets are fixed as a basis for achieving greater effectiveness throughout part or whole of an enterprise. May involve motivation of personnel by involving them in setting targets of performance, etc.

manifest. (mar). A document completed by the captain of a ship before it leaves port, and containing the record of the cargo the ship carries and its destination. It is handed in to the authorities at the port of departure.

manual, departmental, manual (supplies, stores, etc). A handbook detailing procedures, administration, duties, policies and all other information needed by staff for efficient and harmonious working.

manual handling of loads Directive. (90/269EEC) (HS). To be implemented by UK wef

115

1.1.1993. (Manual Handling Operations Regulations 1992). This UK Regulation has wide implications and particularly for storage, handling and distribution embraces a wide range of manual handling practices and risks. Key provisions include three main steps for employers to take to protect the health and safety of their employees: 1. avoid hazardous nanual handling where possible. 2. assess those operations which are unavoidable. 3. reduce the risk of injury as far as possible.

manual, technical manual. BS 4884. Also **BS 3811 (3132).** 'A document providing information explaining use, maintenance and repair of any material or product. Technical Manuals are provided for those involved with management, operation, maintenance and provisioning'. *Also may include* INSTRUCTIONS; INSTALLATION, COMMISSIONING, OPERATING.

manufacturer's agent *See* AGENT, MANUFACTURER'S.

manufacturing resource planning. Usually known as MRP2. This is a development from 'materials requirements planning' and encompasses the planning and scheduling activities associated with production resources to match output needed and supplies available.

marginal costing. CIMA. A principle whereby MARGINAL COSTS of units are ascertained. Only variable costs are charged to cost units, the fixed costs attri-

butable to a relevant period being written off in full against the CONTRIBUTION for that period. *Note:* It is recommended that the term be applied only where the routine system incorporates the marginal principle.

maritime law. *See* LAW, MARITIME LAW.

market, buyer's market. Market conditions where supply exceeds demand and prices tend to fall to the advantage of buyers. Typical of conditions changing from boom to recession in a free market economy. (Seller's market is the converse of a Buyer's market.)

market, commercial market. Place where sellers offer goods and purchasers come to buy. *See also* UNDER MARKETS: COMMODITY, MARKET FUTURES.

market, commodity market. One where (usually) natural products e.g. minerals and crops are bought and sold on the world or regional market basis. Often situated at centres of importation, e.g. London, Chicago, etc. Such 'organised markets' tend to develop when the COMMODITY is fairly durable, traded in large consignments, and subject to price fluctuations.

market, commodity market, auctions at commodity market. Procedures for sales of non-standardised graded natural commodities. Catalogues are circulated and samples made available for inspection. Trade associations set terms and conditions of trading and brokerage charges. The seller's contract takes the form of a 'sold note' against which the broker issues a 'bought note' and delivery is made against a 'warehouse warrant'.

market, the economic market. The trade in commodities and goods for which buyers and sellers are in free competition.

market economy *See* FREE MARKET ECONOMY.

market forces. Forces acting in an economy which affect prices through pressures on demand for the supply of, goods and services. Market forces may include, for example: 1. forces: exerted by marketing activities. 2. demands for changes: in domestic habits, fashion, etc. 3. technological change, development, or obsolescence. 4. State intervention, pressures, Statutes, quotas, controls, etc. 5. International pressures, controls, regulations, Directives, etc. *See also* note at COMPETITION.

market, futures market. Commodity markets where 'futures' contracts are arranged between producers, purchasers and speculators.

market grades and grading. Grading of materials sold on COMMODITY MARKETS. These take place according to recognised and accepted standards using samples in the case of crops and ASSAY in the case of some minerals.

market, hardening of market. A market situation where prices tend to rise and become inflexible to negotiation for reduction, e.g. price will harden if a supplier discovers he is in a monopoly position *vis-à-vis* the market, or his customer or that the purchasing officer is committed to buy from him.

marketing costs. *See* COSTS, MARKETING COST.

market leader. The enterprise with the largest share in the market of a particular product.

market overt (open market). A market open to the public (originally between sunrise and sunset) where goods are displayed in bulk. Gives the purchaser certain rights of the TITLE regardless of the title of the seller.

market, perfect market. A theoretical condition where many sellers and buyers are in continuous close contact so that their combined activities tend to produce a uniform price after allowing for distribution costs.

market research. A systematic investigation into the actual or potential market for a particular product, commodity or service.

market, share of market. CIMA. A firm's share of a market as a percentage of the total market available.

market testing. Using cost analysis to detemine whether an internally provided service might be more economically provided by an external organisation.

market, terminal market. FUTURE MARKETS are sometimes called terminal markets because the dealings in them are for specified 'terms', i.e. in periods of time.

market, the. Economist and business term for trade in a particular commodity, e.g. copper, cotton, sugar, etc.

marketing. The creative management function that promotes trade by assessing consumer needs and initiating research and development to meet them, it co-ordinates the resources of production and distribution of goods and services; determines and directs the nature and scale of effort required to sell profitably the maximum production of goods.

marketing, distance selling. Marketing to (mostly) domestic areas which may then enter into contracts for goods and services at a distance as a result of remotely operated marketing. Domestic postal consumers may expect protection through new DIRECTIVES but these may not apply to business contracts.

marketing, inertia selling. The supply of unsolicited goods or services. Applies chiefly to domestic consumers for whom protection is proposed by a 'Distance Selling Directive' from the Commission.

market value. The prevailing price as determined by MARKET FORCES applied to goods and services bought and sold under free market conditions.

marking (of packages, etc.) BS 3130 (11005). The process of applying to a container such particulars as: 1. destination; consignee and special transportation markings. 2. consignor. 3. quantity. 4. nomenclature. 5. package number. 6. invoice or other document details as may be necessary.

mark up, mark down. CIMA. A term used in commercial business (retailing, wholesaling, factoring, etc.) adding ('up') or reducing ('down') a selling price to effect a sale. Often expressed as a percentage.

mass production. *See* PRODUCTION, MASS PRODUCTION.

master production schedule. The plan for production of completely finished products or assemblies.

material. *See also* MATERIEL. In a supplies context materials are substances in solid, liquid, powder, gaseous or other form and which have a recognisable identity for use in production, process or other function.

material control. BS 3138 (A7002) Procedures and means by which the correct quantity and quality of materials and components (SUPPLIES) are made available to meet production needs.

material costs. *See* COSTS, MATERIAL COSTS.

materials cost analysis sheet. CIMA. A record showing the total materials cost charges for a period and detailing the separate amounts relating to different COST UNITS or COST CENTRES.

materials credit note. A document used internally giving details of surplus materials returned to store from a production department.

materials direct. Those materials consumed or converted which may be traced to a particular job or contract.

materials handling. *See* HANDLING, MATERIALS HANDLING.

materials management. (CIPS). The concept requiring an organisational structure which unifies into one functional responsibility the systematic planning and control of all materials from identification of the need through to delivery to the customer. Materials management embraces planning, purchasing, production and inventory control, storage, materials handling and physical distribution. The objectives of materials management are to optimise performance in meeting agreed customer service requirement at the same time adding to profitability by minimising costs and making best use of available resources.

materials requirements planning. (MRP). BS 5729 Pt.2.(5). A method of provisioning which depends upon a master manufacturing schedule as distinct from statistical predictions. The 'schedule' defines when finished batches and items are needed for production. It is then broken down into components and sub-assemblies, etc. and each of these broken back to provision (purchase or supply) raw materials or parts. *See also* MANUFACTURING RESOURCE PLANNING.

materials requisition. *See* REQUISITION.

materials returned note. A document which records the return of unused material to stores.

materials transfer note. CIMA. A document which records (and may authorise) the transfer of material from one store to another, or from one COST CENTRE to another.

material utilisation control. BS 3138 (A7003). Procedures and means set up to ensure that materials provided for the production plans are used most effectively.

materiel. BS 4778 (10.8). Equipment, stores, supplies and spares that form the subject of a contract, chiefly those used by armed services, e.g. NATO. This generic term is often used for large scale PROCUREMENT and avoids the necessity of repeating items covered in this definition. *See also* MATERIAL *and* SUPPLIES.

maximum stock. *See* STOCK LEVEL, MAXIMUM.

max-min system. *See* STOCK-CONTROL, MAX-MIN.

mean, arithmetic mean. BS ISO 3534–1 (2.26). The sum of recorded values divided by the number of values recorded.

mean, moving, exponentially weighted. *See* EXPONENTIAL SMOOTHING.

mean, arithmetically weighted. BS ISO 3534–1 (2.27). Each of the values in a table of data is multiplied by a coefficient called the 'weight'. The arithmetically weighted mean is found from the sum of the products of each value multiplied by its weight and divided by the sum of the weights. [It is noted in **BS 5532** that the weights are 'non-negative coefficients'.] However in purchasing and supply, the activity of VALUE ANALYSIS, etc. may involve the use of negative weights where account has to be taken of undesirable factors – such as environmental pollution, toxicity, health and safety requirements, etc.

measurement, units of measurement Directive. (89/617. EEC) This Directive (adopted 11/89 by HMG UK) extends the use of metric units throughout the Community for: economic, public health, public safety and administrative purposes. BS 5775 UNITS OF MEASUREMENT.

mercantile agent. *See* AGENT, MERCANTILE AGENT.

mercantile bills. Bills of exchange drawn by one merchant on another.

mercantile law. *See* LAW, MERCANTILE LAW.

mercantile person. One engaged in an area of buying and selling as distinct from manufacturing.

merchandising. The practice by traders, particularly in the retail area, of seeking to increase sales by publicity and attractive displays of goods in shops, market places, etc.

merchandise. A generic term usually applied to commercial goods and stocks of all kinds.

merchant. Strictly a person who imports goods on his own account, applied also to persons in the home trade who buy and sell on their own account, or sell another's goods on commission.

merchantable quality (law). *See* QUALITY, MERCHANTABLE QUALITY.

merchant shipping (Dangerous Goods) Rules 1965. Lays down the classification of dangerous goods under IMO classifications.

merger. The union of two or more enterprises by which either 1. one is absorbed by the other and terminates its separate legal existence, or 2. the identities of the existing enterprises are extinguished and a new combined enterprise is formed.

method engineering. 'The systematic recording and critical examination of the factors and resources involved in existing and proposed ways of doing work, as means of developing and applying easier and more effective methods and of reducing costs *See* **BS 3138 (11007).**' 'Method Study'.

metrology. BS 5233. abb. The field of knowledge concerned with measurement. Legal metrology treats units of measurement, methods of measurement, measuring instruments, in relation to mandatory technical and legal requirements. *See* BSI publication **PD 6461** *and* Handbook 18. Metric Standards for Engineering.

micro-economics. *See* ECONOMICS.

microfiche. Flat filing system for small scale photographic transparencies.

microfilm. Film often used for storing small scale photographic images, often of documents or drawings.

middleman. Any WHOLESALER, MERCHANT, BROKER, AGENT, DISTRIBUTER, STOCKIST, who has to do with the distribution of supplies. *See also* AGENTS.

mid-range BS ISO 3534–1 (2.29). The artithmetic mean of the sum of the greatest and values at each end of a RANGE of values.

milking. The practice of a supplier, who may have a MONOPOLY of supply, who excessively inflates profit by extortionate pricing of his product.

minimum stock level. *See* STOCK LEVEL, MINIMUM STOCK LEVEL.

mio. abb. Currency dealer's abbreviation for million.

mission approach. Management across functional barriers in an enterprise in order to meet and achieve particular organisational goals. e.g. the introduction of specialists in purchasing and supply administration and management in a growing firm so as to co-ordinate the total SUPPLY aspects and needs of the enterprise.

mistake. Legal doctrine recognises three classes of mistake only: 1. *Common mistake* – includes circumstances where for example, unknown to either party, the subject of the contract no longer exists. 2. *Mutual mistake* – here both parties mistake the nature or subject matter of the contract, which may then become void. 3. *Unilateral mistake* – here the mistake may be in the person with whom the party believes himself to be dealing. Lawyers assume that when people enter into a contract they know what they are doing and mean what they say in the contract.

misrepresentation. An untrue statement of fact made by one party to another, e.g. during the course of negotiations, as to some existing fact or past event, and which acts as a material inducement to the other party to enter into the contract.

misrepresentation, fraudulent. A false statement which the representor himself did not honestly believe to be true.

misrepresentation, innocent. A statement made by one party to another in which the party making the statement genuinely believes it to be true.

mnemonic. *See* CODES, MNEMONIC CODE.

mock up. A model (not necessarily 'working') made up to display (usually) physical size and proportions and other characteristics of the final product, e.g. an aircraft fuselage.

mobile machinery and lifting equipment, directives EU. (HS). Wef 1 January 1996, most mobile machinery and lifting equipment made, sold, imported into UK will have to: 1. satisfy wide ranging HS requirements on WORK STATIONS, controls, protection against mechanical hazards, and 2. in some cases be subject to TYPE-EXAMINA-TION by an APPROVED BODY, 3. carry the 'CE'MARK and its relevant information. 4. The manufacturer (or his authorised representative in the Union) must draw up and keep available, a technical file of the MACHIN-ERY. Failure to comply will be a criminal offence.

mobile racking. *See* RACKING, MOBILE RACKING.

mode. BS ISO 3534–1 (1.17). The value of an item which occurs most frequently in a range of observations, or 'the most frequently occuring value in a distribution'. The 'mode' is not suitable for mathematical calculation but may be used as a means of assessing quickly, action required on PROVISIONING, dealing with production rejects in QUALITY CONTROL, etc.

modification. BS 5191 (12013). An alteration made to a physically existing product usually resulting in an improvement in performance and generally carried out as the result of a design change (e.g. replacing a plain bearing by a sealed roller bearing).

modification order. *See* ORDER AND CONTRACTS VARIATION ORDER.

momentum ('P'). The impetus of a body (such as e.g. a fully laden truck) resulting from its motion. Formula:
$$P = Mv$$
Where: P is momentum
M is the mass of the body
v is the velocity

monitoring, health and safety, reactive monitoring. The monitoring of Health and Safety *after* things have gone wrong. (Investigation of cases of illness, property damage, 'near misses!!', – identifying in each case why performance was sub-standard). (bibl) HSE publ:IND(G) 132L.

monitoring and targets, conservation (MIT). *See* CONSERVATION.

monopoly. (econ). A market situation in which an enterprise or a number of enterprises acting in concert control a large proportion of a market in such a manner that they can fix prices and terms of trade to a large extent without regard to competitors. *See also* DUOPOLOY *and* OLIGOPOLY.

monopoly, absolute monopoly. (econ). The control of total output/supply of a commodity or service for which there is no substitute, by a single enterprise, State or CARTEL, etc.

monopsony. The reverse of monopoly, many suppliers but only one purchaser.

Monopolies and Mergers Act 1965. (law). This act extended the functions of the Commission under monopoly investigations to the consideration of supply of services as well as goods. At the same time mergers of business were brought within its scope and the Commission was renamed the Monopolies and Mergers Commission.

Monte Carlo method. BS 3527 A method of obtaining an approximate solution to a numeric problem by the use of random numbers and simulation.

MRP. *See* MATERIALS REQUIREMENTS PLANNING.

multiple sourcing. *See* SUPPLIES, SOURCING OF SUPPLIES.

multipler, the multiplier. The degree to which extra spending power injected into an economy is spent a number of times over, and the proportion saved each time the money passes from one individual to another.

mutagenic substances. *See* SUBSTANCE.

mutual relationship. A relationship between buyer and seller whereby it is felt that mutual support, advice, technology sharing, etc. can create benefits for both cf. PARTNERSHIP SOURCING.

N

National Accreditation Council for Certification Bodies (NACCB). A Council formed in 19865 to recommend to the Secretary of State for Trade and Industry concerning the competence and impartiality of CERTIFICATION BODIES, leading to their accreditation and ability to display the National Accreditation Mark alongside their own certification mark, 071 233 7111.

National Measurement Accreditation Service (NAMAS). A service provided by the National Physical Laboratory to give formal accreditation to calibration and testing laboratories. A list of accredited laboratories worldwide is available from NAMAS and from Department of Trade and Industry.

narcotic. *See* SUBSTANCE.

National Quality Information Centre. The Centre is operated by the INSTITUTE OF QUALITY ASSURANCE in order to assist industry and commerce to obtain information and improve quality in their corporate activities and in the products and services they provide.

'negative clearance', (EU). An individual exemption granted by the Commission of the EU in respect of an article of Community enactments. [May be needed for some special purchasing contract which otherwise may be in breach of (e.g.) Community requirements on competition.] *See also* COMFORT LETTER.

negligence. (law). 1. want of care. 2. 'culpable negligence', a degree of negligence deserving censure and blame. 3. 'gross negligence', the want of even the slightest care.

negotiable instrument. A document entitling the holder to a sum specified upon it. It can normally be transferred to another party, usually by endorsement. Examples are cheques, bills of exchange, etc.

negotiate (v)**, negotiation** (n). To communicate, discuss and bargain with the objective of reaching an agreement.

negotiating bank. SITPRO. The bank specifically nominated in the letter of credit to purchase the bill of exchange (draft) drawn by the beneficiary, or a drawee other than the negotiating bank. If a letter of credit is freely negotiating any bank willing to do so can be the negotiating bank. *See also* ADVISING BANK.

net. The amount of any charge, weight or other measures which remain after all allowances have been made. Also spelt 'neat' and less accurately 'nett'.

net cash. *See* PRICE, NET PRICE.

net present value. *See* VALUE, NET PRESENT VALUE.

net price. *See* PRICE, NET PRICE.

net profit. *See* PROFIT, NET PROFIT.

net registered tonnage. (NRT). The gross registered tonnage (in cubic tons) of a ship less allowance for space not available for cargo (e.g. engine room, crew's quarters, etc.). Usually about 55–65 percent, and used for assessing harbour dues, etc.

net weight. Gross weight of goods less TARE, i.e. after deducting the weight of box and package, etc.

network analysis. BS 3138 (7010). A group of techniques for presenting information to assist the planning and controlling of projects. The information, usually represented by a network, includes the sequence and logical inter-relationships of all project activities. The group includes techniques for dealing with time, distances, resources and costs. *Note:* The term 'critical path analysis' refers

to a particular technique of project network analysis, and should not be used as synonymous. *See* **BS 4335**.

network (project network). BS 4335. A representation of activities and/or events with their inter-relationships and dependencies.

Newton (F). The SI unit of force which imparts to a mass of one kilogramme an acceleration of one metre per second per second. Of importance when calculating the effects of collisions or similar events with moving plant, e.g. fork lift trucks, vehicles, etc.

noise. 1. An 'inhibition' which may induce unwanted signals which intrude into a telecommunications system. 2. Random variations to be discounted in forecasting.

nominal price. *See* PRICE, NOMINAL PRICE.

normal price. *See* PRICE, ECONOMIC PRICE.

noxious substance. *See* SUBSTANCES.

O

objectivity. The study, consideration or discussion of subjects or problems based upon facts, untrammelled by SUBJECTIVE emotional or prejudicial influences. An important characteristic/quality of those engaged in administration and management to ensure that subjective considerations do not override commercial or technical aspects of a problem or a purchase.

obsolescence,   functional obselescence. The measure of loss of value of a FIXED ASSET due to various causes: 1. asset superseded by one which is superior to it, technically or in performance. 2. cessation of need in consequence of change in the market or a change in production method. 3. in the purchasing supply context it may imply that supplies, equipment and spares have ceased to be readily available even although the plant requiring them is still in use. 4. on the way to becoming OBSOLETE.

obsolescent. Not yet obsolete but becoming so.

obsolete. 1. Supplies, plant or equipment which have passed OBSOLESCENCE and are completely out of date, out of use. 2. Supplies which are no longer available and cannot be replaced.

ODETTE. A standardised format for transport labels, employing

bar coding as well as plain language information. Used internationally in Europe.

offcuts. Residual materials left after machining, turning, cutting off, shearing, etc. Represent a loss-centre in supplies and call for effective materials management and control.

offer (in a contract). An offer is a communication of definite intention to enter into a contract; it may be written or verbal for any value under English law. It is a vital component of a contract and must be met by an unqualified acceptance.

offer, by tender. *See* TENDERS AND TENDERING.

offer, counter-offer. An offer made in response to the offer from another party in a negotiation. The communication by an offeree (e.g. a purchaser) to an offeror a (supplier) seeking to modify the terms of an acknowledgement by the latter, is in law, a 'counter-offer' and deprives the contract of an 'unqualified acceptance'.

offer, firm offer. One which has been made by a supplier for supplies of a specified quality, quantity, price or delivery date and which allows of no variation from that stated. It binds both supplier and buyer and as common with most offers is usually open for acceptance for a limited and stated period, usually 30 days.

offer to treat. *See* TREAT, INVITATION TO TREAT.

offeree. A person to whom an offer is made.

offeror. A person who makes an offer.

Office of Fair Trading. The statutory body responsible for oversight of British industrial and commercial life and its 'fair trading'. Examples of its remit include prices charged for supplies and raw materials and the impact of take-overs. It can launch investigations, revoke licences, refer matters to the MONOPOLIES AND MERGERS COMMISSION (MMC), highlight mal-practices and make recommendation to the government. While it must be noted that this and other similar Acts exist primarily to protect the public, they can also have implications for purchasing and supply activities if these impinge upon the domestic supply area.

ogive (stat) (cumulative frequency curve). A curve of characteristic shape, similar to the letter 'Z'. It is used in purchasing and supply when (for example) plotting cumulative values of a range of demands/usages on the vertical axis against time on the horizontal axis in periods of (say) weeks, months, production periods, etc. [In purchasing and marketing e.g. the upper curve can represent the twelve month moving mean of

consumption or sales; the lower curve the monthly take off or sales; the curve sloping upwards from left to right, the cumulative sum of take off or sales.

oligopoly. (econ). The occupation of a market, or a large part of a market, by a small number of enterprises, each of which has significant economic power which it exercises independently, at the same time taking account of the conduct in the market by other enterprises. *See also* DUOPOLY *and* MONOPOLY.

oligopsony. (econ). A buyer's market' situation, where for a certain good (or range of goods) there are so few buyers that they are able to influence the price paid in their favour.

oncost. *See* COSTS, OVERHEAD COSTS.

one-for-one. *See* STOCK CONTROL, 'ONE-FOR-ONE'.

'on line'. The term used in information technology for the immediate access to information through electronic process facilities. [Of particular importance for instantly updating stock control records, movement of transport, etc. immediately as it takes place.]

open access bins. Bins (or other containers) usually at work-centres from which operatives can take supplies without formal paperwork control. The level is usually maintained by visual stock control by imprest and/or by regular (daily) replenishment. *See also* OPEN ACCESS STORES.

127

open credit. Name given to a letter of credit when it contains an unconditional request to pay money to another person. *See also* DOCUMENTARY CREDIT.

open market. *See* MARKET OVERT.

operational research. BS 3138 (11009). 'The application of methods of science to complex problems arising in the direction and management of large systems of people, machines, materials and money in industry, business, government and defence. *Note*: The distinctive approach is to develop a scientific model of the system, incorporating measures of factors such as chance and risk, with which to predict the outcomes of alternative decisions, strategies, or controls. The purpose is to help management determine its policy and action scientifically'.

operating profit. *See* PROFIT, OPERATING. PROFIT.

operating ratio. Operating costs of a (transport) service expressed as a percentage of receipts. The higher the percentage the lower the profitability. Over 100 percent involves a loss. Formula:

$$Or = \frac{Cat}{Rt} \, 100$$

Where:

Or is operating ratio
Cat is total operating costs in given period
Rt is total receipts in period.

NOTES: adjustments may be needed for back and part loads, seasonal and other factors.

operation costing. CIMA (abb). Basic costing methods applicable where standardised goods or services result from a sequence of repetitive and more or less continuous operations or processes to which costs are charged before being averaged over the units produced during the period. *See also* CONTRACT *and* JOB costing.

operator. (adm). The person or persons given the task of installing, operating, adjusting, cleaning, repairing or transporting MACHINERY.

option. The right of choice, particularly in contracts, where an offer (or some part of an offer) may be taken or not taken at the choice or option of the offeree.

opinions. (EU). Such (e.g. from the Union) have no binding force but merely state the view of the institution that issues them.

opportunity cost. *See* COST, OPPORTUNITY COST.

order cover. The sum of stock physically on hand and on order, less any reserved stock.

ordering costs. *See* COSTS, ORDER PREPARATION COSTS, *etc.*

order processing time. *See* LEAD TIME, INTERNAL LEAD TIME, *etc.*

order, production order. BS 5191 (42003). A written internal instruction to proceed with the manufacture of a product or the provision of a service, normally specifying quantity, delivery date, etc. Also referred to as: 'works order', 'manufacturing order', 'factory order', 'shop order'.

order, purchase order (written). BS 5191 (42002). A written * instruction to a supplier to provide a product or service normally specifying: quality, quantity, delivery-date required and price. *Note**: A purchase order does not need to be in writing in order to create a valid contract.

orders and contracts, varieties of.

Definitions in this section refer chiefly to kinds of order and contract. For their administration please check with the section headed CONTRACTS AND ORDERS: ADMINISTRATION OF. ORDERS, (PURCHASE) AND CONTRACTS, VARIETIES OF.

all-in contract. A contract which covers all aspects of a job including, design, provision of prototypes through to commissioning. Also known as 'Turnkey Contract'. *See also* DESIGN AND DEVELOPMENT CONTRACT.

amendment order. See VARIATION ORDER.

automated purchasing. See AUTOMATED PURCHASING *at* A.

barter. Direct exchange of goods without transfer of cash. Goods bartered may be part of a major transaction. Often favoured by states with controlled economies. *See* COUNTER TRADE.

batch and batch schedule ordering. A production, linked ordering system in which purchase orders (and/or their deliveries) are so scheduled that INTAKES are in accordance with the production or process schedule for which they are required. *See also* 'JUST IN TIME' TECHNIQUE.

blanket orders. Orders covering or 'blanketing' a range of goods from a supplier, e.g. an order covering a range of tools from a tool supplier. As with other similar arrangements enables user to obtain goods and services at known price, specification and delivery.

bulk/contract order. 1. A contract for bulk materials. 2. A contract in which a number of requirements are bulked together to achieve price/delivery advantage.

buy, sell and lease back. A form of capital financing whereby the purchaser of a large unit plant (such as a ship) sells the unit at the time of purchase to a finance company from whom he then leases it back for his own use. *See also* LEASE BACK.

call off. See DRAW OFF ORDERS.

cancellation order. Notification to a supplier that the purchaser intends to break the contract by cancelling his order. As with VARIATION ORDERS these should be in writing and agreement of the other party is needed.

cash and carry. Buyer pays cash and collects, loads and carries away the goods he has purchased. More usually applicable to the domestic market.

cash on delivery. Buyer pays cash when he receives the goods. Mostly confined to domestic trading.

cash with order. Goods are only despatched if the buyer sends cash with his order. Generally restricted to retail firms between wholesalers and new retail accounts. *See also* PAYMENT PROFORMA. PAYMENT AGAINST.

cheque-order. System of ordering where the order form has a cheque attached which the supplier detaches and passes to his bank. For security the cheque should have the amount filled in. Restricted to suppliers with whom the purchasing company has regular transactions.

computer ordering. *See* COMPUTERISED ORDERING SYSTEMS AND AUTOMATED PURCHASING.

consignment stock order. The supplier places goods in the purchaser's stores to be drawn off and paid for as used. (For use with forward supply arrangements, etc. on high-use items. Assures supply and saves investment by the purchaser. Supplier may seek to recover his investment costs.

consortium buying orders. Orders by a consortium which shares a secretariat to collate requirements of the members. Enquiries are placed on behalf of the consortium members. Often used to purchase important items common to a number of enterprises.

cost plus orders/contracts. A purchase contract in which final sums invoiced are based on prices paid by the supplier for materials with an estimated or actual addition for cost of labour. Used in construction industries and where the precise estimates of price are impossible.

cost reimbursable. Payments are made against claims for actual costs of work done and incurred in carrying out the work. Costs may be based upon pre-agreed rates or targets, as in the case of contracts on a time and materials basis. Applications are mostly as for lump sum contracts.

delivery note acceptance ordering. The supplier uses specially printed delivery notes for requirements of customer whose authorised named persons collect goods. Delivery notes are priced, and used as invoice *and* order. Used for routine purchases from wholesaler, etc. for (e.g.) spares for maintenance, small tools, resale items, etc. Not for large value items as a rule.

design and development contract. An order or contract placed purely for design and/or development of a complete product, prototype, etc. Used where design, etc. is beyond the capability of the purchaser, and he wishes to retain freedom of negotiation and choice of supplier. Regularises the use of supplier's expertise by the purchaser.

draw-off order, call off order. Order used to 'draw off' requirements from FORWARD SUPPLY CONTRACTS and/or FORWARD SUPPLY ARRANGEMENTS. Branches, stores, etc. authorised to issue these according to need at regular intervals or according to stock levels. Can be used for all classes of supplies from raw materials to miscellaneous but standard factory needs.

enquiry-proceed ordering. An enquiry carrying instructions to put preliminary or complete work in hand. An order number is reserved and mentioned on the enquiry but only released on agreement of quotation. Used in similar circumstances to those for LETTER OF INTENT, but of smaller requirements, such as urgent spares.

fixed order quantity cycle. Method of ordering on a fixed order quantity (e.g. *see* EOQ) when FEEDBACK from STOCK CONTROL or production/process indicates need for further supply.

fixed price order/contract. One which has been subject to a firm quotation and no price variations are allowed for. [For long term contracts some clause for re-negotiation in the event of market changes may be essential.]

forward buying contract/order. One placed in advance of actual need. Delivery may be 'as available' or planned for future. Object may be to secure supply from the source, for seasonal requirements, to profit from seasonal price changes, etc. [This form of contract needs a firm price, otherwise a CONTRACT PRICE ADJUSTMENT formula will be needed. *See also* FUTURES CONTRACT.]

forward supply arrangement (FSA). An arrangement for the future supply of specified goods and services to be drawn off as required. Such arrangements may be open-ended in regard to quantity and/or time. Some commitment on supplier and buyer. Can be used for class 'C' and sometimes class 'B' requirements where quantity and/or time are indeterminate. May have value in pegging price and specifications. *See also* MAIN (and FORWARD SUPPLY) CONTRACTS *below*.

free-issue order. An order raised by a supplier's purchasing department on his firm's customer (in agreement with him) for the procurement from him of embodiment materials to be used in the supplier's production. Often includes details regarding inspection, etc. Regularises the transaction and provides valuable record. Harmonises the supplies procedures with those of all normal transactions.

futures contract. A contract made with a FUTURES EXCHANGE

131

or TERMINAL MARKET for supplies to be available on maturity of the contract. Used for basic raw materials, metals and natural products. Hedging techniques can establish final price.

group purchasing. The channelling of requirements for a group of companies into bulk contracts, etc. Means of gaining improved prices, deliveries, specifications, etc. (May break competition rules of the European Union).

hire contracts (plant). Either a normal style order with special terms and conditions appropriate to hire or more usually a special contract form presented by the plant hire company. Contract conditions should be studied with great care. The hire firm should service and maintain the plant hired.

hire purchase contract (also known as lease purchase contract). The bailment of goods (usually) plant and equipment, under which the hirer becomes the BAILEE and to whom ultimately upon the completion of the contract the property in the goods will pass.

incentive contracts. Contracts which include a clause authorising the payment to the supplier of additional money on the contract price for early delivery, improved performance, etc. For major contracts where completion date, delivery or performance is vital.

in-plant stores arrangement. A kind of forward supply arrangement in which a supplier (sometimes a stockist) keeps a section of his customer's stores replenished at regular intervals, or 'on call', or as stock levels dictate. Employed for small miscellaneous requirements, usually class 'C'. *See also* STOCK, CONSIGNMENT STOCK.

job lot. A term sometimes used for a BATCH ORDER covering requirements for a PRODUCTION BATCH. More correctly, the term should be used to describe a miscellaneous assortment of goods sold as a lot and often of a low price and trivial nature.

leasing (financial) contract. An arrangement whereby a finance house advances cash to the lessee so that the latter can obtain plant, etc. which he retains in possession and full use, but the property in which rests with the lessor during the period of lease.

lease, hire. The hire of plant, buildings or equipment for rent.

letter of intent. A written communication to a supplier leading to a contract and instructing him to take some action such as: 1. reserving production capacity or 2. puting preliminary work in hand, or 3. proceeding with work, etc. The letter of intent must usually be subject to a firm order being placed by a pre-agreed date or to cancellation at that date if work is not to proceed further.

loan order. Used for borrowing tools, jigs or other equipment from a neighbouring factory or a main contractor to whom the user is a subcontractor. Standard small-value or local-purchase order forms can be used.

local purchase order (LPO). As SMALL VALUE ORDERS but restricted to use with local suppliers.

long term contracts. Those contracts for supplies or services which may extend over a number of years as distinct from the normal twelve month period. There may be a number of objectives such as continuity of supplies or services of consistent quality and delivery at agreed prices. Such contracts may include safeguards such as 'quality compliance' with BS 5750, a BREAK CLAUSE in respect of price change, compliance with quality conditions, etc.

lump sum contract. A method of contracting usually restricted to civil and construction works. A single price and payment is quoted and paid for the whole job.

main (and forward supply) contracts (FSC). An order or contract for the future supply of definite quantities of goods and services usually in a predetermined period. May be delivered at an agreed rate or drawn off at a variable rate as required. Full commitments on all parties. Used for major class 'A' requirements particularly where geared to a production plan. Branches or functional divisions may issue draw-off orders or delivery schedule.

measurement contract. Based on a BILL OF QUANTITIES with a schedule of rates, payments being made against certificates at various stages or upon completion of the contract. Used mostly as for LUMP SUM CONTRACT.

memorandum buying. A system of purchasing mainly confined to retailing activities. The system permits the retailer to sell the goods before he pays the supplier. [May be coupled with a 'sale or return' clause agreed in advance with the supplier.]

model/master order procedure. See CONTRACTS, PROTOTYPE CONTRACT.

modification order. See BELOW, VARIATION ORDER.

open-ended order/contract. A form of running order/contract arrangement having no fixed date for termination. [It is usually essential to include a clause (such as a BREAK CLAUSE) enabling the purchaser to terminate or modify the arrangement].

open order. An order wherein one or more features of a full contractual commitment are missing, usually in respect of time of completion, or quantity or both as in many FORWARD SUPPLY ARRANGEMENTS – See ABOVE.

package deal. See ALL IN CONTRACT.

parallel working contracts. A representative part of a project is fully designed with full bills of quantities. Remainder is planned in outline with approximate bills. Details are then worked out and firm tenders obtained. Large projects where it is neither practicable nor desirable to design the whole job from the start e.g. local authority housing schemes.

periodic ordering or batching. To reduce the number of orders per week, or other period, requirements are held and collated into an order placed or reviewed for placing at a fixed rate, or when a viable quantity is reached, e.g. routine items or miscellaneous items on a wholesaler.

petty cash purchases. Purchasing method by which purchases are made for cash and the sum recovered from firm's petty cash fund. Very small low value items in the fixed price range.

pound cost averaging. *(CIPS)* Where regular imports are made at a fixed/stable commodity price the EXCHANGE RATE may vary. Under this arrangement, a fixed sum is allocated for each period. If the exchange rate varies adversely, the intake is reduced so as to keep expenditure within the fixed amount of finance allotted for the period. If the exchange rate varies in favour of the purchaser he may take advantage of this to build stocks to the value of the finance which is allotted. [Such SPECULATION needs close control by the financial management of the enterprise. Also it may not fit production or process demands.]

prime cost contract. One in which the contractor is reimbursed for his proven costs plus an addition to cover his over-heads and profit, either a percentage on that cost or a fixed fee.

priority order. An order which is identified as taking precedence over other orders to ensure its completion in the minimum time or to meet a fixed DEADLINE.

procurement systems contract. An arrangement made between buyer and seller whereby arrangements are made in advance of the actual need arising, enabling the buyer quickly to acquire material as and when required against the arrangement. These arrangements often take the form of the provision of CONSIGNMENT STOCK, held at the customer's premises, and are sometimes referred to simply as 'systems contracts'.

production reservation arrangements. Purchasing arrangements whereby the purchaser earmarks his supplier's production capacity, usually by monetary value or by machine hours, etc. Advance reservation is firmed up before each production period. Used for major requirements often with varying specifications but usually within the same product group.

quasi contract. *See* CONTRACT, QUASI CONTRACT.

reciprocal trading contracts. Purchase contracts which are related to the sales of other goods to the supplier. Each side buys from, and sells to, the other.

requisition/order. A requisition/ order form is so designed that after preparation by the user it may be sent to the purchasing department for editing, signature and forwarding to a supplier. 'Authorised persons' and other limits should be applied. Employed in companies, etc. where requisitioning on a central purchasing department is required. This obviates typing orders.

run-on contracts or serial contracts. Project planned in reasonably continuous phases. The first contract is let against firm details. These give a sound basis for later phases on the same supplier, these are then negotiated with him subsequently for firm contracts, e.g. council house schemes and where advantages of continuous work outweigh the need for fresh competition.

sale and lease-back. A method of acquiring the use of a major asset without owning it. The buyer sells off the asset for cash, thus eliminating any call on his own cash flow or other resources. He then leases back the asset for his own use and takes over the risks in use of it. The technique is used for acquisition of capital items such as factory premises, plant, ship, etc.

sale or return. A purchase on sale or return is an arrangement whereby the purchaser and seller agree that in the event of the goods not being sold they may be returned and the price credited.

sample, order for sample. Order for samples free or on charge. It regularises the transaction and provides valuable record.

self-regulating forward planning. A system whereby orders are placed periodically according to need and monitored against forecast and checked cumulatively. For major class 'A' needs, particularly for process-plant work. May be monitored by means of '2' CHARTS.

serial contracting. A system whereby a contractor (subject to satisfactory service) tenders for a series of projects on agreed terms. The rates of prices on the first job may be used as the bases for the remainder of the programme.

service contracts. As hire contracts as regards type of order. The same warnings apply. Also essential to study tariffs, etc with great care. Used for specified tasks, e.g. to carry out a specific overhaul programme, undertake a specific duty, i.e. security service.

severable contract. One involving deliveries by instalments where failure to deliver any one instalment may render the whole contract broken. Otherwise, in a normal contract a court will treat separate instalments as separate contracts, but in the case of a breach the court will look for the INTENTIONS of the parties.

small value order (SVO). Simplified ordering system. Smaller (usually) order forms in tear-off manuscript pads may be used. Have a limited cash validity. Only issued for use by 'authorised persons', foremen, etc. May be restricted to, say, £25–£30 or other limit. Technique used in non-recurring small value orders, or those drawn from forward supply arrangements and needed for day-to-day or occasional use.

sole supplier contracts. Contract with named supplier to the exclusion of others. A form of restrictive trading. May incur the attention of legal authorities if in breach of state or EU regulations.

standing order or contract. An order for regular delivery of goods or services for an indefinite period. A single original instruction normally suffices.

stock schedule order. A schedule, often of standard parts, used as an order. Schedules sent to suppliers either at regular intervals or on demand for specified materials.

stock production order. BS 5191 (42005). An production order to manufacture a product to replenish stock in a store.

stock purchase order. An order on a supplier for stock replenishment.

subcontracts. Arrangement whereby a main contractor (or supplier) authorises a second (or more) to undertake part of the order he has secured. Or, subcontract for supplies outside the purchaser's own production or because his production is overloaded.

supplier's order form. Order form provided by supplier. The form is completed and signed by the purchasing officer of the purchasing firm. (Not recommended unless full safeguards are applied. Only used in routine and regular orders, if at all.)

supplier's pre-printed order schedule. As above, a pre-printed (or duplicated) schedule of items supplied by a supplier. Employed for miscellaneous small regular items. May be used in conjunction with stock items, consignment stock, inplant stores, etc.

turnkey. *See* ALL-IN.

variation order. A purchasing instruction to a supplier to vary the substance (e.g. the instructions) on a purchase contract, e.g. quantity, specification, delivery, etc. *Note:* A variation order should always be in writing and a price should be agreed at the time of the variation order. The term VARIATION ORDER is preferred to the term MODIFICATION ORDER as this may have a double meaning. It is synonymous with 'amendment order'.

verbal orders. Orders given verbally by telephone or face to face. Legally binding once accepted by the supplier and acted upon. Should always be confirmed by written order unless of totally insignificant value.

volume versus exchange rate contract (= CIPS title 'VOLUME TIMED CONTRACT'). 'For this type of contract a datum rate of exchange is agreed as basic to the contract for importation of supplies. When the exchange rate rises above this level intake may be increased and stocks built up to take advantage of the favourable rate of exchange. When the exchange rate falls below the datum the purchaser reverts to HAND TO MOUTH buying of the minimum possible and using stocks where available'.

volume versus market price contracts. A system of buying in which timing of each contract is adjusted according to the market price forecast. Major raw materials only.

work and materials orders. Those orders which fall outside the scope of a contract for sale or hire-purchase, e.g. a contract for maintenance or installation of plant but not its purchase.

organisation and method ('O&M'). (adm). The application of WORK STUDY to the detailed administration, clerical and office work with the objectives of improved methods and procedures. Methods include examining: 1. needs for and of procedures/operations. 2. effectiveness of procedures/ operations. *See also* BS 3357 PART I. GUIDE TO ORGANISATION STUDY, *and also* WORK STUDY BS 3138 BS 3375: PART 1: 1984. Demonstrates the scope, objectives and procedures for organisation study to all levels of management and employee representatives who may be involved in investigations of organizations in which they operate. *See also* BS 3128.

Organization of Petroleum-Exporting Countries (OPEC). A prominent example of an international commodity PRODUCERS ASSOCIATION.

outage. The state of an item e.g. plant being unable to perform its required function.

outgoings. A term sometimes used for EXPENSES.

outsourcing. Placing responsibility for the provision of a selected service activity with an external provider.

out-of-phase, in supplies. The condition where INTAKES are out of step with DEMAND. This can result in glut when replenishments arrive and yet fail to prevent stock-out later in the production cycle. The difference between stock level and USAGE represents financial loss (usually unseen) to the enterprise.

overcharge. An amount in excess of the sum agreed in a contract. It must be noted that those costing for sales owe the same obligation to their enterprise to avoid an undercharge as does the purchasing officer to prevent an overcharge.

overhead costs. *See* 'COSTS, OVERHEAD COSTS.'

overhaul. BS 3811 (4117). A

137

comprehensive EXAMINA-TION and RESTORATION of an ITEM, or a major part thereof, to an acceptable condition. *See also* REPAIR.

overload. A load, electrical or mechanical, which exceeds the normal (stated/indicated) capacity of the plant or equipment. 'Overload capacity' may be negotiated by the purchaser. In this case the supplier should state the extra capacity above the normal rating which will be available and for an agreed (specified) time under specified operating conditions.

'Overseas Trade Magazine'. A free periodical (ten issues per annum) from the dti. Gives export news and opportunities in European markets.

over-specification. A specification in which TOLERANCES, LIMITS, performance or other features are specified more closely or rigidly than the end-use demands.

overtrading. CIMA. A term applied to a business which enters into commitments in excess of its available resources, e.g. a supplier may accept purchase orders for which he has inadequate means of paying for the supplies needed to execute the work.

own account operator. One who provides his own service, particularly transport, on his own account instead of using other available sources for the service he provides.

owner's risk. *See* RISK, OWNER'S.

ownership. *See* TITLE.

P

PPM. *See* PARTS PER MILLION.

package. Anything in which goods are contained for transit or storage, etc.

package deal. *See* ORDERS AND CONTRACTS, 'ALL-IN' CONTRACT.

package register. A record of movements inwards and outwards of packages (e.g. drums, cylinders, pallets, containers, handling tackle) which are sent by the supplier and will be charged for and invoiced and must be returned for credit and items which are free but returnable. Copies of package notes will be required by the invoice checking section.

packaging. BS 3130 (n). The design of, and the materials involved in, the packing of articles or commodities for carriage, storage and delivery. Some British Standards relevant to packaging, containers, etc. BS 814 sp: Drums, light duty, mild steel and tinplate. BS 1133 The Packaging Code. BS 1596 sp: Drums, fibreboard for shipment overseas. BS 1702 sp: Drums heavy duty, mild steel. BS 3130 gl. packaging terms. BS 4826 Packages, complete, filled for transport. BS 6051 sp: Packages filled for transport, records of distribution trials. BS 6082 Guide to compilation of test schedules for filled transport packages. BS 6720 sp: Packages, distribution, marking, transit information. BS 6837 sp:

Dimensions for rigid rectangular transport packages, distribution, marking, transit information, with modular relationships to suit 1200 mm × 1000 mm and 1200 mm × 800 mm and unit loads.

packing. (v). The operations of packaging whereby articles or commodities are enveloped in wrapping and/or enclosed in containers or otherwise secured.

packing note (packing list). A document packed inside individual packages of a consignment listing the actual goods in that package. cf. **BS 5191 (43007).**

pallet. BS 3810 (abb.). Portable platform with or without superstructure for the assembly of a quantity of goods to form a unit load for stacking and handling by mechanical appliances particularly by pallet truck and fork lift truck. *See also* LOAD BOARD, *also* STILLAGE.

pallet invertor. Device for transferring the load from one pallet to another by making a sandwich then turning it over.

pallet truck. Wheeled device for moving pallets horizontally (but not vertically). May be manual or powered.

palletisation. The arrangement for housing goods and material on pallets for handling, transportation, storage and use.

palletiser. Mechanical equipment for loading and/or wrapping pallets.

pallet loader, lorry bed type. Roller tracks in vehicle beds to facilitate the movement of pallets along the vehicle thus obviating the necessity for lift trucks to operate on the vehicle deck.

pallet racking. *See* RACKING, PALLET RACKING.

paperless trading. (it). The practice of sending trade information by electronic data interchange (EDI) instead of using paper documentation. EDI is claimed to give quicker*, cheaper and more secure communication than paper forms, and to allow traders to reduce LEAD TIMES and thus stock levels (and apply JIT ideas, reducing inventory costs). Requirements are a computer, telephone connection or access to a dedicated computer link. [*A vital caveat for purchasing and supply application is the need for mandatory checks on the data transmitted.]

paperless purchasing. *See* AUTOMATED PURCHASING.

parameter. (stat). A mathematical term, frequently used as a synonym for BOUNDARIES or LIMITS etc. It is more correctly defined as follows: 1. a constant that determines the form of a mathematical expression such as 'p' and 'b' in the formula $£c = pn + b$, where $£c$ is total cost, $£p$ is manufacturing cost per unit, n is number of units, $£b$ is fixed overhead costs. 2. a constant of a statistical POPULATION such as the VARIANCE or MEAN. 3. any constant or limiting factor such as that upon a designer working within the PARAMETERS (more correctly LIMITATIONS) of cost and practical utility.

Pareto's principle. IM. (Guidelines for Smaller Businesses No. 14.) A principle based on a study of distribution of national wealth, Pareto noticed that a large proportion of national wealth was under the control of a relatively small number of people. He therefore enunciated the rule that: 'In any series of elements to be controlled, a selected small factor in terms of the number of elements almost always accounts for a large factor in terms of effort'. *See* ABC ANALYSIS.

part (or component). BS 5191 (12005). A uniquely identifiable product that is considered indivisible for a particular planning or control purpose or purchasing.

partnership sourcing. An approach to sourcing through which mutually profitable long term relationships between suppliers and their customers are sought, based on openness and trust. It is important to note that this approach is not intended to allow the 'partners' to become relaxed and perhaps therefore less competitive, but instead to become more competitive through co-operation in the avoidance of waste. This approach is sponsored and supported by Partnership Sourcing (see list of bodies and associations at appendix). *See also* PARTERSHIP PURCHASING. [note that legislation relating to competition may have a bearing]

parts per million. PPM. Self explanatory; now commonly used (parts per million defective) as an indicator of quality where substandard parts are rarely encountered.

particular average. *See* AVERAGE, PARTICULAR AVERAGE.

particulates. Separate small particles of materials.

parts list (bill of materials, parts schedule). BS 5191 (12010). A list of all parts, sub-assemblies and raw materials that constitute a particular assembly, showing the quantity of each required.

Patent. *See* LETTERS PATENT.

payback. CIMA. A method of PROJECT ASSESSMENT by comparison of investment projects by calculating for each project the periods in which the profits earned will equal the original capital outlay.

payee. SITPRO. The party nominated by the drawer of a bill of exchange (draft) to receive payment.

payer. The person who pays the money due, by initiating a document such as a bill of exchange, etc.

paying bank. SITPRO (abb.). A

bank nominated in a DOCUMENTARY LETTER OF CREDIT to which documents (and sight bill of exchange, if called for) must be presented for payment.

payload. That portion of a load which contributes to revenue for the transport enterprise.

payment. The final stage in a contract whereby the purchaser completes his side of the contract. There may however be residual aspects committing the supplier: MAINTENANCE PERIOD, RETENTION MONEYS, ADJUSTMENT MONEY, etc.

payment against documents (cash against documents). SITPRO. The shipper (exporter) does not release the goods or the bill of lading on arrival until full payment has been made. When a contract includes this clause, the captain of the ship will not, on arrival in port, hand over the bill of lading and documents of title, or the goods until the covering draft from the consignor has been paid.

payment, cash with order. *See* ORDERS & CONTRACTS, CASH WITH ORDER A–Z.

payment, down payment. One made by a purchaser as an initial instalment for a purchase, or as a DEPOSIT. *See also* PAYMENT, STAGE PAYMENT etc.

payment, lump-sum payment. A single payment in cash, usually for a large sum. Also remuneration paid to a shipowner for charter of a ship or portion of it irrespective of the quantity of cargo loaded.

payment, pro-forma payment. Payment made against a PRO-FORMA INVOICE before goods are released or delivered.

payment, pre-payment. CIMA. A clause by a seller that payment is to be made before delivery.

payments, progress payments. Payments which may be made for work done during the progress of a contract. The amounts due are in proportion to the work so far completed, and the proportions are agreed between the buyer and seller at the time the contract is let, or are as laid down in standard national agreements for various trades. Payments are made against certificates for work so far completed at the various agreed stages of manufacture or construction. *See also* PLANNING AND PROGRESSING.

payment, prompt payment. *See* PRICE, PAYMENT AND TIME RELATED.

payment, spot cash payment. Payment to be made on ACCEPTANCE OF CONTRACT for goods wherever they may be lying and not necessarily waiting for delivery to be effected.

payments, stage. Payments made at planned stages of a civil engineering, or construction or plant contract against certificates signed by an authorised person to vouch that the work has been done. *See*

also PAYMENTS, PROGRESS PAYMENTS.

penalty (penalty clause). (law). A term sometimes used for a clause in a contract which stipulates a sum to be paid by a supplier in the event of his default in a contract. A penalty clause ('in terrorem') cannot be enforced in a court of law. *See* DAMAGES LIQUIDATED *and* DAMAGES UNLIQUIDATED. *Note:* On applying a penalty clause a plaintiff can, as a rule, only recover the direct damage resulting from a BREACH of the contract.

perfect competition. *See* COMPETITION, PERFECT COMPETITION.

performance bonds. *See* BONDS, PERFORMANCE.

performance, specific performance. (law). The carrying out of all TERMS and CONDITIONS of a contract. An order by a court may call for specific performance by a supplier, i.e. to complete his contract with the purchaser, instead of awarding DAMAGES to be paid to the latter who has suffered loss.

perils of the sea. (ins). A marine insurance clause relating to dangers which may occur to a vessel and its cargo during a voyage, the risks of which, on being accepted in a bill of lading, is undertaken to cover by the insurers.

periodic stock check. *See* STOCK CHECK, PERIODIC STOCK CHECK.

period, production period. *See* PRODUCTION PERIOD.

perishable goods. Those which deteriorate if not used within their SHELF-LIFE or stored under (special) suitable conditions to preserve them.

permits, bi-lateral transit permits. (EU). Bilateral permits, usually for one 'there and back' trip only, enable transits across EU and non-EU States. Further permits are needed to cross intervening States. Conditions of granting the permits varies from State to State.

perpetual inventory. Americanism for STOCK-CONTROL, CONTINUOUS. *See also* INVENTORY, *and* STOCK-TAKING.

perpetual stock record. *See* STOCK RECORD CONTINUOUS STOCK RECORD.

perquisites. Fees or emolument allowed by law for some specific purpose, usually of a casual nature and beyond normal salary or wages for services rendered.

personal protective equipment. (EC directive (89/686 EEC) (HS). Any device or appliance designed to be worn or held for protection against safety and health hazards. The 'essential requirements' include 'general requirements' such as the suitability of constituent components, and requirements specific to particular risks such as fire, heat, cold, radiation noise and unbreathable atmospheres. It includes hard hats, safety footwear, life-jackets, eye and hearing protection, high visibility clothing and clothing to pro-tect against adverse weather. *Note:* The REGULATION SI 1992/2966 does not cover ordinary working clothes and uniforms or PPE for road transport (e.g. crash helmets or portable devices for detecting or signalling risks and nuisances). *See* HSE PERSONAL PROTECTIVE EQUIPMENT AT WORK. ISBN 0 11 886334 7. Implemented by UK Regulation SI. 1992/2966 w.e.f. 1.1.1993. Involves the provision and use of PPE where risks cannot be avoided or sufficiently limited. Employer must carry out RISK ASSESSMENT, provide free suitable equipment, comply with EU provisions on design and manufacture, maintain PPE in good working order, involve workers and provide information, etc.

photodegradation. (env. ecol. pkg. subs). Degradation of certain substances by absorption of light particularly to ultra-violet rays. Applies chiefly to fibrous textiles, etc. Usually the degradation is accompanied by a loss of strength in the material owing to breakdown of the polymers. Suitable protection from ultra-violet light is therefore needed when storing such materials.

petty cash. (fin). A small sum set aside for minor expenses and purchases. From the standpoint of administration of purchasing and supply the control of purchasing through the use of petty cash is difficult. It can lead to abuse, fraud and error, one solution is the use of LOCAL PURCHASE

ORDERS. *See under* ORDERS & CONTRACTS, VARIETIES OF.

piece goods. Name applied to goods sold by the piece, such as sheetings, canvas, etc.

pie chart. A chart within a circular boundary whose area is the sum of individual amounts (of stock or other measurement) represented by segments within the circle. The area of each of the segments is proportional to the amount (of stock) held.

piece parts. Components manufactured from raw materials, to make assemblies or sub-assemblies. The term is often applied to parts made in a manufacturer's own works.

piece rate. A method of remuneration by which the worker receives a definite sum for performing a stipulated quantity of work. Originally, goods or material made 'in the piece', now applied to components used in manufacture and assemblies.

picking, order picking. Colloquialism for the act of removing goods from their storage location for issue.

picking list. Colloquialism for a parts list or schedule set out in such a manner as to facilitate order picking from stores.

pictogram. Diagram which displays statistical information by pictorial representation of the items under consideration, e.g. in purchasing

and supply. For example, a diagrammatic map showing origins of sources of supply from different areas with colours or shading to indicate (e.g.) pricing or transport, etc.

pilot run and/or prototype. May be required before the start of a major contract.

pipeline. 1. Large diameter tube for long distance conveyance. 2. Used metaphorically for ideas similar to SUPPLY CHAIN.

planning. The setting of targets, whether of production, sales, supplies, profits or other features, or the plant and structures needed for their attainment.

place utility. The value added to a product by moving it to where it can be used.

planning, corporate planning. The study of long term (long HORIZON) objectives and strategy of an enterprise as a corporate entity.

planning cycle. The sequence by which planning, implementation, evaluation and revision of plans take place.

planning, distribution requirements and resource planning. (DRP). A system for forecasting or projecting requirements for finished goods at the point of demand. 'From these projections, aggregated, time-phased requirements schedules can be derived...' DRP is a 'pull' system depending upon assessments of the demands of end-users of the supply concerned.

planning horizon. BS 5191 (22001) (adm). 'The longest time ahead for which production plans are normally made'. *See also* PURCHASING PLANNING HORIZON.

planning, long term strategic planning. CIMA. abb. The formulation, evaluation and selection of strategies involving a review of the objectives of an enterprise, its environment, strengths, weaknesses, opportunities, threats, etc. so as to prepare a long term plan.

planning policy. (adm). Decisions of an important nature usually wider in scope than strategies or tactical planning and of long HORIZON, i.e. a decade or more.

planning, strategic planning. Overall planning to meet main overall objectives and taking account of tactical planning which should contribute to the overall strategy.

planning, supplies. PROVISIONING to suit the planning policies of the enterprise on a time scale to suit the HORIZONS of the main planning policies of the enterprise.

planning, tactical. Planning decisions usually in a particular field or activity and which may be of shorter duration than other planning – a year or less.

plant. The assemblage of tools and equipment to manufacture goods, chemicals, power, etc. and usually situated in a fixed location for a particular operation, or mobile as in the case of handling equipment.

plant numbers, plant numbering. The numbering of units of plant and equipment with individual numbers. These facilitate the keeping of maintenance and performance records. Plant numbers can also assist the functions of purchasing and supply in the provisioning and storage of spares and maintenance contracts.

plant register. CIMA. A record showing the details of each item of plant purchased and used by a business. A valuable record for maintenance purchasing, record and control of spares, etc.

plating, of vehicles. The fixing to vehicles of the various signs showing their size, type, capacity, load, dangerous goods, hazard signs and so on.

Plimsoll Line. *See* LOAD LINE.

policy. The objective, the mode of thought, and the body and principles underlying activities and organisation in the light of changing circumstances.

policy stock *See* STOCK, POLICY STOCK.

population. BS ISO 3534–1 (2.3). The totality of ITEMS under consideration. e.g. The total of all the ITEMS in a RANGE. *Note*: 'Range' may be misleading if used as a measure of demand for future stock building, control or purchasing unless due care is taken regarding exceptions at each extreme of a range.

post date. (v). To date a document with a date later than that upon which it was prepared, or signed, etc. In the latter instance and in regard to contracts and similar documents there may be legal implications. But the action may be warranted where a cheque is post dated to ensure it will not be cashed until funds are available or some other contingency such as delivery has been successfully achieved.

practicable. Able to be achieved at the current state of knowledge bibl. (HSC) 7.

practicable, reasonably practicable. The point at which 'good practice' in the relevant industry at which further improvements simply cannot be justified by the benefits that follow [from such improvements]. bibl. MANUAL HANDLING CD 36 (F) p. 7. (HS)

precision. *See* QUALITY CONTROL.

preferred numbers. A technique devised by Charles Renard using the principle of geometric progression in sizes of particular items of supply. The choice of sizes depends upon the number and range of sizes needed. Applied to plant, preferred numbers provide means to greater interchangeability, e.g. of spares. The technique helps to create uniformity and assists VARIETY REDUCTION. *See* **PD 6481**: recommendations for the use of preferred numbers and preferred sizes.

premium. (fin mkt). A margin deducted from a spot exchange rate reflecting the dearer forward value of one currency against another.

pre-packing. BS 3130. The operation of packing goods ready for sale or issue immediately they are required.

pre-paid. *See* PAYMENT, PRE-PAYMENT.

pre-standards. *See* EUROPEAN PRE-STANDARDS.

preservation. The prescribed protection or other preparation of an item so as to maintain it in good condition during transit and in stores.

prevention cost. *See* COST, PREVENTION COST.

price. Amount of CONSIDERATION to be paid or given for an article, goods, service or something desired, offered or purchased. *See also* COST for which price is not a synonym.

price, all round price. One which covers various costs which would normally be charged as 'extras'.

price analysis. 'The examination of a seller's price without examination of the separate elements of cost and profit making up the price'.

price, at despatch. The normal method of pricing where the purchase order fails to specify an agreed price at the time it is placed. But, *see also* PRICE, PRICE AT INVOICE DATE.

price, average price. A price which represents the average (mean) of a number of prices. This may be based upon the simple or weighted average. *See also* COST, AVERAGE COST.

price, basing point price. A method of pricing so that identical freight charges are made to all customers in a particular area irrespective of their distance from a point selected by the supplier and known as the basing point.

price, basis point. A price taken for the basis of comparison or for further calculation.

price, basis price. The difference between the price of a commodity for a specific future month and the SPOT PRICE for the same commodity.

price, bonded or in bond. The price of goods as they lie in a bonded warehouse, the buyer to pay duty on them.

price break. The point at which a supplier's price changes in response to a change in quantity. (e.g. there may be a reduction in price when a certain quantity of supply is ordered.)

price, cash and carry. Orders priced in this manner require the buyer to pay cash and carry away the goods he has purchased with no credit allowed. *See* ORDERS AND CONTRACTS.

price, cash price. The price at which a vendor is prepared to sell provided the purchaser is prepared to make immediate payment. [In making the DEAL the purchaser may or may not also be required, or wish to take immediate delivery.] *See* PRICE, CASH AND CARRY.

price, cash on delivery. Orders priced in this manner require the buyer to pay cash when the goods are received with no credit allowed. *See* ORDERS AND CONTRACTS.

price, catalogue price. The price quoted in a catalogue or price list as an 'invitation to treat' by the prospective purchaser. Such lists were originally taken as CURRENT PRICES, but this assumption can no longer be made without a specific statement to that effect being given by the vendor.

price, 'conference price'. Adjusted price by means of a rebate given to shippers who agree to restrict shipments to a destination to the sailings of the shipping lines in the conference serving that destination.

price, contract price adjustment price. A final price of a contract whereby the original contract price has been adjusted for changes in wages and materials during the course of the contract and calculated by a formula agreed between the parties to the contract. Also referred to as an ESCALATION CLAUSE.

price, cost insurance and freight. Price applicable to shipping contracts on this basis. *See* COST, INSURANCE AND FREIGHT *and* INCOTERMS.

price, cost price. A price based purely upon cost of goods without allowing profit, etc.

price, current price. 1. The established price 'for the day' in a market. [But *see also* SPOT PRICE]. 2. The up-to-date catalogue/price list. [But note, unless stated otherwise such prices are 'invitations to treat' with no commitment as to the validity of the price shown]. *See* TREAT, INVITATION TO TREAT.

price, cut price. Incentive pricing at a figure usually below true cost and competitor's prices to obtain business or dispose of surplus, etc.

price, discriminatory price. The offering of similar or identical goods at different prices to different buyers.

price, dishonoured price. One where a supplier who has accepted a FIRM PRICE order later claims an increase for which no provision for adjustment has been made in the contract.

price, dumped price. The sale of goods (usually) in an overseas market at a lower price than in the home market.

price, duty paid price. The price of goods (e.g. in a bonded warehouse) including duties.

price, duty price. The price defined by Customs as 'Customs landed price or open market value at the point of entry'.

price, economic net price. A price which results in equilibrium between profit and loss to the supplier.

price, elastic demand price. A situation is regarded as elastic when a small change in price results in significant increase in demand or vice versa. For example, if the price per unit of a commodity is listed in one column and demand in units for each price in the adjoining column (or presented graphically) the optimum policies for selection of appropriate price or target for demand can be assessed. [An industrial purchasing and supply demand is however usually fixed by production/sales needs].

price, equilibrium price. The theoretical price which arises in a 'perfect' market when supply and demand are equal.

price, estimated price. One which is based upon an ESTIMATE and may therefore not be the final price required for the goods or service offered and ordered.

price, fair price. 'The price at which buyer and seller are prepared to do business with each other on a specific deal or a continuing basis': from an economic report by the former Purchasing Officers Association. That price which allows a producer to pay fair wage rates, buy and use the correct materials, carry out adequate research, and maintain adequate capital investment in plant and equipment and earn a reasonable return on capital so invested. 1. Governmental Statutes, EC Directives, CODES OF PRACTICE, etc. 2. Health and safety regulations 3. Environmental control 4. Conservation 5. British, European and international standards. 6. Compliance with the 'Social Chapter' in States which subscribe to its provisions. [Developments brought about by Community membership may entail further disciplines.]

price, firm price. A price which will not be varied during the term of a contract.

price, first-in, first-out price. The price paid for supplies first taken into stock is used for pricing purposes, costing, invoicing, etc. *Note*: Such 'historical pricing' is not reliable for estimating purposes.

price, fixed. A price which cannot be varied by the efforts of the buyer in negotiation as distinct from a price which can be so negotiated in the course of offer and counter-offer between buyer and seller.

price fixing. The process by which prices are set in advance or by agreement between producers, viz. PRICE RING, or by governmental edict, rather than through the operation of a free market. Now illegal in most free market economies.

price, forward price. One offered by a supplier for a supply against an order to be confirmed at a future date. *See also* PRICE, FUTURES PRICE.

price, 'franco'. Free delivery to buyer's warehouse.

price, free alongside, free on board, etc. *See* INCOTERMS.

price, free price. A price which is arrived at by the effects of free unfettered MARKET FORCES.

price, futures price. (fin mkts). Price estimated by brokers for FUTURES based on options to buy and sell a commodity on an exchange.

price index. A figure, usually expressed as a percentage, and showing the relationship between a current price and the price at some pre-arranged date. [*See also* STATISTICS, INDEX NUMBERS.]

price, indifference price. The price at which a buyer, if he has the option whether or not to purchase goods, will be indifferent whether or not to proceed with purchase or seek a better bargain. *See* BREAK-EVEN POINT, COST-BENEFIT ANALYSIS *and* PRICE, EQUILIBRIUM PRICE.

price, invoice date, price at. The order will be priced as at date of invoice not necessarily at date of despatch. [A delayed invoice may thereby include a price increase after the completion of the contract].

price, leader price. A ruse used by a price ring to evade the law. One member's price is followed by others, based on 'reported price' communicated to all members. Illegal in most 'free market' economies. *See also* PRICE, LOSS LEADER PRICE.

price, limits of. The limits, normally above [e.g. a TARGET PRICE] which should be specified on a purchase order so as to avoid overspending on a project or budget.

price list. A vendor's list of articles he has for sale with the prices at which he makes an OFFER TO TREAT with prospective purchasers. In former times a price list was valid until the issue of the next edition.

price, list price. Price given in a supplier's published PRICE LIST.

price, loco price. Price wherever lying – buyer to pack and load.

price, loss leader price. A price applied to a sales item (or line of items) which is near or below COST PRICE in order to induce additional sales.

price, loyalty price. A concessionary price given to a customer in consideration that he will make all or an agreed proportion of his purchases from the supplier who gives the concession. Usually such concessions are in the form of a rebate.

price, marginal price. The price for one more article than the previous quantity quoted for, manufactured or purchased.

price, mark down price. The price which has been reduced from normal selling or list price shown by a retailer or a distributor to increase sales.

price, market price. 1. Current in open market; 2. Economic equilibrium price resulting from supply and demand in open market.

price, mean price. The mean price calculated from a series of values. Used in some stock account valuations.

price, monopolistic price. Price based on ability of monopolist to control price against the natural forces of supply and demand, or the efforts of a purchasing officer.

price, net price. The price at which a bargain may be made with no further discounts or additions. (Old usage was neat price.)

price, nominal price. An arbitrary price [may be a very low one] applied to an item of goods or a service, etc. *See also* PRICE, NOTIONAL PRICE.

price, notional price. A hypothetical price (or cost) taken into account to represent a benefit enjoyed in respect of which no actual known price (or cost) can be ascertained.

price, normal or natural price.

(fin). That price which arises through the interplay of free market forces. But, *see also* PRICE ECONOMIC PRICE *and* PRICE, FAIR PRICE.

price, on rail. *See* INCOTERMS.

price, on site price. A price which includes plant or goods being delivered and set down on a prepared site or hard-standing. The contract must state if other requirements apply such as, if to be 'erected', 'tested', 'set to work', etc.

price, open price agreement. The practice of some businesses to exchange information regarding prices and/or price changes in the field. The method adopted has to avoid the need to report the arrangement to the RESTRICTIVE PRACTICES COURT. Illegal in most 'free market' economies.

price, opportunity price. The price at which the benefit from the purchase breaks-even with the disbenefit of foregoing the acquisition of the item. *See also* COST, OPPORTUNITY COST.

price, overdue account price. A 'penalty' price applied by a supplier upon customers who are 'late payers' – usually claimed by a percentage on the account – but, must be stated when the order is accepted, otherwise it is void.

price, payment and time related price. A price which takes account of time or times at which payment is to be made. *See* PRICE,

PROMPT CASH PRICE. *See also* STAGE PAYMENTS.

price, premium price. A price set above the normal or list price, etc, paid to a supplier so as to gain some advantage.

price, progressive rebated price. *See* REBATES.

price, progress payments. Price structures which contain this clause will require PROGRESS (or stage) PAYMENTS during the term of the contract to which they apply. Such progress or stage payments usually require certificates authorised by the purchaser or his duly appointed agent, to certify that the work has been satisfactorily executed to that stage of its completion.

price, prompt cash price. A price reduce below LIST (or normal) price of the supplier to encourage prompt payment of his account. Usually given in the form of a discount. *See also* PAYMENT.

price, quantity price. One based upon profitability of quantities bought and/or manufactured. Usually offered as an inducement to order in larger quantity. (May be given by discount, rebate, etc.)

price, quoted price. Price submitted in quotation or tender. Usually valid 30 days or other stated period.

price, reasonable price. *See* PRICE, FAIR PRICE.

price, recommended price. A price suggested by a supplier (manufacturer or major distributor) for sale of his goods in the domestic market. The former method of establishing fixed prices for goods has been banned in most free market economies in the interest of stimulating competition.

price, re-opener clause. A clause which a purchaser may write into a contract so that a new lower price can be negotiated if, for example, the quantity required turns out to be greater than the original estimate or an improved method of manufacture, packaging or handling, etc. is discovered; or higher if the purchaser changes his specification, quantity or other factor(s) which may have price-cost implications.

price, replacement price. CIMA. The price at which an asset, identical to that which is being replaced or revalued, could be purchased.

price, reported price. Members of a trade association (or price ring) report quoted prices to one another. Illegal in most free market economies.

price, resale price. Price recommended by supplier for resale.

price, reserve(d) price. The lowest price at which an owner will sell. Term usually applied at an auction.

price, ring price. Price fixed by price ring. Illegal in most free market economies.

price, ruling price. The price generally understood to be that ruling at the date of despatch or other date specified and agreed. *See also* PRICE, INVOICE DATE, PRICE AT.

price, seasonal price. A price (or prices) adjusted to meet seasonal conditions, either variations in seasonal demand or conditions of shortage or glut, or stringency such as difficulties of transport, harvesting or numerous other factors.

price, small quantity price. A PREMIUM PRICE charged (or claimed) for a smaller than normal quantity ordered or delivered in smaller batches than usual, or more frequently.

price, spot price. Price on the day of quotation for immediate delivery. Term used when trading in a commodity market.

price, standard price. BS 5191 (B2005). A predetermined price fixed on the basis of a specification of all the factors affecting that price.

price, station at. *See* FREE ON RAIL.

price, statutory (legal) price. A price set by governmental decree as a form of control.

price, survival price. A special price offered by a supplier to secure an order or contract without which his business will fail unless he secures it.

price, target price. A price given to

a supplier either in an enquiry or purchase order where the precise value of the contract may not be precisely known when the order is given, e.g. an urgent plant repair. It may also be the price given to a purchasing officer to ensure the competitiveness of a sales project or quotation by his company. *See also* PRICE, LIMITS OF.

price, trade price. Price usually given to buyers in same trade or for resale. (Usually given by special discount).

price, transfer price (and transfer pricing). CIMA. The price used when supplies or services are transferred from one department to another in the same plant or between firms within the same group. The extent to which costs and profit are covered by transfer price is a matter of policy. The transfer price may, for example, be based upon marginal cost/full cost/market price/ negotiated price, etc. For further information *see* CIMA MANAGEMENT ACCOUNTING GUIDELINE NO. 1.

price, upset price. The lowest (or reserve) price an owner will accept at an auction.

price, ex warehouse price. Warehouse price includes cost of goods and packing, and loading on to the customer's vehicle but not carriage to the customer.

primage. Percentage on the freight paid to owners of freighters or vessels to cover commission for chartering and other expenses, e.g. lights, pilots, wharves, etc.

prime costs. *See* COSTS, PRIME COSTS.

privity of contract. (law). A legal doctrine which avers that a contract is a private relationship between the contracting parties and that no other person can acquire rights or incur liabilities in it.

Proactive: 1. Tending to initiate change rather than reacting to events'. [der:Latin, 'pro' = 'in favour of'.] From Collins, English Dictionary 1991. 2. An action or condition which may arise in the future. As a medical/'health and safety' application it can refer to the future onset of a disease. e.g. asbestosis from the inhalation and/or ingestion of asbestos dust which may affect the victim some years later. [der: Greek 'pro'='before' – as with 'prognosis' = 'foreknowledge'.]

probability. A measure of the likelihood of an event to occur. Statistically its value lies between the limits of 'zero' and 'one'. '0' represents impossibility. '1' represents certainty. Probability is calculated by dividing the number of favourable events by the total number of possible events considered.

probabilistic systems. Systems with characteristics which are predictable and controllable but only between defined limits, such as maintaining production or supply within limits, e.g. at maximum and minimum stock control levels. *See also* HOMEOSTASIS. Also known as STOCHASTIC SYSTEMS. They are distinct from deterministic

153

systems which have fixed and clearly predictable limits such as an engine (or other prime-mover) controlled by a governor.

process mapping. Investigation and modelling, usually by means of a graphical representation, a process or problem with a view to improvement or solution.

process plant industry. Second stage in overall SUPPLIES CYCLE, where basic materials (usually) from extractive industries (e.g. oil) are converted (usually) for further manipulation and processing before the final END-PRODUCT is reached. The end-products of most process plants provide the raw materials for the next stage in the overall supplies cycle.

process planning. BS 5191 (13001). The activity which determines the operations required, and their sequence to produce a part or assembly [or operate a process].

processing, information processing. (adm). A specialist activity performed by the administrative organisation of an enterprise. It is concerned with the systematic recording, arranging, collating, processing, filing, retrieval and dissemination of facts relating to the physical/financial events occuring in a business. *See also* INFORMATION TECHNOLOGY.

procurement. The obtaining by various means (e.g. loan, transfer, hire, purchase, etc.) of supplies and services with or without CONSIDERATION.

procurement cycle, the. The overall cycle of obtaining supplies from the origin of the need through the purchasing or other means, e.g. loan etc, to the intake of correct requirements and final consumption and disposal.

procurement lead time. *See* LEAD TIME, TOTAL.

'Procurement Weekly'. A weekly publication by the Chartered Institute of Purchasing and Supply. It gives news of developments, new regulations and products.

producer goods. Plant, buildings and equipment, etc. required for manufacturing purposes as distinct from CONSUMER GOODS.

producers' associations. Organisations for co-operation among enterprises producing or marketing the same commodity.

product. BS 5191 (12001). An end item or output from a work station, factory or other organisational group. 'Any industrially manufactured product and any agricultural product'. (dti)

product group. A number of products with one or more common characteristics which make it convenient to combine them for planning and control purposes, for example products using similar resources or products with similar marketing requirements.

product liability. (HS) **BS 4778 (pt.1:3.19).** The onus on a producer or distributer for the condition of a product that causes an event by which someone suffers loss or harm.

product liability Directive. (85/374 EEC). This Directive makes manufacturers and importers liable for injuries caused by defective products. [A UK 'option' provides a balance between the right of compensation to those injured and the need to see that innovation is not hampered].

product safety directive. (92/59 EEC). This directive introduces a general obligation on producers, importers and distributors, to supply safe consumer products. [Adopted by HMG.UK wef 29.6.1994].

production. The creation of goods or materials by manufacture, manipulation and/or process, and also the provision of SERVICES. Production, in the economic senses, involves ADDED VALUE leading to END-PRODUCTS or SERVICES which possess 'money value' known in contract and legal terminology as 'CONSIDERATION'. *Note:* As in the other specialised sections the terms included are restricted to some of those which relate directly or indirectly to purchasing and supply ADMINISTRATION AND MANAGEMENT. For more comprehensive coverage the reader is recommended to consult the BRITISH STANDARDS and EUROPEAN STANDARDS, particularly BS 5191 'GLOSSARY OF PRODUCTION PLANNING AND CONTROL TERMS.'

production: waiting time. BS 5191 (26010). The period of time for which an operator is available for production but is prevented from working by shortage of materials or tooling, or breakdown, etc.

production (and process) capacity. For both the broader and detailed aspects of production and production capacity, a production handbook should be consulted. The definitions given here relate to those of the purchase, manufacture and process. 1. OUTPUT CAPACITY measured in units/ tonnage available for supply in units of time such as 'per production period', 'working week' 'calendar month', or other measure, such as the time-cycle of the purchaser's requirements [a frequent cause of misunderstandings]. 2. OUTPUT CAPACITY (MAXIMUM) in units as above and essential data for the purchaser whose demand varies with peaks which are predictable, seasonal or random. 3. ALLOCATABLE/ RESERVABLE CAPACITY: capacity which a supplier can by negotiation and subsequent contract allocate or reserve for output dedicated to the purchaser. This may be in units of output, or in financial value based on the production costs of the supplier. If, for example, the output comprises equipment or plant which is of a particular type but for which there can be some variations in SPECIFICATION (e.g. electrical switchgear) some flexible order method may be used such as PRODUCTION RESERVATION ORDER/ CON-

TRACT. *See also* PROGRESSING and PLANNING. 4. CAPACITY, PRODUCTION. **BS 5191 (13010).** 'The capability of a production facility under specified operating conditions'.

production: batch production (cf. **BS 5191).** Production of quantities in BATCHES which do not reach quantities needed for mass or continuous production and which may, or may not, be in standardised form. Frequently batch production' is the output of a 'jobbing' production unit. Such units can be more economical for supply than the use of high-output units with greater SETTING-UP COSTS and CHANGE-OVER COSTS.

Production, 'Census of Production'. A summary of information about British industry. It provides valuable statistics on: sales, output per employee, inputs of supplies, usage of energy on all the major industrial product groups.

production, changeover time. BS 5191 (26005). 'The time taken to change a work station from a state of readiness for one operation to a state of readiness for another and different operation.' *Note:* changeover time may be less than the sum of breaking down and setting up times. May incur additional costs to a purchaser where an urgent or emergency measure is needed for supply in crisis.

production, computer integrated production. *See* **BS: DD194.** 'Computer integrated manufac-

turing' (CIM). BS gives 'systems architecture for modelling. Structure for identifying and coordinating standards development for computer based modelling of enterprises. Emphasis on discrete parts manufacturing and relevant to the implementation of computer executable models'.

production cycle time. BS 5191 (26002). 'The time required to complete an operation on a BATCH. = also "floor-to-floor" time'.

production down time. BS 5191 (26008). 'The period of time for which a work station is not available for production due to a functional failure'.

production, flexible manufacturing system (FMS). A system which enables a manufacturer to switch rapidly from the output of one product to another. A common situation in general jobbing engineering. May be helpful to those purchasing urgent and various supplies *but* the manufacturer (supplier) needs close control of stocks and supplies and logistics.

production, flow production. A production/process system (usually large-scale) in which products (or materials in process) flow from stage to stage until they reach the final state. [In both product and process flow BUFFER STOCK may be needed to ensure continuous operation, JUST IN TIME technique may be applicable.]

production, glossary of terms. BS 5191.

production, idle time. BS 5191 (26009). The period of time for which a work-station is available for production but is not utilized due to shortage of tools, materials, or operators. *See also* DOWN TIME *and* WAITING TIME.

production item, an item (of production). An identifiable item, sub-assembly or equipment supported by a manufacturer's part or drawing number.

production, 'just in time'. *See* JUST IN TIME. *See also* KANBAN.

production, lean. A system pioneered by Toyota in Japan whereby production takes place in small quantities as determined by immediate demand only. Skilled and dedicated personnel, using appropriate equipment and methods, avoid defective production and other forms of waste. Facilities are arranged to enable smooth flows of work. JUST IN TIME ideas are employed.

production-line production. The layout of production plant and equipment in the direct line in which the production processes will take place. [May affect the points at which additional supplies are fed into the process from stores].

production, manufacturing resource planning (MRP). This technique is usually known by the acronym 'MRP2'. It is a development from 'materials resource planning' (MRP), and encompasses the planning and scheduling activities associated with the allocation of production resources themselves. *See also* MATERIAL RESOURCE PLANNING.

production, marginal production. Manufacture where the cost of production equals the cost of the goods, i.e. with no profit or other allowance. *See also* COST/COSTING MARGINAL COST.

production, mass production. The production of END-PRODUCTS or COMPONENTS, etc. on an intensive, repetition basis to a standard specification.

production, master production schedule. The plan for production of completely finished products or assemblies.

production, modular production. A method of production by which items are produced to modular dimensions enabling them to be used in a number of applications.

production, operational duration times. BS 5191 (2.6) and Figure 5. **(26001).** 'The period of time required to carry out an operation on a complete BATCH exclusive of SET UP TIME **(26004)** and 'breaking down' time **(26003).** Other factors may need to be taken into account such as: CYCLE TIME **(26002),** 'changeover time' **(26005),** 'transit time' [internal movement within the production process.]

(26006), 'queueing time' **(26007)**. But *see* QUEUEING THEORY UNDER STATISTICS, 'DOWN TIME' **(26008)** AND IDLE TIME **(26009)** *also* 'WAITING TIME' **(26010)**.

production, optimised production technology (OPT). The OPT method seeks the balance of component parts of the manufacturing process through control of flow by technological means. OPT can avoid bottlenecks common to batch production if numerous different products are in course of manufacture simultaneously.

production overheads. Indirect materials, supporting goods, indirect wages, and expenses incurred in production.

production period. The length of time which forms the basis for production or process plant operation. May be the number of hours, days weeks, etc. the plant will operate continuously, e.g. on one production run or one batch of feedstock in a process plant.

production pilot run. The initial throughput of units or process material to check 1. suitability for manufacture, 2. costs, 3. tooling, 4. robotics, 5. material supplies, etc.

production planning and control. BS 5191 (11001). Procedures and means by which manufacturing programmes and plans are determined, information issued for their execution and data collected and recorded to control manufacture in accordance with the plans.

production, pre-production/ assembly operations. Operations, which in the context of purchasing and supply administration may be performed prior to and in preparation for production/process, within a stores complex, e.g. cleaning of components, removal of spew from plastic mouldings, deburring of castings, counting and weighing batches, loose assembly and other operations of a preparatory nature.

production programme. BS 5191 (22003). A list or chart showing products and quantities which are to be produced in a given time.

production resource planning. *See* MANUFACTURING RESOURCE PLANNING 'MRP2'.

production, set up time. BS 5191 (26004). 'The time required to prepare a work station from a standard condition to readiness to commence a specified operation'. Also has implications for purchasing and supply. *See also* COSTS, SET UP COSTS.

production, stock production order. BS 5191 (42005). 'A production order to manufacture a product to replenish stock'. The same desciplines regarding STOCK CONTROL will usually apply to both manufacturer as to purchaser.

production, work centre. BS 5191 (13006). 'A set of WORK STATIONS grouped for convenience of PLANNING or work-flow'.

production, work cycle. BS 3138 (22096). Work study. Work cycle is the sequence of elements which are required to perform a job or yield a unit of production output. The sequence may include 'occasional elements'. Such occasional elements are intermittent and may not occur in every work cycle of a job, but, may occur at regular or irregular intervals. [e.g. Stores staff may be required to leave stores from time to time to assist incoming traffic to unload, etc.]

production, work measurement. *See under* WORK.

production works order. BS 3811. A written instruction detailing work to be carried out. *Note:* BS 3811 depreciates the use of the word 'job card' for this.

production, work in progress. BS 5191 (23004). Stock (or other supplies) upon which work has been performed or has been made ready for work to be started, but which is not available for supply to an external consumer.

production, work station. BS 5191 (3005). The smallest set of resources for the purpose of planning and control that form a productive unit at a particular location.

production, 'zero defects' in production. A motivating discipline which encourages the sense of responsibility and pride of achievement in production staffs when producing output with ZERO DEFECTS.

profit. CIMA. The financial gain resulting from a transaction or combination of transactions, being the excess of sales revenue over related costs. *See also* PROFITABILITY.

profit, profit attributable (on contracts). CIMA. That part of total profit currently estimated to arise over the duration of the contract (after allowing for likely increases in costs so far as these are not recoverable under terms of contract) which fairly reflects the profit attributable to that part of the work performed at the accounting date. There can be no attributable profit until the outcome of the contract can be assessed with reasonable certainty.

profit centre. A division of an organisation to which both expenditure and revenue are attributed and in respect of which profitability can be assessed.

profitability. Actions or transactions which tend to lead to profit, or the 'ability' to produce a profit. The term profitability as defined here is an important element in the economics of purchasing and supply. Savings in costs of supply or service used in an enterprise can feed directly into the profits it is able to make. [The converse also is true]. Increase or decrease of profitability can be expressed by the formula:

$$Pn = Pi \pm (Si \times c)$$

Where:
Pn is the new profit after change in supply costs.

159

Pi is the initial profit with original supply costs.
Si is the original supply cost.

All the above costs are expressed as decimal fractions of selling price.
c is the decimal fraction by which supply costs have increased or decreased.

examples:
a) A product is made to sell at £100. Supply costs are £60, costs of administration, labour and other overheads are £30 and profit is £10. The supply costs are reduced by 2%. How much extra profit does this change generate?

$$Pn = .10 \pm (.60 \times .02)$$
$$= .10 + .012 = \underline{.112}$$

A 12% increase in profit has arisen from a 2% decrease in supply costs.

b) In a process plant with 90% material content (supply costs of .9) with the same initial profit of 10% and the same saving of 2% on supply costs, Pn would be .10 + .018, giving a new profit of .118.

An 18% increase in profit has, in this case, arisen from a 2% decrease in supply costs.

profit, net profit. CIMA. 1. The profit remaining after all expenses and/or losses have been deducted from the OPERATING PROFIT and further revenues added. 2. The profit of a business before distribution but after deducting from net sales all direct and indirect costs incurred in making the sale. Net profit can be stated 'before' or 'after' taxation.

profit, operating profit. Profit arising from the normal activities of an enterprise, such as the sale of manufactured goods and services, before taking account of extraneous transactions such as those of a purely financial nature, e.g. interest on bank loans, etc.

pro-forma. *See* INVOICE.

program(me) evaluation and review technique (PERT). A form of NETWORK ANALYSIS used to programme, progress and review the stages of a complex project towards its final completion.

progress chaser. A person engaged in PROGRESS CHASING (PROGRESSING).

progressing. BS 5191 (32001). Production progress control. The function that is concerned with: 1. recording of actual production progress, its comparison with planned production, and the feedback of warnings, and/or instructions to enable the correction of deviations; 2. the EXPEDITING (hastening) of production orders which have to be fulfilled in less than the normal LEAD TIME. The production definition is equally applicable in the fields of purchasing and supply and marketing. Note also the following definition, abbreviated from **BS 5191.** They are included because they can have implications in planning and progressing purchasing and supply as well as production – especially where closely integrated with the production system, and where 'JIT' and PURCHASING PARTNERSHIP operate. **32002**, 'sequencing': production sequence selected for best use of resources. **32003**, 'batch splitting': division of batches to hasten one portion. **32004**, 'parallel splitting': work stations share same operation to speed output. **32005**, 'sent ahead splitting': portion of a batch split ahead before entire batch, subsequently designated separate batches. **32006**, 'overlapping': starting a portion of a batch before completing previous operation but not to form a separate batch. **32007**, 'divergent materials flow': transfer of parts from one batch to others without intermediate stocking activity.

progressing, 'progress chasing'. The activity of monitoring the progress of purchase orders with suppliers to ensure that delivery to the purchaser is as-and-when needed and in the quantities required. The activity may involve EXPEDITING or retarding delivery or re-scheduling to suit production or sales programmes. *See also* CONTRACT MANAGEMENT. *and* **BS 5191 (32001)**, pre-production progressing.

progress payments. *See* PAYMENTS, PROGRESS PAYMENTS.

progressive rebate. *See* REBATE, PROGRESSIVE.

prohibited goods. Those which are forbidden to be exported from or imported into a country.

prohibition notice. (HS). A notice issued by an inspector of the Health and Safety Executive who discovers a contravention of one of the provisions of the Health and Safety at Work act or related legislation. The notice is issued if there is a risk of serious injury or pollution etc., to stop the activity giving rise to this risk until remedial action specified in the notice has been taken. It can be served on the person undertaking the activity, or on the person in control of it at the time the notice was served. *See also* IMPROVEMENT NOTICE.

project. BS 4335. An enterprise involving a number of interrelated activities.

project assessment. The assessment of the viability of a project.

project network techniques (PNT), project network analysis. BS 4335 (abb). The use of NETWORK ANALYSIS for planning and control of projects to consider the logical inter-relationships of all project activities. The group includes technique concerned with time, resources, costs and other influencing factors, e.g. uncertainty. *Note*: program evaluation and review techniques (PERT), critical path analysis (CPA) and critical path method (CPM) are not synonyms for PNT.

promissory note. CIMA. A signed unconditional document containing a written promise to pay a specified sum on demand, or on a certain date to a specified person.

prompt cash payment. *See* PRICE, PAYMENT AND TIME RELATED PAYMENT.

property, intellectual property (protection of) (EU). Any material, written, drawn or otherwise produced and which is the unique result of intelligent, intellectual effort. In the industrial field this includes such items as engineering drawings and layouts, specifications (technical or other), detailed quotations or estimates, letters or other documents which fall, or appear to fall, within the same category. [It should be noted that, as with copyright, any abuse of such material (copying it and presenting it as one's own when it is not) is an actionable offence under copyright protection. It is also contrary to the Spirit of the Codes of Ethics and good business of the Chartered Institute of Purchasing and Supply and of the Institute of Management. The community laws governing intellectual property (ie patents, industrial designs, trade marks and copyright) are a departure from the operation of the free market; a departure, intended to stimulate and protect innovation. Patents are covered by the European Patent Convention and there will later be Community Patent Courts in each member State to handle patents. *Note*: The Patent Office comment as follows: 'In the UK, copyright protection is automatic . . . there is no registration system, no forms to fill in or any fees to pay. Copyright protects original literary . . . works . . . etc. . . . Technical descriptions b10.5

and engineering drawings are both examples of materials which qualify for copyright protection'. SCI (PO IPP/100/94/2, 20.4.94).

proposals. (EU). Proposals are made by the Commission of the Community to the European Parliament and to the COUNCIL OF MINISTERS for discussion and implementation by the latter, if approved. Proposals have no legal force until and unless passed by the Council of Ministers.

proprietary goods. Goods manufactured and sold and distributed under a trade name, brand, trade mark, etc.

pro rata. 'At a certain rate of' and 'in proportion to in a total'. e.g. 50p in the £1.

protective and preventive measures. (HS). Those measures which can be identified by the employer or by the self-employed person in consequence of the assessment of the measures he needs to take in order to comply with his duties under the relevant Statutory Provisions for health and safety.

protective personal equipment. (PPE). (HS). Includes all equipment designed to be worn or held to protect against one or more risks to health and safety. It includes hard hats, safety footwear, life-jackets, eye and hearing protection, high visibility clothing and clothing to protect against adverse weather. *Note*. The REGULATION SJ.1992/2666 does

162

not cover ordinary working clothes and uniforms or PPE for road transport (e.g. crash helmets or portable devices for detecting or signalling risks and nuisances). Bibl: HSE PERSONAL PROTECTIVE EQUIPMENT AT WORK ISBN 0 11 886334 7 BSI – protective clothing: **BS 1771** Fabrics for protective clothing. **BS 1547** Flameproof & heatproof materials. **BS 6249** Flameproof & heatproof materials. **BS 6629** High-visibility clothing (optical performance). **BS 4973** Interlinings. **BS 3791** Protection against intense heat. **BS 4724** Resistance to permeation by liquid tests). **BS 4526** Workwear and career wear.

prototype. A full-size working and fully operational model made for appraisal and which when improved, modified, tested and approved can be used as a type for future reproduction.

provisioning. The first step in the SUPPLIES CYCLE which relates to the act of providing, particularly the steps taken beforehand to lay in stocks and provisions for production or for a project. *See also* PLANNING.

provisioning level. *See* STOCK CONTROL, RE-ORDER LEVEL CONTROL.

purchase. (n). The article, goods, material, substance or service which has been purchased in exchange for CONSIDERATION. A similar definition applies to PROCUREMENT

except for the lack of 'consideration' in that case.

purchase. (v). To acquire supplies and services by paying money or other CONSIDERATION. (Where acquisition is without passage of CONSIDERATION the term PROCUREMENT can be used).

purchase order. *See* ORDERS & CONTRACTS A–Z.

purchase requisition. *See* REQUISITION, PURCHASE.

pull. In purchasing the term is applied to systems whereby material is brought into the organisation or production area to replace material already allocated or used.

purchasing. 1. The obtaining of supplies of goods and services by PURCHASE. 2. To required specification. 3. To British, European, international, company or other STANDARD as appropriate. 4. To comply with Health and Safety regulations, codes of practice, etc. 5. In accordance with COMMUNITY DIRECTIVES and REGULATIONS. 6. In compliance with environmental controls and **BS 7570**. 7. From reliable suppliers – where appropriate those holding CERTIFICATION to **ISO 9000**. 8. In quantities as demanded/scheduled, etc. 9. Delivered at date and address, loading bay, dock, etc. 11. Suitably packaged for safe transit, ease of loading/unloading, storage and handling, dispensing at work stations. 12. Clearly marked with: destination(s) as above, hazard marks (where required), lifting and handling instructions, order number, or other identification. 13. All as required at lowest total costs of acquisition and use. [der. 13C old French 'porchasier' – to strive to obtain, from 'por' – for, and 'chasier' – to chase. *See* Collins' softback English Dictionary, 1993 reprint]. *See also* PROCUREMENT.

purchasing analyst. A member of purchasing and supply staff who is responsible for those aspects of purchasing and supply requiring technical and statistical expertise. Responsibility for PURCHASING RESEARCH, VALUE ANALYSIS, and liaison with technical departments of an enterprise.

'Purchasing and Supply Management'. (monthly CIPS). News of the Institute, and articles on a wide range of topics in the purchasing and supply field.

purchasing audit. An in-depth investigation into every aspect of departmental efficiency and operations. It may be carried out by an internal audit committee or by external auditors usually firms of accountants or management consultants. The audit examines purchasing records and procedures in order to protect the organisation against fraud or waste, to ensure the company policies are being adhered to and identify ways in which performance can be improved. The audit should consider every aspect of purchasing activity and present its report to senior management. SC (CIPS).

purchasing, automated. *See* AUTOMATED PURCHASING.

purchasing, backward integration. The acquisition of suppliers by an enterprise wishing to expand or (e.g.) to control the source of supply.

purchasing, central purchasing. 'The steering of demands into prescribed channels, all terminating in one AUTHORITY to ADMINISTER the purchasing and supply function'. *See also* PURCHASING: BULK PURCHASING.

purchasing, forward purchasing. *See* CONTRACTS/ORDERS (FORWARD) *also see* FUTURES UNDER TRADE/ TRADING/MARKETS.

'Purchasing Manager's Index'. *See* REPORT ON BUSINESS.

purchasing officer. An official in charge of the whole procurement operation from the receipt of the requisition, through all the stages of negotiation and placing the order, to the final clearance of the related invoices after price checking.

purchasing order. *See* CONTRACTS: ADMINISTRATION OF *and* ORDERS VARIETIES OF.

purchasing, paperless purchasing. *See* INFORMATION TECHNOLOGY.

purchasing, partnership purchasing. The concept of purchasing as a partnership between enterprises, as, for example, between supplier and manufacturing purchaser. The partnership may be extensive and include the fields of 'design and research', 'value engineering', 'value analysis', etc so as to gain maximum advantage for each party. *See* PARTNERSHIP SOURCING.

purchasing power, economic purchasing power. The quantity of a good which may be purchased at a specified time by a unit of currency compared with the quantity obtainable from the expenditure of the same unit of currency in another period. *See also* NEGOTIATION, LEVERAGE.

purchasing power parities. (econ). The actual worth of currencies in terms of the real amount of goods and services they will buy.

purchasing, preclusive purchasing. The purchasing of supply, service, or production capacity as a deliberate means of depriving another enterprise from acquiring those supplies, services or production capacity.

purchasing, public procurement – works & supply Directives. (EU). These Directives apply to central and local governments and certain other bodies which are funded by such authorities. Above certain value limits they: 1. lay down criteria for qualitative selection of tenderers and TENDERS.

2. restrict the use of non-competitive tendering. 3. require reference (where relevant) to national/European STANDARDS. 4. the advertising of contracts in the OFFICIAL JOURNAL OF THE EUROPEAN COMMUNITY. 5. enforcement of the Compliance Directive. (This requires States to provide legal redress for EU contractors/suppliers harmed through breaches of the Works and Services Directive.) 6. the Utilities Directive. This imposes similar but more flexible rules for works and supplies procurement by the public and private sector bodies in: water, energy, transport and telecommunications. 7. the Utilities Remedies Directive. This requires legal redress to be available as (5.) above. (6.) the Services Directive (wef 1.7.93) This applies rules similar to those in the Works Directive to the purchase of services. *Note:* At the time of preparing this edition consideration was being given to the consolidation of these directives into a single text. For UK the contact point is HM Treasury PSP Division.

purchasing, public procurement: attestation. (EU). The examination of public procurement purchasing procedures by an independent examiner to ensure that the European Standards for such procedures are adhered to by public authorities.

purchasing, public purchasing directives. (EU). The directives applicable to public bodies, except some nationalised industries, are intended to open up procedures

165

throughout the Community. The directives include: Supplies Directive wef 1.1.1989, Works Directive wef 19.7.1990, Service Directive wef 1.7.1993 1.7.1993, Compliance Directive wef 21.12.1991, Utilities Directive (90/531 EEC) wef 1.1.1993, Remedies Directive wef 1.1.1993. [A guide to public purchasing is available from the DTI.]

purchasing research. Investigations into improved and more cost-effective purchasing throughout all areas of the supplies/supply cycle. *See also* SUPPLIES RESEARCH.

purpose, fitness for purpose. 'The totality of features and characteristics of a product or service that have a bearing upon its ability to satisfy a given/stated need'. Where goods are sold in the course of business and the buyer makes known to the seller the particular purpose for which the goods are being bought, there is an implied CONDITION that they are fit for that purpose.' Sale of Good Act 1979 Cl.12/11.

purpose made. Goods made specially for a specific job or distinct from standard items 'off the shelf'. [Also referred to as 'bespoke'.]

push. In purchasing and supply the term is applied to systems whereby materials are 'pushed' forward to production areas in anticipation of need, as opposed to 'pull' systems where the material is called up to replace material already earmarked or used.

Q

quality. BS 4778. BS 5191 (A0001).
The totality of features and characteristics of a product or service
that bear upon its ability to satisfy
a given need. *See also* QUALITY,
MERCHANTABLE, BSI.

**quality, acceptable quality level.
(AQL). BS 4778 pt.2 (8.2.1)** The
maximum percent defective (or
the maximum number of defects
per hundred units) that, for the
purposes of (acceptance) SAM-
PLING, can be considered satisfactory as a process average.

**quality, acceptance number/
quantity**. The maximum number
of rejects to be permitted should
be so specified in a SAMPLE
LOT if the total quantity is to be
accepted.

quality acceptance sampling. *See*
QUALITY CONTROL, SAMPLING.

quality accuracy. BS 4778 (8.3).
The closeness of an observed quality to the defined or true value.
Note: accuracy is usually
expressed in terms of error or
uncertainty.

**quality approval, type approval.
BS 4778 (21.6).** The status given
to a design that has been shown by
type tests to meet all the requirements of the product specification
and which is suitable for a specific
application.

**quality assurance. BS 5750. (ISO
8402)** (EU). All those planned
and systematic actions necessary
to provide confidence that a product or service will satisfy given
requirements for quality. *Notes:*
[Based on BSI publications (cf)]
1. Unless given requirements fully
reflect the needs of the user, quality assurance will not be complete.
[This comment by British Standards Institution reflects the need
for accuracy in purchase specifications.] 2. For effectiveness, quality
assurance usually requires continuing evaluation of factors that
affect adequacy of design or specification for intended application
as well as verification and audits of
production, installation and
inspection operations. Providing
confidence in quality may also
involve the production of evidence. 3. Within an organisation,
quality assurance serves as a management tool. In contractual
situations, quality assurance also
serves to provide confidence in the
supplier. bibl: **BS.PD3542** The
Role of Standards in Company
Quality.

**quality attribute, an attribute. BS
4778 (21.23).** A characteristic that
is appraised in terms of whether it
meets or does not meet a given
requirement (e.g. 'go' or 'no go').

quality audit/assessment. (EU).
Audits/assessments made to ver-
ify that applicable element of
QUALITY ASSURANCE prog-
rammes have been developed,

documented and effectively implemented by the supplier so as to ensure that contractual requirements have been met.

quality certificate of conformity. BS 4778 (24.4). A document signed by a qualified person affirming that, at the time of assessment (or INSPECTION) the product or service met the stated requirements. *Note:* 'release certificate', 'release note', 'certificate of compliance' are considered to be synonymous with certificate of conformity.

quality, certificate of quality. (Supplier's certificate). A written warranty by a supplier that supplies from him conform to the purchaser's specification and requirements, etc.

quality, conformance of quality with specification. The extent to which supplies received match the quality specified.

quality certification. BS 4778 (24.1.1). The authoritative act of documenting compliance with requirements. *Note:* the requirements can relate to personnel, processes, organisations and services.

quality compliance. BS 4778 (9.1). An indication or judgement that the product or service meets the requirements of the relevant specification or regulation; also the state of meeting the requirements.

quality circles. (adm). A participation technique where groups of (usually) eight persons from similar working backgrounds meet regularly to: identify quality problems, analyse cause, recommend solutions and in some cases affect implementation of the recommendations. *See also* BRAINSTORMING.

quality, costs related. *See* COSTS, QUALITY RELATED.

quality defect. BS 4778 (3.21). Any non-conformance of an item to specified requirements. *Notes* 1. Defect is restricted to the requirements of manufacturing, assembly, installation, and final test. 2. This term may require a different definition when applied in connection with product liability. *See also* FAILURE.

quality defect, latent defect. A hidden defect which could not be revealed by reasonable inspection. The purchaser is (usually*) protected by the law if the defect is revealed later. [*i.e. unless an agreed contractual clause has relieved the supplier of this obligation].

quality defect prevention analysis. The analysis of defects found in an item of supply from past data providing statistics for improvement in future specifications.

quality economic. BS 4778 (pt.5.5). The economic level of quality at which the costs of securing higher quality would exceed the benefits of the improved quality.

quality, economic quality. BS 4778 (12.8). The economic level of quality at which the costs of securing higher quality would exceed the benefits of the improved quality. *See also* BREAK-EVEN.

quality failure analysis. The study of potential failures that might occur in any part of a system in order to determine the probable effect of each on all other parts of the system and on probable operational success. **BS 4778 (17.8).**

quality failure costs. *See* COSTS.

quality failure mode and effect analysis. (BS 4778 17.7). Study of the potential failures that might occur in any part of a system to determine the probable effect of each upon all other parts of the system and upon probable operational success. (*See* BS 4778 for further details), *also see under* HEALTH AND SAFETY.

quality inspection. BS 4778 (3.14). The process of measuring, examining, testing, gauging, or otherwise comparing the item with the applicable requirements.

quality inspection and test. A technical process which uses a specified procedure to measure one or more characteristics of a product [or service]. A major activity undertaken during design, product development, manufacture and product [service] use. Based on ECdti.

quality inspection and test, 'hold point'. The stage during a contract beyond which the supplier must not proceed without the operation being overseen by the designated inspector.

quality inspection and test, surveillance. Progressive inspection which takes place during the production/process cycle up to the final inspection and release for shipment of the product, or completion and acceptance of the services provided for in the purchase contract.

quality inspection, variables inspection. BS 4778 (21.26 & 21, 24). Inspection whereby certain characteristics of an item are evaluated against a numerical scale and are expressed as points along that scale.

quality limits, control limits. BS 4778 (19.11). Limits on control charts that are used as criteria for action, or for judging whether a set of data does, or does not, indicate a lack of control.

quality management. BS 5750/ISO 9000/EN 29000. 'That aspect of the overall management function that determines and implements the quality policy'. *Notes*: [Based on BSI publications] 1. The attainment of desired quality requires commitment and participation of all members of the enterprise, whereas responsibility for QUALITY MANAGEMENT belongs to top management. 2. Quality management includes strategic planning, allocation of resources and other systematic activities for quality, such as 'quality planning', 'quality operations' and 'quality evaluation'.

This Standard (British, International, European) provides criteria for management systems capable of assuring production or service in accordance with specifications decided between purchasers and suppliers. The application of **BS 5750** is supported by REGISTRATION of suppliers whose quality capability has been externally assessed by accredited bodies to meet its provisions . . . *Notes* particularly relevant to purchasing and supply: 1. A claim that a product or service meets **BS 5750** is invalid. This is because **BS 5750** does not specify particular products or services. Members of the ASSOCIATION OF BRITISH CERTIFICATION BODIES are careful to ensure that their **BS 5750** REGISTRATION SYMBOLS are not misused in this way. Such misuse can be actionable under the TRADE DESCRIPTION ACT. 2. Under European Community procurement rules public bodies and utilities wishing to maintain lists of suppliers for contracts, above certain financial thresholds, are expected to recognise registration to European Standard (EN 29000 **BS 5750**) criteria by ASSESSMENT BODIES whose own activities are governed by the relevant European Standard **EN45000.**

quality, merchantable quality. Sale of Goods Act 1979 14(6). 'Goods of any kind are of merchantable quality within the meaning of the Act if they are fit for the purpose or purposes for which goods of that kind are commonly bought as it is reasonable to expect having regard to any description applied to them, the price (if relevant) and all other relevant circumstances'. *See note at* 'INTRODUCTION'.

quality, physical quality control. BS 4778 (19.1.1). The operational techniques and activities that sustain the product or service quality to specified requirements. It is also the use of such techniques and activities.

quality policy. BS 5750/ISO 8402. The overall quality intentions and direction of an enterprise as regards quality, as formally expressed by top management. *Note:* (Based on BSI publication) 1. The quality policy forms one element of corporate policy and is authorised by top management.

quality precision. BS 4778 (8.4). The closeness of agreement between the results obtained by applying defined procedures several times under prescribed conditions. *See* notes 1 to 4 in BS 4778. 'Precision' can relate to 1. 'precision of statement', 2. 'repeatability' and 'reproducibility' and 3. 'relative precision'.

quality reject note. A note completed as a result of a quality control inspection. It should give details not only of the failure but also of action to be taken, e.g. remachine, scrap, etc. and if supplies are involved a copy to the purchasing department for replacement supplies to be provisioned.

quality sampling (inspection). The inspection of a limited number of items or of a limited quantity of material, taken at random from the lot or batch according to a prescribed sampling plan.

quality, scrap note. A document authorising the discarding of products or supplies after inspection or test as unsuitable for the intended purpose for which they were bought or manufactured and which are economically incapable of being rectified or salvaged. [In the interests of CONSERVATION to be sorted and classified as WASTE or SCRAP.]

quality statistical. BS 4778 (19.9). That part of quality control in which statistical techniques are used. *Note:* these techniques include: the use of frequency distributions, measures of 'central tendency' and dispersion, control charts, acceptance sampling, regression analysis, tests of significance, etc.

quality, statistically controlled during production. A production/process control procedure whereby quality control data is obtained during production/process in relation to the quality of supplies used in the actual manufacture.

quality system, a quality system. BS 5750 (3.3). 'The organisational structure, responsibilities, procedures, processes and resources for implementing QUALITY MANAGEMENT'. *Notes:* 1. The quality system should only be as comprehensive as is needed to meet the quality objectives. 2. For contractual, mandatory and assessment purposes, the demonstration of the implementation of identified and specified elements in the system may be required in order to comply with Standards.

quality tests. BS 4778 (21.3). Critical trials often involving stress or examination of one or more properties or characteristics of a material, product, or set of observations.

quality test, type tests. BS 4778 (21.5). A series of tests directed towards approval of design, conducted to determine whether an item is capable of meeting the requirements of the product specification.

quality, total quality management. BS 4778 includes the following within quality management: 11.1A Quality Manual for policy, procedures and practices. 11.2 quality system to meet BS 5750 requirements. 11.3 programme: activities, resources, events. 11.4 plan as 11.3 relevant to a particular project/product. 11.5 audit, independent examination of quality. 11.6 product quality audit. 11.7 process quality audit. 11.8 quality system audit 11.9 verification – evidence that requirements are met. 11.10 quality engineering – to achieve correct quality. 11.11 vendor appraisal, capability for quality control. (before ordering). 11.12 supplier evaluation, assessment of supplier's quality control (after placing order). 11.13 supplier rating – index if supplier's performance. 11.14 design review – systematic critical study of design. 11.15 calibration of measuring instruments, etc. All the above abb from **BS 4778**

quality, verification of quality. BS 4778 (11.9). The provision of evidence or proof that requirements for policy have been met.

quality vocabulary. BS 4778.

quality, 'zero defects'. *See* ZERO DEFECTS.

quantity. The designation of measure for supplies to be provided under a contract. Unless specified on an order a court would look for a 'reasonable quantity within the contemplation of the parties to the contract'. *See also* ECONOMIC ORDER QUANTITY, BULK QUANTITY, FORWARD SUPPLY ARRANGEMENT.

quantity, batch quantity. 1. The number of parts or other units of material in a batch. 2. The number of parts or other units of material in each of the batches into which the production programme is divided for processing. 3. The number of parts or other units of material in each of the batches into which a purchase order quantity is divided for deliveries.

quantity, bulk quantity. A quantity which can be handled, transported and stored in bulk, and for which the shape and sizes of individual pieces may be of no great

consequence: e.g. coal, coke, limestone, pig iron, etc.

quantity, custom of the trade. The units of quantity fixed by a particular trade as the standard (maximumm or more usually minimum) unit of supply they will normally provide.

quantity discount. *See* DISCOUNT, QUANTITY DISCOUNT.

quantity, economic order quantity. (abb. **EOQ**) cf. **BS 5729 Part 3 (3.2).** That quantity, which having regard to the actual USAGE of the enterprise results in the lowest total of ACQUISITION COST plus HOLDING COSTS.

$$EOQ = \sqrt{\frac{2AS}{CI}}$$

Where:

EOQ is the theoretical economic order quantity.

A is annual usage quantity.

S is order processing (= 'set up') cost per order.

C is the value of the item bought/produced.

I is the stock holding (or 'inventory carrying') cost per annum as a decimal point of the value of the item (e.g. if %age is 25 'I' would be 0.25).

Notes:

Although the formula is widely used, it should always be remembered that there are limitations to its application' [e.g. production, seasonal and other variations.]

* The usage quantity 'A' and holding quantity 'I' need not be annual values but have to be expressed consistently in the same units.' **BS 5729 part 3 (3.2)**

quantity, fixed order quantity. 'A quantity of supplies which may be fixed as to quantity on an order from which the supplier shall not deviate (*see* SALE OF GOODS ACT,) or one for which the supplier shall deliver fixed quantities at intervals as specified on the purchase order, or the same or programmed quantities on a sequence of orders to, follow one another.' *Note:* the former **BS 5729 Part 3 (3.2)** commented that modern systems pay increasing attention to quantities being supplied when they are needed by techniques such as MATERIALS REQUIREMENTS PLANNING and 'JUST IN TIME', etc.

quantity, supplier's quantity. A quantity which may be negotiated by a supplier because it is his economic batch quantity, the CUSTOM OF THE TRADE, his maximum output or some other constraint.

quantity surveyor. A qualified person who measures the work to be done, prepares the BILL OF QUANTITIES for TENDERS. On the contract he checks work done and advises the client on STAGE PAYMENTS.

quantity, units of quantity. A primary component of purchase orders, contracts, stock-control, production and sales. An aspect of supplies and materials administration requiring continuous checking, co-ordination and updating, with supplies, production and sales.

quantum meruit. (law). ('how much it deserves'). A party may sue in *quantum meruit* for a reasonable sum for work done, goods supplied, or services rendered where 1. a contract is at an end through default of one party or because it is unenforceable, 2. one party asks someone to do them a service and expressly indicates he is to be paid, although no price is stated or agreed.

quarantine store. *See* STORE, QUARANTINE STORE.

quasi. Something which resembles a recognisable object but it is not actually what it appears. *See* CONTRACT, QUASI CONTRACT *at* ORDERS & CONTRACTS, LETTER OF INTENT, INADVERTENT CONTRACT.

queueing theory. This theory, also known as 'theory of congestion' and 'theory of waiting lines', deals with the problems of congestion and waiting. It has important implications in respect of 1. arrival and handling of transport at transport loading and unloading bays, 2. arriving and serving of personnel at stores serveries, 3. production planning and machine loading. 4. supply of materials at work centres, particularly where 'just in time' procedures are in operation.

questioning technique (*see also*

INQUIRY) **BS 3138 (21064).** A technique used in inquiries where intensive investigations are needed. The process is in two stages: 1. 'primary stage': question the need for each activity, its means, sequence, place and person(s) and justification sought for each reply, 2. 'secondary stage': the remaining essential activities are further questioned to determine alternatives and select those which are practicable and preferable. [BS 3138, suitably modified, can be applied to purchasing negotiations and to work-study in stores.]

quota system. 1. Fixed total amount of a commodity to be imported. 2. The maximum to be imported from each country. 3. In trading between enterprises quota may refer to a proportion or quantity of a commodity or service fixed or shared between the parties by agreement. Usually it relates to production or sales, but in the case of GROUP PURCHASING it could refer also to purchases. May well conflict with UK law and EU DIRECTIVES AND REGULATIONS. *See also* COMPETITION LAW.

quotation. Information from a seller to a buyer (usually the result of an enquiry from the buyer – but may be unsolicited) and an INVITATION TO TREAT (i.e. negotiate). *See also* ESTIMATE. A quotation should give an accurate price for the goods or services offered and should be valid for the period stated by the offeror, or for a reasonable period. *See also* ESTIMATE.

R

ROT. *See* RETENTION OF TITLE.

racking, pallet racking. Steel (usually) framed racking designed to house pallets and similarly other unit containers and loads.

racking, mobile racking. Racking designed so that it can be moved horizontally thus requiring less aisle space than conventional fixed racking.

random access. A storage system whereby incoming materials are allocated the next available space. Space is more fully utilised. Tracking of materials needs to be carefully considered, controlled and coded for identification.

range. BS ISO 3534–1 (2.3). The difference between the greatest and smallest values of a quantitative CHARACTERISTIC in a range of data. *Note:* Range may be a misleading statistic if used as a measure of, for example, demand for future action (e.g. stock-building, purchasing, energy consumption) unless care is taken regarding exceptions at each extreme of the range, e.g. minima and *particularly* maxima of usage or demand etc.

rate of return, annual. A method of PROJECT ANALYSIS by assessing the annual rate of return on the capital invested, over the LIFE CYCLE of the project.

rate of stock-turn. *See* STOCK-TURN, RATE OF.

rationalisation. In the business context rationalisation entails the application of rational decision-making to problems of trade and industry, where for example there is 1. overcapacity, 2. plant no longer produces competitively, 3. market has shrunk. In all such cases, and others, rationalisation calls for reorganisation, and the application of remedial actions.

ratios, management ratios. Ratios used in management to establish aspects of management and control such as profitability, efficiency and so on. Reference should be made to Centre for Interfirm Comparisons.

raw materials. CIMA. Unprocessed stocks awaiting conversion into saleable/usable products (part of CURRENT ASSETS). **BS 5191.** Materials used as input to a production process resulting in finished products. *Note:* The finished product from one organisational group may be the raw material of another.

raw material stock. *See* STOCK, RAW MATERIAL.

real time (computer). (it). A computer is said to be operating in real time when it is connected ON LINE to a data processing system and

175

records and processes the data as it is generated, e.g. such a computer may update stock-control records immediately each stock movement occurs.

reasonable care and skill. (law). In a service (or other contract) 'the supplier shall carry out the service with reasonable care and skill'. (Supply of Goods and Services Act 1982 Sect 13). 'It is sufficient if he exercises the ordinary skill of an ordinary competent man exercising that particular art'. (High court judgment).

reasonable price. *See* PRICE, REASONABLE.

reasonable, reasonableness of terms in contract. (law). Tests for: 1. what are the relative bargaining strengths of the parties? 2. could the goods have been bought elsewhere without the terms being applied? 3. did the purchaser know of them, or should he have known? 4. was the clause involving liability of the contractor reasonable? 5. were the goods 'manufactured, processed or adapted to the special order of the purchaser?' (Unfair Contract Terms Act 1977 Schedule 2.) *See also* DEALING, A COURSE OF DEALING.

rebate. A financial allowance on a contract usually based on some relationship to turnover of business over a given period or other conditions. *See below.*

rebate, deferred rebate. A rebate, the credit in respect of which is not paid, or allowed, until an agreed time has elapsed, or a target of expenditure or volume of through-put has been achieved. *See also* REBATE, PROGRESSIVE REBATE.

rebate, flat rebate. A rebate paid at the end of a trading period at a pre-agreed rate regardless of the amount of business.

rebate, loyalty rebate. A special rebate given by a supplier to a purchaser in consideration of some agreement to purchase all (or an agreed proportion of) total intake from that supplier, or for a long term contract. [May or may not be tied to target quantities of business].

rebate, progressive (sliding scale rebate). Rebates paid at the end of a trading period and based upon the amount spent. e.g. £5000, 5%; £5001–£10,000, 7½%; over £10,000, 10%. The supplier benefits by deferred payment as distinct from STEPPED REBATE where he pays directly each step is reached.

rebate, retrospective rebate. The usual arrangement whereby a rebate is paid at the end of a trading period or when a financial or quantitative target is reached rather than at the outset of the trading period.

rebate, stepped or sliding scale rebate. A rebate paid directly each step or target of business is reached. The purchaser receives his rebate immediately instead of waiting until the end of the trading period as in the case of the PROG-RESSIVE REBATE.

rebuilding, rebuilt, etc. A term which should commit the supplier to the dismantling and entire rebuilding of equipment completely – or at least substantially, so far as working parts, worn and faulty components are concerned – and of providing a unit in near new condition. *See also* RECONDITIONING.

receipt. A written acknowledgment of having received a sum of money or money's worth.

receipt, clean. A term used when goods put on board a ship agree with the wharfinger's delivery sheet.

receipt, foul. A term used if the goods put on board a ship do not agree with the wharfinger's delivery sheet.

receipt, mate's receipt. (ts). Receipt given by the mate of a ship when goods are put on board ship as she lies in mid-stream, or offshore.

receiver, a receiver. A person appointed by a court to administer the financial affairs of a bankrupt company. He takes into his custody all assets including any which belong to the firm's customers, e.g. free issue materials, tools, etc. The receiver may combine his role with that of manager of the firm.

receiving. *See* GOODS INTAKE.

reciprocal trading (reciprocity). The practice (sometimes under a company policy directive) of placing purchase orders with suppliers which are customers of the purchaser. *See also* CUSTOMER-TRADE.

recommendations. (EU) See OPINIONS (EU).

reconditioning, reconditioned. Unlike REBUILDING this term may imply merely the replacement of worn and broken parts, cleaning and perhaps testing. It may not include diagnostic work to ascertain causes of failure, etc. It is important that purchase orders are clear in this and in REBUILDING contracts.

record(s). BS 4335. Collection of related data, e.g. that representing an activity.

record, documents of record. Documents which although not necessarily of legal effect may have implications as evidence in a legal dispute, e.g. a purchase order, goods received note, a reject note, a consignment note and so on.

recovery. *See* SALVAGE AND RECYCLING.

rectification note. BS 5191 (43009). A document which authorises additional operations to bring a substandard product up to specification.

rectify, to rectify. BS 5191 (A0007). To perform additional operations to bring a substandard product up to specification.

177

rectilinear. (stat). *See also* CURVI-LINEAR. A straight line graph in which a direct simple relationship exists between variables. e.g. HOLDING COSTS in the formula of ECONOMIC ORDER QUANTITY.

re-cycling. 1. To pass (a substance) through a system again for further treatment and use. 2. To reclaim for further use, e.g. to recycle waste water.

reefer. Refrigerated vehicle or ship.

registered stockist. Registered firm, symbols. *See* appendix C.

Regulation. (n) (EU). Regulations issued by the Union are directly applicable in all member States. They do not have to be confirmed by national parliaments in order to have binding legal effect. If there is any conflict between a regulation and existing national law, the regulation prevails.

regression. A term used in statistics to describe the CORRELATION between one VARIABLE and another variable, or variables, which are related to the primary variable.

regulation(s), health and safety regulation(s). (HS). Regulations on health and safety are made by the Secretary of State upon advice from the HEALTH AND SAFETY COMMISSION. They may relate to any of the purposes of part 1 of the Health and Safety Act including any matters set out in Schedule 3. They may be 'gene-ral in scope', 'limited', 'functional' or 'industry related'. They may be detailed in form incorporating references to documents, such as CODES OF PRACTICE, or STANDARDS.

rehabilitation. BS 3811 (4118). Extensive work intended to bring plant or buildings up to current acceptable functional conditions, often involving improvements. *Note:* BS 3811 deprecates the use of the word 'refurbishment'. *See also* REBUILDING and RECONDITION-ING.

reject note (rejection note). BS 5191 (43008). A document which records that an item or batch does not conform to specification. A note completed as a result of quality control inspection. It should give details not only of the failure but also of action to be taken, e.g. re-machine, scrap, etc, and if supplies are involved a copy to the purchasing department for replacement supplies to be provisioned. *See also* SCRAP NOTE.

reject, to. To designate an item or batch as not conforming to specification.

relationship management. The relationship between buyer and seller is now seen as being of key importance. Attention now focuses on achieving and monitoring the right relationship rather than simple performance measures. *See also* PURCHASING, PART-NERSHIP PURCHASING.

release note. BS 5191 (43004). A

document recording that products conform to specification and authorising subsequent issue or processing. **BS 4778** gives the following as synonymous with release note: 'release certificate', 'certificate of compliance' and 'certificate of conformance'.

reliability. BS 4778 (8.2) and **6.1.1)** and **BS 3811(04).** The ability of an item (or service) to perform a required function under stated conditions for a stated period of time.

reorder interval. BS5191 (33004). The fixed interval of time between placement of order, used in a reorder system of type **BS 5191 (33002(b)).**

re-order level (provisioning level). The stock level at which a purchase (or production) order must be placed if replenishment is to take place before STOCK-OUT occurs provided demand remains reasonably steady and lead time for supply is also reliable and/or steady. Formula:

$$ROL = Lt \times Ult + Ss$$

Where: ROL is re-order level
    Lt is units of LEAD TIME.
    Ult is usage per unit of lead time
    Ss is safety stock where needed*

[* Safety stock may not be needed where demand is steady or predictable and delivery is assured.]

reorder systems. BS 5191 (33002). The methods used to regulate the placing of orders for replenishment of stock. 1. Fixed quantity reordering at variable intervals of time. 2. Ordering at fixed intervals of time, with varying order quantities 3. Ordering at varying intervals and in varying order quantities (e.g. MATERIALS REQUIREMENT PLANNING).

repair. BS 3811 (4119). To restore an ITEM to an acceptable condition by the renewal, replacement or mending of worn, damaged or decayed parts. *See also* OVERHAUL, RESTORATION, REHABILITATION, RECONDITION, REBUILDING.

replacement cost, (accounting by). *See* COST, REPLACEMENT COST ACCOUNTING.

replenish (v). Renew or replace stocks or supplies which have been issued or used.

reports. (adm) (HS). Accounts of an INQUIRY or study, for consideration by an authority, also required in certain instances (e.g. 'accidents' **BS 5729 Pt. 5 tbl. 3)** which are required under statutory obligations.

requisition, purchase requisition. cf. BS 5191 (42010). A document making a formal request to purchase, issued by the person or department requiring supplies to the purchasing department.

requisition, stores/stock requisition. BS 5191 (42011). An inter-

179

nal document to request the issue of product or raw material from a store.

requisition, travelling. A requisition (usually) for replenishment of stock which circulates to and from the purchasing department automatically when REORDER LEVEL is reached without other clerical work being necessary, e.g. ONE-FOR-ONE, or RESERVE PACKAGE CONTROL may use such a document.

Resale Prices Act (1964). (law). The Resale Prices Act (1964) sought to bring under control the application of resale price maintenance. This is a practice whereby a manufacturer sets the price at which a retail shop which he does not own must resell his products to the public, or at which a wholesale business he does not own must sell the product to a retailer. The object of the Act is to prohibit resale price maintenance, thereby enabling goods to be sold by retailers at whatever prices they think fit except where goods have been exempted from the provisions of the Act by order of the Restrictive Practices Court. It also makes unlawful various methods of enforcing resale price maintenance by withholding goods from a dealer or discriminating against him, except where the goods have been used as a 'loss leader'. The Act only affects the fixing of minimum prices. *See also below.*

resale price maintenance. A practice whereby an enterprise endeavoured to enforce a mini-

mum price for the resale of its product. The Resale Price Maintenance Act (1964) rendered void any agreement to fix resale prices unless approved by the Restricted Practices Court and registered with the Director of the Court.

research, pure/basic research. (adm). Experimental or theoretical work undertaken primarily to acquire knowledge of the underlying foundation of phenomena and observable facts. Basic research is not primarily directed towards any specific aim or objective. *See also* RESEARCH, APPLIED RESEARCH *below.*

research, applied research. Original or critical investigation undertaken in order to gain new scientific or technical knowledge and directed towards any specific aim or objective. *See also* DEVELOPMENT.

research cost. *See* COST, RESEARCH.

research operational. *See* OPERATIONAL RESEARCH.

reserve price. *See* PRICE, RESERVE PRICE.

reserve package control. *See* STOCK CONTROL, VISUAL CONTROL.

reserved stock. *See* STOCK RESERVED.

residual value. *See* VALUE, RESIDUAL VALUE.

response. (v). The act of responding, replying or reacting to a message, communication or FEED-BACK, etc. [i.e. an important factor in purchasing and marketing].

response time. The length of time taken by a system to respond or react to an instruction, input, FEEDBACK, or other communication.

responsibility. An obligation upon a subordinate, to whom AUTHORITY or duties have been delegated, to use such delegated powers purely for the purposes for which they were intended and in accountability to the person who delegated them. *But note:* the 'superior is always responsible for the activities of his subordinate and cannot escape this responsibility by delegation'.

responsiveness. The rate at which a system of information technology, or an individual in administration, reacts or replies to a stimulus or communication. Responsiveness in the supply chain is receiving scrutiny as a possible source of advantage. The faster a supply chain can respond to the needs of customers the more potential for cost savings.

restoration. BS 3811 (4121). MAINTENANCE intended to bring an *item* back to its original appearance or state. *See also* REPAIR. *Also* REBUILD, RECONDITION, REFURBISH.

restraint of trade. 'Any contract which interferes with the free exercise of trade or business by restricting the work done for others, or, arrangements made with others in a contract, is a restraint of trade. It is invalid unless reasonable as between the parties and not injurious to the public interest'. Petrofina v Martin (1966). *See also* COMPETITION, COMMUNITY RULES. HORIZONTAL RESTRAINTS: those which operate across the board of all products generally. VERTICAL RESTRAINTS: those restraints that apply to a particular or type of goods.

restrictive trade practices. 'Any agreement by two or more firms to fix common prices for a particular commodity or to limit the quantities by the manufacturer or the channels through which they will sell'. Restrictive Trade Practices Act 1976, which consolidated the previous enactments.

retention money or merely **retention.** CIMA. A sum of money representing an agreed proportion of a price for goods supplied or work completed, such proportion being withheld by the purchaser from the contractor for an agreed period of time as security against failure by the supplier or contractor to fulfil his obligations under the terms of the contract.

retention of title. *See* TITLE, RETENTION OF TITLE.

retrospective rebate. See REBATE, RETROSPECTIVE REBATE.

return on capital. The fundamental ratio for determination of success of an enterprise or plant or other project.

$$R\% = \frac{Pr}{Cap} \times 100$$

Where:

R% is percentage return generated by capital employed*.

Pr is profit generated before interest and tax.

Cap is average capital employed.

* Usually taken at successive year-end or other datum.

return, internal rate of return (IRR). A percentage discount rate used in capital investment appraisal. It brings the cost of a project and its future cash inflows into equality. (CIMA).

returns book. CIMA. The record of details and amounts of goods returned to suppliers. Also, a register of goods returned to a firm e.g. for repair, rectification and so on.

return load. An arrangement for goods to be brought to the factory by a BACK HAUL.

returns, physical returns. In supplies, goods which are returned by a purchaser to the supplier, or from a customer to the factory of the purchasing officer for treatment or due to rejection by the customer, etc.

returns, clerical returns. Collections of data or statistics such as weekly stock issues, etc.

review. A general survey or report, such as review of performance of a supply department, performance of handling plant and future requirements, etc.

rider. An addition to a document, after its completion; an additional clause to a resolution or verdict.

right first time. *See* ZERO DEFECTS.

ring price. See PRICE, RING PRICE.

risk. BS 4778 pt.3.1 (7.2.1). The combined effect of the probability of occurrence of an undesirable event, and the magnitude of the event.

risk, buyer's risk. If goods are consigned 'carriage paid', then buyer's risk commences on delivery. If consigned 'ex works' or 'ex wharf' or 'ex depot' the risk commences where lying.

risk, carrier's. A term in a contract for carriage under which the carrier undertakes the risk of loss or damage in transit. *See also* RISK, OWNER'S.

risk. (health and safety) (HS). The likelihood of the potential of a HAZARD being realised. The risk from a substance is the likelihood that it will harm a person in the actual circumstances of use.

risk, process risk. (health and safety) (HS). Risks of outbreak of fire, [explosion or other similar dangerous occurrence] associated with particular substances [or processes] HSC2 p. 10 HSWA Section 78.

risk, in property of goods. 'Unless otherwise agreed, goods remain at the seller's risk until the property in them is transferred to the buyer . . . whether delivery has been made or not'. Sale of Goods Act 1979 Sec. 20 (1).

risk, owner's. A term in contracts applied to the carriage of goods. In such cases (e.g. as applied to a COMMON CARRIER) where the consignor agrees to relieve the carrier of all liability, save the wilful misconduct or negligence on the part of the carrier's employees, the owner is responsible for the loss and a lower rate of carriage charge is then applied.

roadstead. (ts). A place where ships can ride at anchor some distance from the shore at whatever state of the tide.

robot. A machine controlled by computer and INFORMATION TECHNOLOGY so that it can sense, grasp, locate and move objects (e.g. tools, work pieces, etc.) in the course of manufacture and process. A similar, but not precise, analogy is the automatic storage and retrieval plant in an AUTOMATED WARE-HOUSE/STORES. robotics: the study design and use of robots, particularly for industrial purposes in the present context.

robotics. The study, design and use of robots – particularly for industrial purposes, including storage and handling.

roll-over credit. See CREDIT, ROLL OVER.

Romalpa case. See TITLE, RETENTION OF TITLE.

Ro-Ro (ship, berth, terminal). Designed so other vehicles can 'roll' on and off. See BERTH, RO-RO BERTH. Vehicles on ro/ro ships **BS AU 240: Part 1: 1991 = ISO 9367-1.** Specification for securing commercial vehicles, excluding semi-trailers

Royal Society for the Prevention of Accidents (ROSPA). See Appendix.

royalties. A percentage of (annual) revenue from sales paid to the person to whom they are due in respect of his invention, patent, proprietorship, authorship, etc.

rummaging. 1. Search by a Customs' officer for dutiable goods. 2. Search for packages bearing certain marks and numbers from a pile of landed goods. See also JERQUER.

running days. Consecutive days (cf. WORKING DAYS in shipping) without regard to Sundays or holidays.

S

SCM. *See* SUPPLY CHAIN MANAGE-
MENT.

SWL. *See* SAFE WORKING LOAD.

safe, intrinsically safe. (MS) The
design or construction (etc.),
chiefly of plant and equipment, so
that in the event of MALFUNC-
TION, however caused (e.g. overload, operator error, breakdown,
etc.) it will FAIL SAFE or otherwise avoid any hazard.

safety. BS 4778 pt.3.1 (11.2.1).
The freedom from unacceptable
risks of personal harm.

safety mark. (BSI). A triangular
symbol authorised by the British
Standards Institution to appear
only upon products which conform to British Standards specifically concerned with safety or to
safety requirements of standards
which cover other product characteristics. *See* appendix C.

safety signs. (EU directive). Under
this directive, safety signs for
industry include not only written,
printed, diagrammatic or other
signs of that nature, but also
include other means of communication, such as: hand signals, verbal signals, accoustic signals (e.g.
fire alarms) and illuminated signs.
The Directive requires employers
to use safety signs whenever there
is a hazard that cannot be avoided
or adequately reduced by alternative means. (Member States may
'derogate from hand and verbal
signals provided adequate measures are taken to protect health
and safety'.)

safety stock. *See* STOCK, SAFETY
STOCK.

safe working load (SWL). The load
or capacity which plant or equipment can safely carry, as determined by design and test. Used in
the case of lifting tackle regularly
tested and clearly marked on the
plant or equipment concerned. *See
also* OVERLOAD.

sale, contract of. 'A contract of sale
of goods is a contract by which the
seller transfers or agrees to transfer the property in goods to the
buyer for a money CONSIDERA-
TION, called the "price".' Sale of
Goods Act, 1979.

Sale of Goods Acts. Acts consoli-
dating relevant enactments
between the date of the original
Sale of Goods Act (1893) and the
current Act.

sale and lease back. *See* ORDERS &
CONTRACTS A–Z.

sale or return. *See* ORDERS AND CON-
TRACTS A–Z.

sales order. CIMA. A document
(usually internal) to factory or
warehouse to proceed with the
customer's purchase order. A
copy may be issued by a supplier

to the purchaser as an acknow-ledgement of his customer's order. *See* ACKNOWLEDGEMENT OF ORDER.

salvage. (v). Rescue goods or prop-erty from loss at sea or from other hazard. (n) Goods, property, scrap materials from production, plant or equipment which can be recovered and disposed of, or recy-cled or otherwise used. *See also* WASTE. *See also* ARISINGS, SCRAP, WASTE, RECYCLING, BY-PRODUCT, etc. and **BS 6543** Guide Use of Industrial By-products and Waste Materials in Building and Civil Engineering.

salvage money. A reward paid in recognition of the services rendered in saving a ship or its cargo at sea.

salvage note. A document which authorises the use of a product for a purpose for which it was not originally intended.

sample. cf. **BS 4778 pt.2 (8.1.2).** 1. A small quantity drawn at random from bulk and taken as represen-tative of the whole. 2. An item held out as an example.

sample size. (stat). The quantity drawn from a LOT that will be inspected in order to determine the quality of the entire lot.

sampling. *See* QUALITY CONTROL, SAMPLING INSPECTION.

sanction, financial sanction. The formal arrangement whereby those in charge of the financial affairs of an enterprise control

expenditure on major capital pro-jects, such as plant extensions, etc. The manager of supplies should be involved in costs, delivery, etc. of the plant, also of the supplies needed to feed the new capacity involved.

scale, economy of scale. The gain expected from large scale produc-tion, process or purchases. *See also* LEARNING CURVE.

scattergraph (scatter diagram). A graphical representation of data which results in a number of points scattered over a wide area instead of a linear curve. A LINE OF BEST FIT may be found by observation (or calculation). Also, there may be valuable information to deduce from the range between lines marking the boundaries of the maximum and minimum data on the scattergraph.

scheduling. BS 5191 (24001). 'The process of setting operation start-ing dates and/or finishing dates for jobs'. Applicable also to pur-chasing and supply and market-ing. May also involve component BATCH SCHEDULING, to ensure quantities of components for other supplies arrive precisely when required, particularly where 'JIT' procedures are in operation. *See also* PLANNING AND PROGRES-SING.

Scissor lifts. *See* LIFT TABLES.

scrap. CIMA. Discarded material, having some recovery value, which is usually either disposed of without further treatment (other

185

than reclaiming and handling) or re-introduced into the production process in place of fresh raw material. *See also* BY-PRODUCT *and* WASTE.

scrap note. A document which authorises the discarding of a product as economically incapable of being rectified or salvaged.

seal, container seal. A uniquely numbered seal attached to a *TIR* vehicle or CONTAINER for through transit across frontiers and which must be seen to be unbroken upon arrival at its destination.

seasonal adjustment factor. A factor introduced into statistical supply calculations so as to take account of and make allowances for regular seasonal fluctuations, such as rate of usage, demand, price, etc.

seasonal index. BS 5191 (21010). A set of numbers, giving relative values e.g. of demand during the periods of a year, which is used to modify forecasts obtained from any forecasting technique which ignores seasonal effects.

secrecy clause, in contract. A clause (where appropriate) inserted into a contract to prevent suppliers (and/or sub-contractors) from divulging any information regarding the subject of the contract to a third party. *See* TERMS AND CONDITIONS OF CONTRACT.

security, in stores and purchasing. (BS 5729 Pt. 5(0.3). British

Standard includes: 1. locking of stores when unattended, 2. protection of contents from damage/deterioration, 3. contents only issued as required and authorised, 4. properly accounted for. In purchasing, security includes: 1. abiding by the ethical codes of the Chartered Institute of purchasing and Supply and the Institute of Management, 2. avoiding release of trade/industrial secrets to others, 3. maintaining security of supply – quality/delivery, 4. avoiding the influence of any VESTED INTERESTS. The following British Standards apply: **BS 4737–1:** Intruder alarm systems, remote centres. **BS 5872:** locks and latches for doors in buildings. **BS 5979:** Remote centres for intruder alarms. **BS 6100 (3.2.1.)** Internal communications. **BS 7230:** for article theft detection systems. **BS 8220** Guide for security of buildings. *See also* GOODS, ATTRACTIVE GOODS *and* ACCESS.

seizure note. (law). A note issued by Customs officer and attached to goods placed in a Customs warehouse, when the officer has good reason for believing that such goods were not properly acquired.

seller. The person who sells, or agrees to sell, goods. Sale of Goods Act. Later Acts refer to 'transferor'.

seller's market. One in which MARKET FORCES tend to be to the advantage of the seller who can dictate price, delivery, quality and so on.

seller's option. The right of a seller to require a buyer to purchase merchandise or other property at an agreed price and within an agreed period.

sellers, over. (com. fin. mkts). A situation in a commodity market where there are only sellers or more sellers than buyers.

selling cost. *See* COSTS, MARKETING.

SEMA. Acronym for Storage Equipment Manufacturers Association.

semantics. The meanings of words, their development and changes in meaning. In so far as semantics affect supplies activities they relate to the careful use of words when framing purchase orders, specifications, and (especially) major contracts. In some contexts it also deals with symbols used in communication and in formulae. The latter is of increasing importance with the opening of the European Economic Area and the need for accuracy and clarity in communications within the Union. (No British Standard at the time of writing).

semi-manufacturers. Products, such as rubber and steel, which have been processed from raw materials and are intended for use in manufactured articles, such as tyres and car bodies.

semi-variable costs. *See* COSTS, SEMI-VARIABLE.

sensitive commodities. *See* COMMODITIES, SENSITIVE COMMODITIES.

service. BS 3811 (n). A supply of air, gas, electricity, water, etc. (also used in connection with factory cleaning, waste disposal, etc). (v) To replenish the consumables needed to keep an item in operating condition and to make routine adjustments.

service departments. (In industry). Those which provide for the running of an enterprise (particularly one engaged in manufacture, e.g. accounts, stores, maintenance); drawing and design, purchasing (supplies) personnel, transport, safety, materials handling.

service factor. *See* SERVICE RATIO.

service industries. Those which provide supporting services to industry, and those which as part of the national INFRASTRUCTURE control or enhance the quality of life.

service level. The measure of actual success in an operation such as number of successful issues from stores, or supplier's number of occasions when delivery was on time. *See also* STOCK, SERVICE LEVEL.

service ratio (also service factor) The ratio of DEMANDS met to total demands made. e.g. Requisitions submitted for 10,000 of an item but only 9,000 available for issue = service ratio of 90 percent, or if 10 requisitions presented only 8 fully met = 80 percent service ratio.

settlement terms. Terms offered by a supplier in respect of payment for goods and services. *See* DISCOUNTS, SETTLEMENT.

set-up time (make-ready time). BS 3138 (22069). The time required for preparing a machine (or process) for production. It may affect VALUE ANALYSIS when buying machines, tools, fixtures, jigs, etc.

severable contracts. *See* ORDERS AND CONTRACTS A–Z.

shelf-life. The length of time during which supplies do not deteriorate beyond acceptable limits under suitable conditions of storage (and in the domestic market) display.

ship's clearance, inwards. A customs certificate to certify that a ship arriving in port has satisfied all dues. This is now waived throughout the Community for Community internal trading.

ship's clearance, outwards. The converse of ship clearance inwards. (Community note above applies).

ship's protest. A statement made before a notary declaring damage to a ship and its cargo.

ship brokers. Those who transact business affairs of a ship, finding and arranging cargoes from port of departure to, and at, the port of arrival.

ships cellular ships. Container ships fitted with modular vertical guides etc so as to accept loading of ISO CONTAINER from cranes direct into the holds.

ship's chandler. One who provisions ships for their voyage. (Originally the provisioning of candles for a voyage).

shipping agent. *See* AGENTS, SHIPPING.

shipping bill. Manifest of goods on board.

shipping conference. Meeting of the owners of liners with a view to fixing uniform freight rates.

shipping marks. Marks which an importer instructs the exporter to show on his packages (case, crate, plant bale, etc). Usually: the importer's initials, the port of entry, the package number and number of packages in the shipment. SITPRO endorses and recommends the simplified four line mark introduced by The United Nations.

ship's manifest. Details of the cargo for Customs offices.

ship's papers. Documents establishing ownership, nationality, the nature of the cargo, the CHARTER PARTY, and bills of lading, contract with the seamen, manifest, official log, bill of health, certificate of registry, together with all other papers necessary to comply with the regulations of the governments concerned. Most of the above terms are entered separately.

shipment, short shipment. The goods which cannot be loaded on board either because of lack of space or, through an accident or, for internal transport, the delivery of less than quantity specified.

shipping note. Delivery or receipt note for goods to be placed on board a ship.

shipping terms. Terms used in the regulation and conduct of transactions for shipment by sea. (*See under relevant sections, such as* FREE ON BOARD, EX WORKS, etc.) The term has also come to include other forms of transit by land surface (rail and road etc.) and by air. *See* INCOTERMS.

shipping weight. The actual weight of a ship's cargo.

shop order. *See* ORDER, PRODUCTION ORDER.

shortage, supply shortage. BS 5191 (33031). A shortage of supplies due or overdue demands(s), or part of such demands(s), which cannot be fulfilled from stock. Applies also to direct infeed of supplies to production where JUST IN TIME system is in operation.

shortage cost. *See* COST, SHORTAGE COSTS.

shortage-time. BS 3811 (4122). The period of time during which an ITEM (e.g. plant) is unable to perform due to shortages of labour, spares, facilities, movement, (supplies), etc.

short termism. (econ). Actions based on decisions taken for immediate gain. It usually implies that little, or no, consideration has been given to long term effects or results. It is included here because it can have important implications in purchasing policy. These could include finance and economic considerations, effects upon long term health and safety of workers and/or the public, environmental long term effects, scientific effects, metal fatigue, wear, corrosion, chemical action etc.

shrink wrap. Plastic sheet which can be shrunk by heat to wrap and protect and stabilise goods stacked on some form of *loadboard*. *See also* STRETCH WRAP.

SI Units. Metric units with scales in decimals or sub-decimals employed internationally, e.g. joules, newtons etc.

sight draft. SITPRO. A BILL OF EXCHANGE which is payable on demand, instead of on a time or term.

signs, hazard and warning. Signs often in the form of 'pictograms' or 'ideograms' (*see* CODES AND CODING) and used for transit of goods and hazards at the workplace to workers and/or the public. Many are increasingly required under statutory provisions, EU regulations and subject to BSI and ISO standardisation.

simplification. The process of eliminating complexities of design by streamlining features or components by their omission or their combination with other features without impairing the functional use of the article. *See also* VARIETY REDUCTION *and* DIVERSIFICATION.

simulation. A decision making approach whereby a mathematical or other model is made of the system under scrutiny.

simulation. (stat). **(BS 3527).** The representation of a feature of the behaviour of a physical phenomena by means of a physical or abstract system by the behaviour of another system. 1. (mathematical). The use of a mathematical 'model' which represents in numerical terms, a process or other problem to be solved. e.g. The behaviour of stock movements in purchasing and provisioning. 2. (physical). The use of a physical 'model' to study the operation of the handling system in a storehouse or stockyard.

sinking fund. (fin). A fund into which sums are paid (usually) at annual intervals to provide for meeting a future commitment such as the repayment of a loan or the replacement of machinery or of some other asset and to cover DEPRECIATION.

site. 1. The place where some project (e.g. building or plant) is situated, or to be situated. 2. To erect or set down the building or plant which is the subject of a project. *Note:* In contracts, some points to cover include: inspection of site, safety of personnel [and public], security, stores, payment and control of site

labour. *See* TERMS AND CONDITIONS OF CONTRACT. CIPS.

SITPRO. Acronym for 'Simpler Trades Procedures Board', formerly 'the Simplification of International Trade Procedures Board'. SITPRO is sponsored by the Department of Trade and Industry. It works nationally and internationally to remove barriers to trade by the simplification of documents and procedures involved in international trade. Include: advice on simplified commercial, official and transport procedures; export, practice, documentation, finance and payments, advice on standards and techniques for the exchange of information by on-line computers. SITPRO promotes the use of information technology in trading, distribution and payment process.

skewness. (stat). The degree to which a FREQUENCY CURVE is asymmetric. [This is an important characteristic in many frequency distributions associated with purchasing and supply.

slow-moving. Supplies, such as stocks which may have a slow turn-over rate or which are seldom called for. *See* STOCK, TURN *and* STOCK THROUGHPUT.

social audit. An audit of the social balance that results from activities (e.g. purchases) by an enterprise. It may be associated with VALUE ANALYSIS and COST BENEFIT ANALYSIS.

sortation systems. Systems designed to divert materials or packages to their appropriate storage
or despatch location. Usually
based on ramps or roller conveyors making use of divertor
gates and bar coded labels.

source documents. Those (such as
PURCHASE ORDERS,
REQUISITIONS, 'GRNS', etc)
which can be used to record physical and financial movements/
commitments, etc.

sourcing. A term coined by supplies
staff to cover their activities in
locating satisfactory and economical sources of supply of goods and
servies. *See also* SUPPLIES, SOURCING
OF SUPPLIES.

sourcing of supplies. *See* SUPPLIES,
SOURCING OF SUPPLIES.

spares, strategic spares. Those
which are vital for the functioning
of plant or equipment. [May be of
relatively low price and quantity
in classification 'C' of 'ABC
ANALYSIS' but require priority
treatment in the stock control system to ensure continued availabil-
ity].

spares stock. *See* STOCK, SPARES

'Spearhead'. A database operated
by the Department of Trade and
Industry. It summarises all measures in the European Community
Programme and in other areas
which have substantial implications for business. e.g. Collabor-
ative research and development
programmes, measures for Health

and Safety at Work, the environment and the social aspects of the
Common Market.

specific duties. Customs duties
which are levied on weight or
other measure of quantity instead
of on value. *See* AD VALOREM.

specific goods. *See* GOODS, SPECIFIC.

specific performance. *See* PER-
FORMANCE, SPECIFIC.

specification. 1. 'A statement of the
attributes of a product, process or
service'. [These attributes may be
performance or conformance
requirements, depending upon
the use to which the specification
is put]. The attributes may be
descriptive of a product or service,
identifying for the user or prospective user its likely fitness to fulfil
the purpose. If, however, the purpose of the specification is to
establish a basis for conformity to
design or to manufacture, the
attributes become requirements'.
BS 7373 (1.2.1.) 2. This term is
also used to describe the document which carries details of the
requirements.* 3. The specification document may not only bear
the actual requirements but may
also be accompanied by drawings,
patterns or other relevant documents appertaining to but outside
the scope of the specification on
which the contractual agreement
is based.** 4. The specification
document may also indicate the
criteria whereby conformance of
the object, substance, service, etc.
can be checked.
NOTES: * Those engaged in

buying, selling and trading should note that under definition '2' every purchase order bearing requirements is a 'specification'. ** It is essential that the governing contract document shall enumerate all the documents etc. which relate to the contract and are conditional upon it. **BS 7373** is The Guide to the Preparation of Specifications. *See section headed* QUALITY.

specification, functional specification. BS 4778 pt.1 (3.22). 1. Document that describes in detail the characteristics of a product with regard to its intended capabilities. 2. The description of any object, material or process in sufficient detail to enable its manufacture, or procurement, to be identically produced, reproduced or procured. 3. A detailed statement of a set of requirements to be satisfied by a product, material or process, indicating, whenever appropriate, the procedure by means of which it may be determined whether the requirements given are satisfied. **BS 5532 (4.9).** 4. 'Open specification': one which does not fully specify a need but which leaves a latitude for the supplier(s) to provide variants or alternatives.

specification, over-specification. Specification for dimensions, quality or other description of supplies or services beyond that needed for the satisfactory performance of the supplies or services. [Over-specification may arise from a number of causes: designers may overspecify to ensure their designs are effective,

e.g. unnecessarily close LIMITS and TOLERANCES on fits. *See also* **BS 4500** ISO LIMITS AND FITS. Or designers and draughtsmen may specify special items where a standard item may be just as good and probably not a lower price.

specific goods. *See* GOODS, SPECIFIC GOODS.

specimen. BS 4778 (10.7). A representative single item or a measured quantity of material. *Note:* The term is often used in the formation of a SAMPLE.

'spend'. Jargon speak for 'expenditure' or 'spent'.

spot cash. *See* PAYMENT CASH, SPOT.

spot goods. Goods actually available and ready for delivery.

spot price. *See* PRICE, SPOT.

spot sale. Goods which were in stock and have been sold for immediate delivery.

spreadsheet. An electronic device using a computer program. It comprises the well known matrix tabulation layout prepared electronically.
Vertical columns relate to headings such as periods (months, years, etc.) or alternative quotations, distribution networks, routes, projects, etc. Horizontal lines define the PARAMETERS which affect the data which appears in the vertical columns opposite each parameter, such as costing details of quotations, costs

of different routes in distribution, etc. Where the lines intersect is termed a 'cell' and this under the appropriate column states the figure calculated by the computer from the parameter at that line and under the appropriate column. The Chartered Institute of Purchasing and Supply cite the following applications for spreadsheets in their field: evaluation of bills of materials, phased purchasing based on product related leadtimes, EOQ Models, comparing suppliers' offers, effects on total cash-flow of projects to meet cash restraints, stocktaking evaluations, planning stock levels in relation to predicted demand, evaluation of stockholding and purchase strategies.

stage payments. *See* PAYMENTS, STAGE PAYMENTS.

standard. 1. The establishment of a unit of measurement, or reference instrument or component for use in the calibration of other instruments. 2. A standard may be a specification or practice adopted formally (See definition 3, below) or informally by established usage, for example 'A COURSE OF DEALING', or other informal but regularly used commercial or technical practice.* 3. 'A standard, in the sense of ISO/IEC/CEN/CENELEC or BSI, is a document established by consensus and approved by a recognised body, and that provides common and repeated use, rules, guidelines or characteristics for activities or their results, aimed at the achieve

ment of the optimum degree of order in a given context.'** (Notes: * Those engaged in buying, selling and trading, particularly overseas, should be alert to the possible problems which may arise when they encounter practices, conditions, etc. with which they are unfamiliar. ** A standard may be a code of practice, a guide, method, specification, etc. A standard may become binding only if it is made mandatory by legislation, if a party is contracted to work to it or once a claim for compliance with it has been made). 4. *See also* the following relevant British Standards: **PD 6489:** guide to the Preparation of a Company Standards Manual. **PD6495:** IFAN Guide 1, Method of determining the advantages of (Company) Standardization. PD 6515: IFA Guide 2, Company use of International Standards.

standardization. 'The activity of establishing, with regard to actual or potential problems, provision for common and repeated use, aimed at achievement of the optimum degree of order in a given context'. NOTES: 1. In particular, the activity consists of the processes of formulating, issuing and implementing standards. 2. Important benefits of standardization are improvements of the suitability of products, processes and services for their intended purposes, prevention of barriers to trade and facilitation of technological cooperation.

standards, assessment policy on (EC) conformity assessment.

193

The policy adopted by the Council of Ministers (1989). Their resolution aims to: 1. assist in replacing national rules by Community Rules by means of DIRECTIVES, 2. encourage mutual recognition of test reports and certificates and develop Europe-wide certification. Five guiding principles laid down are: 1. a coherent approach to conformity assessment, 2. promotion of (i) the **EN29000** series of STANDARDS for QUALITY MANAGEMENT, (ii) **EN45000** STANDARDS on the competence of test laboratories and certification bodies, (iii) development of national accreditation systems, (iv) intercomparison techniques between test laboratories, 3. set up a flexible non-bureaucratic European body for testing and certification, 4. studies to deal with different levels of development in national quality infrastructure, 5. mutual recognition agreements with non-EU States.

standards, 'conformity'. (EU). 'Conformity' in the single market implies to producers, suppliers, purchasers and users that a product [or service] does in fact conform to a STANDARD or SPECIFICATION, which in some cases may be a legal requirement. Both kinds of requiremen, purely commercial or legal, are met by ASSESSMENT OF CONFORMITY and the granting of a CERTIFICATE OF CONFORMITY. [*See* UNDER QUALITY]

standard, certificate of conformity. The certificate: 1. specifies the tests to be carried out in the course of manufacture, and the procedures and frequency of such tests. It includes undertakings that: 2. all tests will be carried out as specified, 3. by appropriately qualified independent personnel and 4. will be subject to written reports by those persons. Application for the certificate must be accompanied by the design and manufacturing schedule and a document which: 1. describes the manufacturing processes, 2. and all measures to ensure conformity with a relevant national standard or prototype, 3. specifies where the goods are to be manufactured and stored and 4. states the proposed date for commencement of manufacture.

standard costs. *See* COSTS, STANDARD.

standard deviation. A measure of the VARIANCE of individual ITEMS of DATA from the MEAN of all the items of data. It can be calculated by taking the square root of the sum of the squares of all the deviations from the mean divided by their frequency. The result can then be manipulated mathematically in further statistical calculations. It is a very important tool in purchasing and supply. Provided that its basis is a NORMAL FREQUENCY curve its mathematical properties enable it to be used for planning stock control levels, etc.

standard, European standards, ('EN'). (EU). Such standards, designated by the prefix or suffix

'EN' carry the obligation on the members of CEN and CENELEC to implement them at national level by giving them the status of national standards and by withdrawing any conflicting national standards. The technical content of an 'EN' is identical in each country *and is of equal validity. (*There may be exceptions for some EFTA countries).

standard, harmonisation documents ('HD'). (EU). A harmonisation document constitutes a CEN/ CENELEC standard. It (an HD) carries the same obligations to withdraw any conflicting national standards. *But*, the public announcement of its number and title is otherwise sufficient. Harmonisation documents are established if transposition into national standards is unnecessary if [for example] a CEN or CENELEC member has already adopted an ISO or IEC being endorsed in Europe, or impracticable, and particularly if agreement is subject to the acceptance of national deviations.

standards in the Community, 'the new approach'. (EC) [Resolution adopted by the Council of Ministers 7.5.1985]. 'New Approach' Directives set out 'essential requirements' (for safety, for example) written in general terms, which must be met before products may be sold in the United Kingdom or anywhere else in the European Union. Standards fill in the detail and are the main way for business to meet the 'essential requirements'. The

Directives also say how manufacturers are to show that products meet the 'essential requirements'. Products meeting the requirements are to carry the CE CONFORMITY MARK, which should mean that they can be sold anywhere in the Community.

standard price. *See* PRICE, STANDARD.

standard. pre-standards, ('ENV'). These are standards for provisional application similar to BSI 'drafts for development'. [They are subject to consideration and comments and are available for provisional application whilst conflicting national standards may remain temporarily in existence in parallel].

standing order *See* ORDERS & CONTRACTS A–Z, STANDING ORDER.

standing order, banker's standing order. Instructions to a bank by a depositor to pay a stated sum at set agreed intervals to a stated payee.

standing order (purchase). *See also* ORDERS AND CONTRACTS A–Z.

standing order(s). Rules governing conduct, procedures, etc., usually for a public authority or similar body.

statics, electrical. The charge of electricity which may be produced in numerous ways and which can produce serious hazards in storage and handling through sparks resulting from discharge of stored static energy.

statics, mechanical.. The branch of physics that deals with the ways in which forces act together (usually) so as to produce, or destroy, equilibrium. e.g. the stability of stacked goods, racking, floor loading, etc. Important considerations in health and safety in storage.

statistics. The collection and analysis of data which may be classified and interpreted with deductions made (usually on the theory of probability) with the assumption that the relationships between data of a large random sample are typical of the relationships between the whole POPULA-TION of data. 'A function of observed values derived from a sample'. (**BS 5532**) 1. DESCRIPTIVE STATISTICS, deal with methods of describing a large mass of DATA [e.g. PIE CHARTS, SPREAD SHEETS, etc.] 2. ANALYTICAL STATISTICS, deal with methods that enable conclusions to be drawn from the DATA. [e.g. BREAK-EVEN CHARTS, HISTO-GRAMS, etc.]. For more detailed information, the British Standards Institution recommend the use of **BS 5532 part 1 (ISO 3534)** the terminology from which will be used throughout this volume. Reference may also be made to the section headed INFORMATION TECHNOLOGY.

statute barred. (law). A transaction, contract, or other act which is forbidden by statute.

statute law. *See* LAW, STATUTE LAW.

stillage. A workshop or storage platform on legs, transportable by stillage truck. *See* BS 3810.

stochastic. (stats). The statistical situation in which targets are set, based upon estimates which are themselves based upon variable data, e.g. RE-ORDER LEVEL based upon varying demand as distinct from a 'deterministic' system where all the data can be determined precisely. The word is frequently used as a synonym for a target or guess.

stock. BS 3811 (4265) and **BS 5191 (23001).** All the tangible material assets of a company other than the fixed assets. Comprises all the finished or saleable products, all the items to be incorporated into the finished products, and all the items to be consumed in the process of manufacturing the product or in carrying out the business. **BS 3811** deprecates the use of the word inventory as a synonym for stock.

stock, accomodation stock. Stock provided by a supplier to a purchaser. The latter usually holds it in his stores. He may pay for it as it is used, or 'part on delivery' and the balance as it is used, or other arrangement.

stock account, One of the control accounts kept to reconcile the various accounts which flow into the main stock accounts, which finally contribute to the balance sheet.

stock, accounting/accountancy

stock. CIMA. Includes current assets at the end of an accounting period. Includes: raw materials, work in progress, finished goods, and goods in transit or on consignment (i.e. to a customer).

stock, allocated stock. *See* STOCK, PRE-ALLOCATED STOCK *and* STOCK RESERVED, STOCK *or* PHYSICALLY ALLOCATED STOCK.

stock audit. A physical count made by an agency external to stores to ensure veracity of records against physical stock. *See also* AUDIT *and* STOCK-TAKING.

stock, buffer stock. BS 5191 (33011). A proportion of work-in-progress stock held because of varying production rates, not necessarily planned and usually held on the shop floor. *Note:* It is *not* a synonym for SAFETY STOCK and should no longer be used in the context of stock control. For this, the term 'safety stock' should be used. *See* also STOCK, UNCOUPLING EFFECT OF STOCK.

stock check, periodic check. BS 5191 (33026). A stock check which involves the physical check of all stock at one time and which is performed periodically, e.g. annually by annual stock take.

stock check, physical stock check. BS 5191 (33025). A check on stock by direct measurement or scrutiny together with the subsequent comparison with and reconciliation to the stock records. Synonymous with: 'physical stock count', 'stock

audit'. May be continuous or periodic.

stock, consignment stock. Stock (supplies) provided 'on consignment' in commercial trading and to be paid for as used or sold. *See also* STOCK, SALE OR RETURN *and* STOCK, ALLOCATION STOCK *and* STOCK, ACCOMMODATION STOCK.

stock, consumable stock. BS 5191 (23010). That portion of INDIRECT STOCK which consists of items which do not form part of the saleable product and are not normally used in the manufacturing process [e.g. stationery, oil, etc.].

stock control. BS 5729 Pt.3 BS 5191 (33001). The system whereby the levels of supplies in stock are regulated to maintain quantities required without STOCK EXCESS or STOCK DEFICIENCIES. CIMA. 'The alternative term "inventory control" is common in USA', but *see also* BS 3811 of stock. *Note:* for physical control of stock *see* STORAGE. *See also* HOMEOSTASIS.

stock control, audit of stock. An accounting check on the accuracy of stock-control records for INVENTORY or accounting purposes. Involves reconciling the stores accounts, vouchers, printouts, etc. with stock control records. Sometimes used (incorrectly) as a synonym for STOCK-TAKING which may or may not be carried out at the same time.

stock control, base stock control.

A system of stock control, whereby in a sequence (usually) of major projects (e.g. ships), PROVISIONING stock for each next unit is undertaken at a suitable time in advance of its commencement to ensure a smooth and accurate stock level of supplies at the starting date. (Application of NETWORK ANALYSIS is appropriate).

stock control, bin card control. The recording of stock movements on record cards attached to or located at the location of stock. Formerly the most popular method of stock control prior to the introduction of centralised control. Now largely abandoned in favour of the latter thus avoiding clerical work at the storage points (bins). Still used for special applications, such as valuable goods requiring frequent checks at the bin (e.g. jewellery) or strategic spares under ONE-FOR-ONE control, etc.

stock control, continuous control. Stock control in which the stock balance is continuously updated promptly, e.g. by *on-line* computer at each transaction. (If valuation of the stock is simultaneously recorded, the term 'perpetual inventory' (used by the Americans for all stock control) can be correctly applied.

stock control, coverage analysis. A control technique which aims to maximise the use of capital invested in stock. This is done by making a quantitative assessment of likely throughput of the various

stock lines and adjusting intakes to minimise investment (inventory) whilst assuring continuity of supply for production/process.

stock control, cyclical timing. The control of stock by review of stock levels at predetermined time intervals. *See also* STOCK CONTROL, RE-ORDER LEVEL CONTROL METHOD AND STOCK, CYCLE STOCK.

stock control, imprest. A method of controlling stock without the necessity of records. It is usually based upon a pre-determined maximum stock level. This is checked at regular intervals and made up to the maximum level required.

stock control, max-min method. *See* STOCK CONTROL, RE-ORDER LEVEL METHOD.

stock control, 'one-for-one'. A system of stock control where one of the following methods is applied: 1. A new item is only issued upon the return of the old one, e.g. protective clothing, small tools, etc. 2. Directly an item is taken from stock a new one is ordered, e.g. spare parts for plant, etc.

stock control, pre- (or forward) allocation method. BS 5729 Part 3 Fig. 6. Known forward requirements are pre-allocated on the stock records and a 'cover' known as 'forward balance' is maintained. *See* STOCK, RESERVED STOCK.

stock control, re-order level control method. A method of stock control in which the level is maintained by setting a re-order level. Directly this is reached a replenishment is put in hand. *See also* RE-ORDER LEVEL.

stock control, 'reserve package' method. Quantities of stock, e.g. stationery) are made up into suitable size packages and when the 'reserve package' (so labelled) is removed and used last. The label is then detached and sent to the central stores, or to purchasing, for replenishment.

stock control, three bin system. As 'two bin' system described below but with the provision of a third bin for SAFETY STOCK. Former **BS 5729 Part 3, Fig. 7.**

stock control, two bin system. A system of visual stock control by means of two bins (or two levels) so arranged that when one bin is empty (or the lower level is reached) a replenishment is called for from main store, or ordered by purchasing. The term is sometimes used to describe control by RE-ORDER LEVEL – the level of the second bin (or second level) is determined in the same manner. *See* BS 5729 PART 3.

stock control, visual control. General term for a number of methods of controlling stock by visual examination of levels, in some cases avoiding the necessity of any clerical work. *See* IMPREST; 'ONE-FOR-ONE'; OPEN ACCESS BINS; STORES, OPEN ACCESS; RESERVE PACKAGE; TWO-BIN SYSTEM, *etc.*

stock, costs of holding. *See* COSTS, STOCK HOLDING COSTS OF.

stock, costs of investment. *See* COSTS, STOCK, INVESTMENT, COSTS OF.

stock cover. (prod). **BS 5191 (33006).** 1. The sum of stock physically on hand, less any reserved stock. 2. The length of time that a given supply or level of stock will satisfy a given production or process demand at a given rate of consumption for production or process.

stock, cycle stock ('active stock'. 'live stock', 'working stock'.) BS 5191 (33009). That portion of stock available (or planned to be available) for normal demands, excluding 'excess stock' and 'safety stock'. So called because it tends to move in cycles in phase with the demands of production or sales.

stock, 'dead stock'. Stock which never turns over or does so so slowly that it is unprofitable to carry it.

stock deficiency. Situations where demands upon stock result in an actual failure to supply and make a production stoppage imminent.

stock, direct stock. BS 5191 (23008). That which is incorporated directly into an END-PRODUCT.

stock, dues-in. Supplies which are due to arrive in stock either from purchase orders or production orders IN HOUSE, or from a branch stores or depot. *Note:* stock records must be adjusted to allow for quantities to be received from outstanding purchase or production orders. Usually shown in a special column.

stock, dues-out (allocated). Quantities, usually shown in a special column, on stock control record indicating known future demands which must be met. These are often associated with a 'forward allocation system'.

stock evaluation. The evaluation of stock for the preparation of the financial accounts. *See* STOCK VALUATION.

stock, excess stock. cf. **BS 5191 (33008).** A situation where stock exceeds maximum permitted stock. Warrants immediate investigation of DEMAND rate, INTAKE rate, size of purchase order QUANTITIES, PROGRESSING action, etc. *See also* SURPLUS STOCK.

stock, fast moving stock. Stock (or direct supplies) for which there is a frequent or continuous demand. Usually needs special consideration in respect of physical MATERIALS MANAGEMENT such as location in stores, special packaging, and administrative materials management in respect of ordering and stock control, etc.

stock, finished-goods, parts, products. BS 5191 (23006). Stock which is available for supply to an external consumer, including items which have been supplied but not invoiced, but excluding items which have been invoiced to the external consumer. *Note:* A product which may be both

INTERMEDIATE STOCK and FINISHED GOODS STOCK is considered as INTERMEDIATE STOCK until such time as a quantity is physically reserved for external consumption. The quantity reserved then becomes FINISHED GOODS STOCK.

stock, free stock. Stock which is uncommitted and available for use, i.e. after allowing for allocations and reservations.

stock, free issue stock. 1. Stock received from a customer for use in producing goods against his purchase order. 2. Stock of low value made freely available. *See* STORE, OPEN ACCESS STORE.

stock handling cost. *See* COSTS, STOCK HANDLING COSTS.

stock holding costs. *See* COSTS, STOCK HOLDING COSTS.

stock, idle stock. Stock which fails to move through lack of demand. e.g. SAFETY STOCK which only moves occasionally e.g. to meet an emergency. *See also* STOCK, DEAD STOCK.

stock, indirect stock. BS 5191 (23009). Stock which is not incorporated in an end product but comprises SUPPORTING GOODS, e.g. stationery, tools lubricants, etc. *Note:* stock which is incorporated in the end-product but is of indefinite quantity is sometimes regarded as indirect stock, e.g. paint, solder, etc.

stock, intermediate stock. BS 5191

(23005). That portion of WORK IN PROGRESS STOCK which consists of completed parts subassemblies and assemblies which are held available in stores.

stock-keeping unit. The measure by which the quantity of stock is recorded on the stock record, e.g. each, metre, kilogram.

stock levels. The quantities of stock carried, normally controlled by stock control systems.

stock level, balance level (physical). Physical balance: actual quantities of supplies in stock as determined by count, measurement, stock check, etc.

stock level, excess stock level, indication of. A level set in stock control records which will alert those responsible for the maintenance of stock levels when excess stock is indicated. Also indicated as 'maximum stock level'.

stock level, exhaust stock or exhaust bin level. Stock completely exhausted including safety stock.

stock level forward stock balance level. Stock balance based on PHYSICAL BALANCE and 'dues in'. It equals 'physical balance + (dues in – any forward allocation.)

stock level, free stock balance level. Physical stock balance minus forward allocations.

stock level, maximum level. cf. BS

5191 (33014). The planned highest level of stock, above which is considered to be in excess and is normally flagged for management attention. *See also* STOCK LEVEL, EXCESS STOCK LEVEL *above*.

stock level, minimum level. A level below which stock quantity should not be permitted to fall. Sometimes used as a synonym for RE-ORDER LEVEL but may not always be identical with that level.

stock level, opening stock level. Stock level at the commencement of a particular period. Usually taken at beginning of financial year or budgetary period or, in the case of a project, may be at the time work starts on the project.

stock level, progressing. The level at which PROGRESSING action should take place to ensure delivery is on target. May be earlier than that given by a STOCK WARNING LEVEL so as to leave time for provisioning if the reply is unsatisfactory. *See also* PLANNING AND PROGRESSING.

stock level, re-order level. *See* STOCK CONTROL, RE-ORDER LEVEL CONTROL.

stock level, stock-out level. *See* STOCK CONTROL, RE-ORDER LEVEL CONTROL.

stock level, stock-out level. Stock-out level is that at which ACTIVE (OR CYCLE) STOCK is exhausted and SAFETY STOCK is called upon. Sometimes referred to as MINIMUM STOCK

LEVEL but this can be ambiguous and should not be used as a synonym for STOCK OUT.

stock level, warning level. A level intermediate between RE-OR-DER LEVEL and STOCK-OUT LEVEL which although seldom expressed in formal terms can be very important in high priority stock. It is the point after which it will be too late to take alternative action to avoid a stockout if replenishment orders outstanding arrive late or if there is a sudden surge in demand.

stock life. Stock life should be measured from the instant of INTAKE to that of arrival at the WORK-CENTRE or other point of use. [Supplies management must ensure that stock-life never exceeds SHELF-LIFE. *Note*: Batch life should not be used as a synonym for stock-life since it is a production term which implies the length of time a batch of material will last during the production work-cycle]. *See also* BATCH LIFE.

stock optimisation. Reduction in total STOCK HOLDING COST by looking at raw materials, materials stock, work in progress and finished goods to ensure that any stocks are held at the appropriate point in the sequence of conversion or production. As a general rule it is preferred to carry stocks of pre process or partly processed materials rather than finished goods, thereby postponing value adding activity and avoiding the costs associated with tying up high values of stock.

stock order. *See* ORDERS & CONTRACTS – STOCK ORDER.

stock-out or exhaust stock. BS 5191 (33030). The occurrence of a zero stock balance, not necessarily reflecting a shortage if safety stock or other is advisable.

stock, policy stock. BS 5729 Pt. 1. (3.6a). Stocks held for investment or speculation. [Buying or manufacture may be more advantageous now than later because of expected price arises].

stock pre-allocated stock. *See* STOCK CONTROL, PRE (OR FORWARD) ALLOCATION CONTROL. *also* STOCK, RESERVED STOCK.

stock, pricing of stock. The method of pricing of stocks for financial purposes requiring policy decision and must be consistent in method on all matters such as inclusion or exclusion of discounts, carriage, packing, insurance.

stock, 'promotion stock'. Stock of finished goods provided for a specific sales promotion where demand is expected to exceed capacity during the life of the promotion.

stock, raw material stock. BS 5191. Stock which is not part of WORK IN PROGRESS, i.e. is held in the raw materials store.

stock, purchased parts stock. BS 5191 (23002). Stock which is held in the same state as when purchased and has not yet been issued 'from stores', i.e. is held in a purchased parts store.

stock record. A record of the quantity of stock of a single item, often containing a history of recent transactions and information for controlling the replenishment of stock.

stock record, perpetual/ continuous. CIMA. The recording as they occur of receipts, issues and calculations of resulting balances of individual stock items in quantitative measure, and, (if including price) comprising an INVENTORY.

stock relief. An allowance against taxable profits given by the Inland Revenue, to offset increase in closing value due to inflation of stocks of saleable goods.

stock requisition. *See* REQUISITION, STOCK REQUISITION.

stock, reserved stock. BS 5191 (23012). (also known as allocated assigned, earmarked or appropriated). Material committed to specific orders, usually but not necessarily, physically separated from other stock. Where physically set aside it is usually segregated in a RESERVATION STORE or reservation area. *See also* STOCK CONTROL, PRE (OR FORWARD) ALLOCATION CONTROL.

stock rotation. BS 5191 (33034). A procedure which attempts to ensure that supplies do not remain in stock longer than their SHELF-LIFE. *See* FIFO.

stock, safety stock. BS 5191 (33010). A proportion of stock planned to be held to protect against unforeseen circumstances (increased usage, lengthened lead times, etc.) and normally held in store.

stock, seasonal stocks. BS 5729 Pt. 1 (3.6d). Stocks to enable production or purchasing to be carried out at a more constant rate throughout the year when customer demand (or supply) is seasonal.

stock, service level (or factor or ratio). BS 5191 (33013). 'A measure of the achievement of success in satisfying demand for stock during a pre-determined period'. Usually expressed thus:

$$Sl = \frac{Dfs}{Dn} \times 100$$

Where   Sl is service level (percentage)
Dfs is demands fully met
Dn is demands made.

When included in stores performance reports the data. May be further expanded to reveal the degrees to which issues fall below demands. This may be further analysed into individual items demanded versus those available.

stock, slow moving stock. Stock which is only issued occasionally or continually but in very small quantities. It may need special attention for obsolescence, excess build-up, exceeding SHELF-LIFE, provisioning for emergency use, etc.

203

stock, spares stock. BS 3811 (4264) and **BS 5191 (23011).** 'Items which are held available for MAINTENANCE purposes or for the replacement of defective parts', or for supply to customers.

stock, surplus stock. Stock in excess of requirements.

stock-taking. CIMA. Checking of stocks and verication of stock records against physical quantities held in store and also those at WORK-IN-PROGRESS stage and FINISHED GOODS on hand. Stock-taking may be 1. continuous, 2. cyclical (i.e. at regular intervals – as at the end of the financial year, or, 3. random. It may be over the entire stock or a section at a time. *See also* STOCK-CONTROL CONTINUOUS, and STOCK-CONTROL, AUDIT OF.

stock throughput ('turnover', 'usage'). The total volume or value of a commodity (or all commodities) of stock passing through stores during a given period (usually 12 months). It should include all issues, plus *wastage*, loss, deterioration, spillage, etc., but allowing for returns to stock from work-centres, etc.

stock, transport stock. BS 5729 Pt. 1 (3.6c). Stock held because of the time taken to transport goods. Often a significant cost in wholesale/retail distribution costs.

stock, uncoupling effect of. The degree of freedom provided by stockholding to a consuming department or other user to cover variations in demand or supply. It is a direct function of stock levels, intake and consumption rates. *See also* STOCK, BUFFER STOCK *and also* STOCK, BUFFER STOCK *and* STOCK, SAFETY. *Also* HOMEOSTASIS.

stock turn, a stock turn. The complete cycle of use of a quantity or batch of stock, from receipt to exhaustion of the quantity or batch. An important statistic of physical stock control since it involves shelf-life and stock life. Not to be confused with *rate* of turnover. *see* STOCK-TURNS, RATE OF.

stock turns, rate of stock turns. BS 5191 (33091). The rate of consumption of stock. Calculated by dividing the annual (or other chosen period) total THROUGHPUT by the average level of stock.

$$St = \frac{Tp}{St}$$

Where: St is the number of stock turns in period.

Tp is the total throughput in period.

Sm is mean stock carried throughout period.

BS 5191 (33019). cf. *Note:* Make sure data used throughout in preparing statistics are all in the same units, e.g. denominations of money, quantities, volumes, weights, degree of metrication, etc.

stock utilisation ratio. An important ratio affecting profitability of supplies management. It is particularly relevant in class 'A' supplies.

$$Sur = \frac{Tp}{So + In}$$

Where: Sur is stock utilisation ratio.

Tp is total throughput in period.

So is opening stock including safety stock at commencement of the period.

In is intake during period.

Note: Comment at 'stock usage rate' **BS 5191 (33018)** below:

stock, usage rate of stock. BS 5191 (33018). The rate of consumption of stock. The use of the data requires it shall be related to some time scale, viz. production period, accounting period, weekly, monthly, annual periods, etc.

stock valuation. BS 3811 (2214). The total value of stock, usually measured in monetary terms.

stock valuation, first-in, first-out (FIFO). (historical cost. *See* COSTS, HISTORICAL COSTS, CIMA.) BS 5191 (B2001). The price for the material first taken into the stock from which the material to be priced could have been drawn. *See also* FIRST-IN, FIRST-OUT, PHYSICAL CONTROL.

stock valuation, last in first out. abb. **LIFO.** CIMA. and **BS 5191 (B2002).** The price paid for the material last taken into the stock from which the material to be priced could have been drawn.

stock valuation, replacement price. CIMA. and **BS 5191 (B2003).** The price at which mate-rial could be purchased, identical to that which is being replaced or revalued. *See also* PRICE, REPLACEMENT PRICE.

stock valuation, standard price. CIMA. & **BS 5191 (B2005).** A predetermined price fixed on the basis of a specification of all factors affecting that price. Where supplies departments are involved, the standard price may be (in the first place) provided by, or agreed with, the purchasing department based on their experience and statistical analysis of price trends and also estimates from suppliers.

stock valuation, average price. (avco). CIMA & **BS 5191 (B2004).** A price which is calculated by dividing the total cost of materials in stock (from which the material to be priced could be drawn) by the total quantity of materials in that stock. [For sales and estimating purposes 'first in price' may lead to an 'other than current market price' and thus to an error in a sales ESTIMATE or QUOTATION.]

stock verification. The procedure whereby stocks are verified against records and for serviceability, obsolescence and methods of storage.

stock, warehouse stock. BS 5191 (23007). The portion of finished goods held at a warehouse.

stock-wastage. *See* WASTAGE, DAMAGE AND LOSS.

stock, working stock. *See* STOCK, CYCLE STOCK.

stock, work-in-progress stock. (WIP). (Or work-in-process). **BS 5191 (23004).** Stock upon which work has been performed or has been made ready for work to be started, but which is not available for supply to an external consumer. *Note:* it is important when subdividing WORK-IN-PROGRESS that adequate description is made, e.g. shop work in progress, sub-contracted work in progress.

stockist. A MIDDLEMAN who agrees to maintain an agreed level of specified manufacturer's goods in return for special trading terms.

stockyard. An outdoor compound (or other enclosure) usually with a prepared surface with access roads, for storage of materials which do not require protection from the weather or are improved by weathering.

stoppage *in transitu.* (law). The right of an unpaid seller to stop delivery being taken of the goods, if, after shipment but before arrival at the buyer's works, he discovers the customer is insolvent.

stop list (or 'black list). A register. 1. of suppliers who are not acceptable to the purchaser, 2. of particular supplies which are not to be purchased or used because they are not acceptable for technical reasons. *See* VENDOR RATINGS.

storage. Within the context of this dictionary, the term storage is taken to include the housing of supplies of all kinds, and also the physical handling associated with their stowage, retrieval from storage and their distribution.

storage costs. *See* COSTS, STORAGE.

storage, life. *See* STOCK-LIFE *and* SHELF LIFE.

storage stacks and stacking. The stowage in stacks, of supplies usually on pallets by means of lift trucks. Stacks may be handled from aisles or 'block stacked' in bulk without aisles in situations where first-in, first-out (FIFO) practice is not needed.

storage, utilisation factors. The utilisation factors for storage can be apportioned as follow: 1. Building utilisation factor: this factor is obtained by measuring the volume of space actually occupied by storage equipment – racks, shelves, etc. and expressing this as a percentage of the total volume of stores which could be used. 2. Storage equipment utilisation factor: this should be assessed as indicated under UTILISATION FACTOR. In this case the factor is calculated on the volume actually used as a percentage of total usable capacity. 3. Value to volume factor: this factor expresses the relative value of stock in terms of value per unit volume occupied and may be used when considering items of considerable value and the costs of security, etc.

store (n) **or stores.** A place equipped and suitably maintained for the housing of supplies and for keeping them in a condition suitable for use when they are required. The varieties of store are as numerous as the industrial and commercial activities which require them. Some of the principal types of store are given, not in alphabetic sequence below in order of importance. *See also* WAREHOUSE/ STORE, WAREHOUSE BONDED/STORE.

store, allocation store. A store set aside for housing supplies which have been PRE-ALLOCATED to specific jobs. Enhanced security and other steps may be needed to ensure that such pre-allocated stocks are not taken for jobs other than those intended. Such stock is IDLE STOCK and may thus attract added costs. The term BONDED STORE is sometimes used (incorrectly) to describe an 'allocation' or 'reservation' store. The use of this term should strictly speaking be reserved for stores subject to one described here under WAREHOUSE (OR STORE) BONDED WAREHOUSE.

store, bonded store. *See* WAREHOUSE BONDED WAREHOUSE.

store, central store. 1. One from which are supplied all the main needs of a single perimeter enterprise. 2. One supplying a group of industrial units which are geographically separated.

store, concentration store. Stores at geographically dispersed plants of a large enterprise (or GROUP) whereby each store concentrates upon the main requirements of its plant and serves the others with the supplies in which it specialises.

store, departmental store. A store specialising in supplies for main materials peculiar to the department it serves. In this case SUPPORTING GOODS may be provided from a CENTRAL STORE 2. A large retail establishment with several departments.

store, finished goods store. A store (usually located near the despatch area) where the END-PRODUCTS of an enterprise are housed. Such a store may be specially equipped and secure to protect goods which may have a final finish and possibly pre-packed for prompt delivery as spares or for distribution for the domestic market. Security may also be necessary if ATTRACTIVE finished goods are stored.

store, free issue supplies store. A store for housing FREE-ISSUE SUPPLIES. Because the enterprise managing this store is BAILEE for the free-issue goods it is important the stores be SECURE and suitably equipped and maintained in such a way as to preserve these supplies in (at least) the condition they were in when received.

store, general store. Store for GOODS needed throughout an enterprise. Most of the supplies will be Class *C* and UNIT CONTAINERS may be appropriate. Many of the items carried may be ATTRACTIVE.

store, group store. Store serving a group of enterprises which may or may not be in the same PRODUCT GROUP. The actual operation may vary therefore in the supplies held and in the distribution and control systems. *See* CENTRAL STORES and CONCENTRATION STORES.

storekeeping. BS 5729 (Part 5. (3). Those procedures and means whereby goods are received, identified, stored, issued, accounted for and replenished in accordance with defined levels of service and with due regard for the statutory requirements for health and safety.

store, open access store and open access bin. Stores and bins where the normal rules of restricted access are relaxed in favour of operatives helping themselves to supplies as and when required. In some cases omitting any clerical control. Open access bins may be located within stores or at work-centres.

store, maintenance store. *See* STORE, PLANT ENGINEER'S STORE.

store, packaging store. One set aside for packaging materials. Some of these may be ATTRACTIVE and many are subject to the need for humidity control. This store is (usually) within or adjacent to the package or despatch bay.

store, pattern store. One reserved and equipped for housing patterns. Whether part of a main store, or separate, humidity control is essential for wooden patterns and special binning may be needed owing to their (often) awkward shapes. Close control of issues and intakes and pattern number records are very important.

store, piece parts store. A store for PIECE PARTS whether BOUGHT or made IN HOUSE are used in most assembly type industries. Provision of UNIT CONTAINERS, PRE-ASSEMBLY or KITTING are often profitable activities.

store, plant engineer's store. A special store for plant maintenance and similar requirements usually situated within or adjacent to the plant engineer's department for housing strategic and fast-moving spares and consumables used in plant maintenance.

store, processed materials store. An important store in process plants (usually) closely integrated with the process and process control and also with laboratory and batch testing.

store, production store. A store specialising in supplies required specifically for production.

store, quarantine store. cf. **BS 4778 (10.10).** A stores for housing supplies which are awaiting inspection, rectification, return to suppliers or other action. Such stores must be specially SECURE so as to avoid any possibility of their contents circulating or from entering the production or process system without authority. Sometimes referred to (incorrectly) as *bonded stores*. See WAREHOUSE, BONDED.

store, raw material store. A main store housing a major part of the enterprise's assets. Usually storage is in bulk. Special binning, racking, hoppers, silos, etc. may be warranted with their associated handling and control equipment.

store, reservation store. A store in which supplies are held which have been physically RESERVED for a future known (or anticipated) demand. *See also* STOCK PRE-ALLOCATED STOCK.

store, salvage store. A very necessary area for the reception, sorting and despatch of ARISINGS for disposal as WASTE or sale or RE-CYCLING as SCRAP. Should be outside the production area and made secure if arisings include valuable materials eg copper cable. Part of the CONSERVATION SYSTEM.

store, secure store. One where more than normal security is provided for supplies held against unauthorised access or removal. They may be kept there for special reasons such as value, hazards, property of a customer, etc. The term bonded store is not a synonym for secure store and should only be so used if a bond

has been entered into. *See* WAREHOUSE AND STORE, BONDED.

store, site stores. Stores set up by contractors and construction firms for servicing their teams on site. Security and safety at unattended site stores must be carefully worked out.

store, sub-store (satellite store). A general term applicable to many types of stores which are subordinate to another which supplies it. e.g. an OPEN ACCESS STORE at a work centre supplied from a main store.

stores. Stock, items held in store. *Note:* the term STOCK is widely preferred.

stores catalogue. A list of all items held in stock on a regular basis. It must be compatible with the COMMODITY CATALOGUE, where such exists, and use the terminology of the VOCABULARY. The stores catalogue may be incorporated into the COMMODITY CATALOGUE.

stores control account. The control account in which the totals of transactions shown on stock records are entered.

stores ledger. CIMA. A subsidiary ledger containing an account for each separately indentifiable class of material handled by the stores organisation. It is controlled by the STORES CONTROL ACCOUNT in the principal ledger. It is sometimes referred to as the RAW MATERIALS LEDGER.

209

stores, main store. *See* STORE, CENTRAL STORE.

storeman. A employee working within a store whose activities are chiefly confined to manual operations.

stores, management functions. BS 5729 pt 5 (0.2). Main functions in stores are: receiving supplies; identifying supplies; storage of supplies; issuing of supplies; accounting for supplies; replenishment of supplies. But *see also* SECURITY IN STORES (BS5729). *Also* other functions in this section: health and safety, environmental control, conservation of resources, etc.

stores manager. The person who controls and administers the whole of the store's operation and function.

stores requisition. *See* REQUISITION STORES, REQUISITION.

stores reports. *See* REPORTS.

stores, service factors in stores. *See* STOCK, SERVICE LIFE.

stores vocabulary. *See* VOCABULARY.

stores, wastage in. A significant contributor to costs enumerated under STOCK, COSTS OF HOLDING. Allowance may be needed when provisioning if wastage cannot be reduced or eliminated.

straddle carrier. A mobile handling device for the movement and stacking of freight containers (usually of the ISO type fitted with twistlocks for use with the standardised carrier equipment) which suspends the container between the 'goliath' type wheeled legs upon which the vehicle travels. In common use, worldwide at dockside and transport distribution centres. *See also* HANDLING, STRADDLE HANDLING *and also* TRUCK, STRADDLE TRUCK.

strategic gap analysis. *See* GAP ANALYSIS, STRATEGIC GAP ANALYSIS.

strain. The result of stress which, when applied to an object or solid substance, causes its deformation, e.g. bending or stretching (e.g. the deflection (bending) of a storage beam or shelf which has been subjected to strain through being overloaded.

Formula:

$$\text{Strain} = \frac{\text{change in length}}{\text{original length of object}}.$$

There are no units for strain, it is a ratio. It is the product of STRESS.

strategic spares. *See* SPARES, STRATEGIC SPARES.

stress. 1. Force, or system of forces, which produce deformation (i.e. STRAIN in the object or system to which it is applied.) 2. Force expressed in terms of the force applied per unit area of the substance or item to which it is applied.

Formula:

$$\text{stress} = \frac{\text{force}}{\text{area over which force supplied.}}$$

Force is typically stated in Newtons, and area in mm^2.

Lifting and handling equipment is subject to stress.

'stuffing'. A colloquialism for the loading of freight containers. The term is 'non-preferred' by some authorities owing to its implication of possible overloading and bad loading of transport containers. The term LOADING is preferred.

sub-assembly. BS 5191. *See* ASSEMBLY.

sub-contracts. *See* ORDERS & CONTRACTS A–Z.

subject to being unsold. A clause frequently inserted in quotations for SPOT GOODS and in this case the would-be buyer may purchase the goods provided that they have not been sold elsewhere in the mean-time.

subjectivity. Emotional or prejudiced considerations which proceed from, or relate to, the mind of a person and not the basic facts or nature of the subject under consideration. Although inimical to value analysis or value engineering, in some areas 'subjective aspects' are important.

subsidiarity. (EU). The principle of devolving powers to the lowest appropriate level of government so as to take decisions as near as possible to the people. *Note:* similar principles can be applied in the field of administration and management.

subsidisation. The terms applied to a variety of forms of direct or indirect financial assistance which governments may give to exporters.

substance. Any kind of matter, in any form (e.g. solid, liquid or gas, etc.) which has clearly recognisable characteristic properties, and, composition independent of its origin.

substances, carcinogenic substances. (HS) Those which if inhaled, ingested or penetrate the skin may induce cancer in the individual or may increase the risk of it. *See also* PRO-ACTIVE.

substances, controlled substances. (HS) In the context of environmental control (may also have implications for health and safety), a substance which is ozone depleting (e.g. CFCs, halogens, CTC, trichlorethane, etc.) and which under the Montreal Protocol (to which the UK is a party) must be phased out by 31.12.1995.

substances hazardous to health, control of. (COSHH) (HS) Statutory regulation, enforced 1988 onwards requiring that wherever there is a potential for exposure to HAZARDOUS SUBSTANCES during work, a suitable and sufficient ASSESSMENT OF RISKS is made, and the necessary pre-

211

cautions are to be completed before the work is carried out. bibl: HSE Ref: PM(L)46, COSHH an Open Learning Course, ISBN O 11 885434 8; A step by Step Guide to COSHH Assessment ISBN 0 11 886379 7; Health Surveillance under COSHH ISBN 0 11 885447 X.

substances, package of dangerous/hazardous. (HS) Criteria for packing and packaging dangerous substances. 1. flammable solids, 2. spontaneously combustible substances, 3. substances which, on contact with water, emit flammable gas, 4. organic peroxides.

substances, explosives. Substances – solids, liquids, gases, powders or particulates, or other forms of substance – which undergo rapid chemical (or nuclear) change. The former producing gas in high volume compared with the volume of the original substance(s) when heated, struck or energised in some other way. Great pressure is generated if the explosion occurs in a confined space. [Hence, the need to avoid storage of explosives such as LPG within a closed space, or installation of dust containing silos, etc. without explosion vents.]

substances, hazardous substances. (HS) Those which have potential to cause HAZARDS and which may, in transit, storage, handling, etc. present a danger to other goods, property or persons. [In purchasing and supply due regard must be paid (particularly

under EC DIRECTIVES and corresponding enactments within the United Kingdom) to scientific MATERIALS MANAGEMENT with full documentation, labelling, safety instructions for storage, handling, packaging and transportation. *See also under* SUBSTANCES VICE, INHERENT VICE.

substance, immiscible substances. (tec). Substances (usually refers to liquids) which cannot readily be mixed eg oil and water.

substance, mutagenic substance. (hs). A substance which may result in risks of hereditable genetic defects if INHALED or INGESTED.

substance, narcotic. (HS). A substance (a drug) which tends to induce sleep if taken into the bodily system.

substance, noxious substance. (HS) One which is nauseous and may, or may not be harmful, *but* may give rise to industrial disputes working conditions.

suitability for purpose. (law). *See* QUALITY, MERCHANTABLE.

supplier. A general term used by supplies staff for all kinds of providers of goods and services purchased or procured by them.

supplier appraisal cf. **BS 4778 (11.11).** Assessment of a potential supplier's capability of controlling quality (delivery, quantity, price and all other factors to be embodied in a contract). Appraisal is carried out *before* placing orders.

supplier approved list. BS 4778 (11.12). List of approved suppliers. May also include a blacklist of non-approved suppliers with any comments kept under strict security.

supplier assessment. *See* VENDOR APPRAISAL.

supplier association. A group of suppliers to a single customer organised, with the customers assistance, to share ideas and information on working more efficiently.

supplier development. The provision of advice, finance, technology or other forms of assistance by a buyer to a supplier to enable the supplier to offer a product or service which meets the buyer's needs, or to interface with the buying organisation in a mutually appropriate way.

supplier evaluation. Assessment of a supplier's control of quality and other factors under consideration carried out prior to placing orders.

supplier rating. An index of the actual performance of a supplier.

supplier, first tier. A direct supplier.

supplier, nth tier. A supplier to a supplier in the n-1th tier.

supplier, second tier. A supplier to a first tier direct supplier.

supplies. All the materials, goods and services used in an enterprise, regardless of whether they are purchased outside, transferred from another branch of the company or manufactured IN HOUSE.

supplies, classification of supplies. Classification (classes) of supplies in most enterprises fall into three main classes. *See* ABC CLASSIFICATION. 'A' main requirements; raw materials, etc. 'B' secondary requirements; some raw materials, EMBODIMENT GOODS, plant equipment and spares. 'C' minor needs; supporting goods and consumables.

supplies, consumable supplies. BS 5191 (23010). All supplies consumed in an enterprise which are classified as INDIRECT and which do not form part of a saleable product and are not normally used in the manufacaturing process, e.g. stationery.

supplies/supply cycle. 1. Internal: that including the entire field of supplies from intake to despatch (excluding the actual production phase) and covering in particular PROVISIONING, PURCHASING, MATERIALS MANAGEMENT, RESEARCH, etc. 2. External: the supply cycle between trading enterprises. 3. Economic (national) cycle: trade in supplies from EXTRACTIVE INDUSTRIES, to DOMESTIC CONSUMER, through MARKETS, PROCESS PLANTS, MANUFACTURING and serviced by WAREHOUSES, transportation and the (national) INFRASTRUC-TURE. 4. Global: trade in supplies between independent states.

supplies, free issue supplies. Supplies provided by a purchaser to the supplier for use in the manufacture or assembly of the product he has ordered.

supplies/supply management. All aspects of administration and management of the entire SUPPLIES/ SUPPLY CYCLE, including formulation of and/or the carrying out of company policy on supplies. *See also* MATERIALS MANAGEMENT.

supplies, rate of turnover of supplies. BS 5191 (33018). The rate at which supplies are consumed per unit time, e.g. per annum, per production period, etc. *See also* SUPPLIES TURNOVER RATIO.

supplies, ratio of turnover of supplies. BS 5191 (33019). The ratio of mean stock held to the total throughput per annum or other period.

$$Srt = \frac{Ttp}{Sm}$$

Where:

Srt is turnover ratio e.g. of supplies or stock.
Ttp is total throughout (e.g. per annum).
Sm is mean stock throughout period.

e.g. given: Ttp = 5000 units
Sm = 500 units
then Srt is $\frac{5000}{500}$ = 10 stock turns.

supplies research. Research into all the supplies needed by an enterprise, particularly those used in production and processing, raw materials, parts, etc, as regards: specification, quality, quantity, transport inwards, packaging, dispensing, storage, handling, etc.

supplies, sourcing of supplies. The investigation and selection of sources of supply which meet the criteria of quality, price, delivery and other requirements of the enterprise needing them.

supplies, sourcing of supplies (multiple sources). The selection of more than one source of supply. A primary source may be given the task of a major proportion of demand, say 80%, and a secondary source the lesser quantity as back up or to maintain a competitive edge.

supplies, sourcing of supplies (single source). The restriction of intake of supplies to a single source. Usually restricted to cases where there is no alternative source, or where single source trading benefits outweigh risks of loss of supply through shortage or financial benefits outweigh those of competition in the market.

supplies throughput. The measure of total supplies obtained and/ or used in a given period expressed in money, quantity, volume or other measure for various categories of supplies or for total of all supplies. The term 'throughput' is preferred to 'turnover' in this context, but *see also* SUPPLIES, TURNOVER RATE *and* RATIO.

supply and demand, 'law of' or principle of. An empirical rule relating supply and demand whereby if price falls demand may increase, or if supply increases price may fall, with (in theory) price equilibrium at the point where supply and demand break-even. The basis of much economic theory.

supporting goods. Goods (supplies) used directly to support production or process but not directly accountable to specific end-products, etc. Usually Class *C*, and CONSUMABLE and EXPENDABLE.

supplies officer (or supply officer). An officer, usually of executive status responsible for obtaining and management of supplies.

surplus stock. *See* STOCK, SURPLUS STOCK.

supply. 1. The amount of an item of goods that will come onto the market over a given range of prices. 2. Within the context of the Chartered Institute of Purchasing and supply the following meanings apply: (v) the provisioning, administration, service, stock control, storage, handling and distribution and all associated operations connected with supplies, services and materials management. (n) all goods, materials and services which come into the possession of an enterprise as the result

of contracts for purchase, hire or procurement by other processes and for which the enterprise has responsibility.

supply chain. The chain of operations and centres through which supplies move from the source of supply to the final customer or point of use.

supply chain management. The management of materials and services whilst 'upstream' in the hands of suppliers (or their suppliers), and 'downstream' whilst in distribution or the possession of customers.

supply, essentiality. A term sometimes used in supply terminology to describe the degree to which the availability of an item of supply (such as a plant spare) is essential to the successful operation of the plant. [We suggest the use of the more usual words, e.g. 'important', 'critical', 'vital' according to the degree of urgency].

supply, inelastic supply. A situation where a large change in available supply only induces a small change in demand. *See also* DEMAND, INELASTIC DEMAND.

supply, lean. The approach to supply employed where LEAN PRODUCTION takes place. The use or consumption of materials or parts brings new materials into existence, thereby avoiding stocks or unnecessary work. Suppliers are expected to provide defect free materials at the right time to meet customer requirements, and to employ lean supply ideas themselves.

supply: planning of *see* PLANNING.

suspense. A state of insecurity and uncertainty, hence, a decision whether to cancel an order or eliminate a stock item, or in the case of an account, to make an entry in a suspense account until the proper determination of the entry can be decided.

SWOT. Acronymn for 'Strengths, Weaknesses, Opportunities and Threats' (SWOT analysis). An approach employed where a brand, product or organisation is being assessed, each of the four points being considered in turn.

synergy. A biological and medical term currently used in management and kindred subject areas. In those contexts, its meaning should be used to imply 'the working together of two or more forces (etc) to produce an effect greater than the sum of their individual efforts.' Can have serious implications in health and safety and accident research and prevention. The combined effects of two or more forces (or chemicals) may produce results far exceeding their individual capacities for action, damage, danger or hazard. *See also* FACTORIAL.

systems contracts. Sometimes known as stockless purchasing. Systems whereby users can call off materials directly from the supplier. *See* ORDERS, VARIETIES.

T

tachographs. (ts). 'Devices which record upon removeable discs – (usually card) the speeds, movements, mileage, standing times, etc. of the vehicles to which they are fitted. Obligatory on goods vehicles over 3½ tonnes under European Community Regulations.

take-over, in contracts. The stage in a contract (usually buildings, plant, etc.) at which, when final test and COMMISSIONING are completed, the subject of the contract is handed over to the purchaser. *See* TERMS AND CONDITIONS OF CONTRACT IPS.

tally. (v). To check that goods being unloaded from a ship correspond to the documentation under which they were shipped. The person who makes the check is a tally clerk.

tare. Allowance made for case, crate, or other container in which goods are packed. There are five sorts of tare. 1. Real, the actual measured weight. 2. Customary, the amount normally allowed in the CUSTON OF THE TRADE. 3. Average, the mean or average weight of containers used. 4. Estimated, where it is either not practicable to weigh the containers used. 5. Super, where packages are beyond a certain weight set as a limit by the carrier for example; the excess weight is termed super tare. Used in transportation for the unladen weight of a vehicle, or railway truck, etc. and where certified and shown on the vehicle can be used as a basis for charging in conjunction with a certified weighbridge ticket.

target price. *See* PRICE, TARGET PRICE.

tariffs. 1. Taxes imposed by a country on imports so as to restrict or otherwise control the level of importation. *See also* DUTIES. 2. Rate of charges for a supply or service, e.g. gas, electricity, etc.

tariff, block tariff. A method of charging for services, such as energy, whereby the price varies for different 'blocks' of usage e.g. a higher price up to a certain quantity and a (usually) lower price thereafter.

tariff, two part tariff. A method charging for service where (for example) a 'standing charge' may be made representing the interest on capital investment in providing the supply. The price per unit of supply may then be by a BLOCK TARIFF, single fixed rate charge per unit, or other means.

TDC (total distribution costs). (IM). Costs incurred from the end of a production line to consumers (or industrial users).

'T form' procedure. EU transit documents which indicate to cus-

217

toms officers the status of goods in the Community but also permits sealed container goods to cross the Community frontiers without inspection.

technology transfer. The practice of organisations passing technical knowledge to those with whom they deal. For example to facilitate more efficient supply.

Technical Help to Exporters. A service by engineers and information specialists of the British Standards Institution who provide advice on European Community requirements. These include State laws, particularly in relation to: 'safety', 'environmental protection', 'technical standards'. Contact: **BSI (0908) 226888.**

tender bonds. *See* BONDS, TENDER.

tender negotiated procedures. (EU). National procedures whereby contracting Authorities consult suppliers of their choice and negotiate the terms of the contract with one or several of them.

tender negotiation, pre-tender negotiations. Discussions with, and questions to, proposed contractors clarifying what is expected of their best offer in their final sealed tender.

tender, open tender. One where the original enquiry has been open and free for all to enter and make offers, as distinct from a closed or restricted list of those invited to tender.

tender negotiations, post tender negotiations. A tender procedure whereby tenderers are met individually or together to discuss details of offers which may affect the purchaser's final selection of the best bid. *See below*, TENDERS, NEGOTIATED PROCEDURES.

tender, restricted procedures. (EU). All who apply to tender must be given an equal opportunity to qualify. The contracting entity must generally complete qualification within six months but may then invite selected tenderers.

tender, single offer tender. One for a single project. The unqualified acceptance of such an offer constitutes a contract.

tender, standing order tender. One for the supply of goods and services 'as required'. The tenderer is obliged to supply as orders (i.e. demands) are received but he cannot insist that orders shall be given to him. *See also* ORDERS AND CONTRACTS *section*.

tenderer. A party who submits a tender to another party at the invitation of the latter to carry out work, supply goods or service, etc.

tendering, compulsory competitive. An approach to purchasing whereby organisations [usually public sector] are compelled to seek TENDERS from more than one SUPPLIER.

tenders and tendering. Offers from tenderers without collusion, usually in sealed envelopes, delivered by a time and date specified in the invitation to tender, for the supply of goods or services. Such tenders are opened only at the time and date specified by a tender panel of qualified persons who record the necessary details. Late tenders are not considered.

tenders, invitation to tender. An invitation to prospective suppliers (may be on an 'approved list') to submit tenders for, the supply of goods or services. The procedures are intended to safeguard the expenditure (particularly) of public moneys and on large projects and items. Community Regulations and Directives apply over this field.

tenders: open tenders. (EU). The use of OPEN TENDERS called for by the Commission. Generally a notice inviting tenderers should be advertised in the Official Journal of the Communities, where the likely value of the contract is over a certain amount. Technical specifications must not mention 'goods of a specific make or source, or of a particular process which may have the effect of favouring or eliminating certain undertakings'.

tenders, post tender negotiations. Negotiations after receipt and opening of tenders and before the letting of contract(s) with the supplier(s) who submit the lowest acceptable tenders. The purpose is to obtain an improvement of price, delivery or other factor. It is a rule that this shall not put other tenderers at a disadvantage or adversely affect their confidence or trust in the competitive tendering system.

terms, conditions, warranties. Terms in the context of purchasing and supply management comprise the substantive components of a contract which create contractual obligations the breach of which may lead to action. Terms are, broadly speaking, of two kinds: 1. 'conditions'. These are essential terms which go to the heart of a contract. The breach of a 'condition' entitles the injured party to treat the contract as at an end. e.g. failure to meet a delivery date if this was stated as a 'condition of the contract'. 2. 'warranty', a subordinate term in a contract. *See* WARRANTY.

terminal market (mkt). *See* MARKET, FUTURES MARKET. A synonym for futures market. Called a terminal market because dealings are specified in terms of periods of time in the future.

terms, express terms. (law). Express terms are clear statements communicated by the parties and by which they intend to be bound.

terms, implied terms. (law). Implied terms are those which have been implied by 1. statutory provisions or 2. the manifest INTENTIONS of the parties.

terms of shipment. *See* INCOTERMS.

terms of trade. A term used to indicate the current situation of a

219

country in respect of its international trade. For a good situation input prices should be low in relation to exports so that imports can be financed.

terotechnology. BS 3811 (1101). A combination of management, financial, engineering, building and other practices applied to physical assets in pursuit of economic LIFE CYCLE COSTS. Its practice is concerned with the specification and design for RELIABILITY and MAINTAINABILITY of machinery, equipment, buildings and structures, with their installation, COMMISSIONING, operation, MAINTENANCE, modification, and replacement, and with FEEDBACK of information on design, performance and costs.

test. *See* QUALITY CONTROL, TESTS.

testing, 'witness testing'. Certain pre-agreed tests to be witnessed by the representative of the purchaser. Such tests usually include performance tests to simulate or exceed normal working conditions.

third country. A country other than a member state of the European Union. *See also* INTER-STATE *and* INTRA-STATE.

third party. A party other than the principals involved in any proceedings. For example, a 'third party' inspector may be appointed by an importer to check goods prior to shipment.

three-bin system of stock control *See* STOCK-CONTROL, THREE BIN.

throughput. 1. The amount of goods and/or materials which pass through a plant and usually expressed in physical units. May be used as a measure of productive efficiency. 2. Applies also to materials and supplies passing through stores, etc. The term preferred to TURNOVER which has important accountancy implications.

through transit concept. The system whereby goods are packed in unit loads, e.g. palletised or containerised in such a manner that they can travel from supplier to user point with minimum (or nil) disturbance en route.

through-transport. (IM). Concept of moving cargo on a door-to-door basis in trucks, containers or other units, without unloading (or transfer of load) en route.

tie-in sales. A practice of some suppliers to tie the sale of one product to the sale of another. *See also* FULL-LINE FORCING. *and* NEGOTIATION.

tied sales conditions. Conditions by which a seller seeks to enforce the commitment of his customer only to use his materials, services, etc, by introducing CONDITIONS into the contract which have this effect. [e.g. A typical example is to introduce a clause which revokes a guarantee if materials or services are employed by the purchaser other than from that supplier]. *See also* NEGOTIATION

tilt. (ts). A cover of fabric or similar material over a frame which is secured to the bed of a vehicle. For TIR compliance it must be capable of being sealed and be free from tears or repairs except those which comply with TIR regulations.

time, periods of time. The time intervals in industry and commerce may be expressed in: 1. chronological time; hours and minutes or days, weeks, months, years, 2. accountancy/ budgetary periods, 3. production periods. [Important measurements for PROGRESS CHASING, PLANNING PRODUCTION CONTROL, etc.] For numbering of weeks see **BS 4760/ISO/R2015.**

time charter. The hire of a vessel for a contracted period of time, with or without specified routes and destinations which may also be specified in the CHARTER PARTY.

time cycle. The period of time occupied by a series of events, e.g. production periods, seasonal demands, etc. which will continue to recur in similar overall periods. e.g. 'long horizon' (say) 5 years, 'medium horizon' (say) 1 year, and 'short horizon' (say) 3 months. *See* also PLANNING AND PROGRESSING.

time, 'the essence of contract'. A clause which may be inserted into a contract where delay could result in significant consequential loss to the buyer. *See* SUITABLE CLAUSE, 'TIME OF PERFORMANCE SHALL BE OF THE ESSENCE OF THIS CONTRACT'.

time study. (BS 3138). (adm). A work measurement technique for recording the times and rates of working for the elements of a specified job carried out under specified conditions, and for analysing the data so as to determine the time necessary for carrying out the job at a defined level of performance. The 'element' is a distinct part of a specified job selected for convenience of observation, measurement and analysis. Manual element = one performed by a worker. Machine element = one automatically performed by a power-driven machine (or process).

time to market. The time taken to convert an idea into a product or service available for sale to customers.

time utility. (econ). The value associated with having a product at the time needed, rather than later.

time window. The difference in lead times between the shortest lead time a supplier can offer and the longest lead time he can guarantee for delivery.

TIR (1), Transport Internationaux per Route. The international road ·carnet system which enables goods in sealed, approved vehicles or containers to cross frontiers without inspection by Customs, so long as the seals are unbroken and the tilts, if employed, are undamaged.

TIR (2). Acronym commonly used for the vehicles approved for TIR operation and suitably plated.

title, (ownership of goods). The legal entitlement to goods or property of any kind by their possessor. Also, documentary evidence of the right of ownership, e.g. a receipt for payment for the goods. UK law tends to support the owner of goods against all comers including buyers, hence *caveat emptor*.

title deed. A document establishing the right of ownership.

title, retention of title. The establishment of legitimate rights under which a supplier may exercise rights over goods he has sold by clauses in the contract of sale. May be in 'small print' on his acknowledgement. Such as: 1. property in the goods shall not pass until payment in full has been made. 2. the seller reserves interest in the goods or the proceeds of any sale if the buyer sells them on before payment has been made in full. Leading case, Romalpa Case 1976.

tolerance, specification tolerance. BS 47780–2 (7.1.18). The permitted variation in a process or a characteristic of an item. *Note:* the relationship between the process variability and specification tolerance is termed 'relative precision'. *See* **BS 2564.**

tonnage. The freight-carrying capacity of a vessel expressed in 'ocean tons'. *See* TONNAGE, DEADWEIGHT TONNAGE.

tonnage, dead weight tonnage. The total load-carrying capacity of a vessel expressed in tons weight calculated at 100 cubic feet per ton. ['Registered tonnage' is usually much less than 'dead weight' tonnage because few cargoes stow at less than 100 cubic feet to the ton, e.g. iron ore about 20 ft^3 per ton].

tonnage, deadweight tonnage (registered). The weight of cargo a vessel can (is registered to) carry and which will take its level in the water to the maximum LOAD LINE.

tonnage, gross registered tonnage. ('GRT'). The cubic capacity of a vessel taking one ton as being equal to 100 cubic feet. *See* DEADWEIGHT TONNAGE.

tonnage, net registered tonnage. The measure used for port/ canal dues, etc. It is calculated as GROSS REGISTERED TONNAGE less the non-earning portions of the vessel (engine room, crew space, etc). Usually about 55–65% of GRT.

tort. A civil wrong (not being a breach of contract or trust) in respect of which there lies an action for damages.

tote. A box-type container designed for the storage and movement of (usually) small parts. Often used for work in progress.

tote pan. *See* CONTAINERS.

totology. The technology of optimizing the overall performance of a manufacturing company or sector by minimizing the number of products, component parts, manufacturing processes and materials consistent with satisfying reasonable present and foreseeable requirements. BS PD6470. *See also* VARIETY REDUCTION.

traceability. Systems designed to ensure that the origin and manufacturing history of parts or materials can be discovered.

tractive force, effort. The force/effort which a locomotive or tractor unit can exert at its drawbar for pulling (or pushing) vehicles to which it is coupled. The limiting value is given by the weight on the wheels of the tractor unit and the coefficient of friction between the wheels and the rails, or the roadway.

tractive resistance ('coefficient of traction'). The frictional resistance per unit of weight being moved, e.g. the resistance encountered when moving cases, or plant by sliding along a surface in the absence of mechanical aids such as a roller, trolley, conveyor or other means.

trade association. An association of traders or producers to co-operate on questions affecting their interests.

trade, balance of trade. (econ) The difference, usually expressed in financial terms, between exports and imports of a country.

trading down (to trade down). Trading down, or 'down market', by selling low priced goods and relying on high turnover to secure profit, or in order to penetrate an existing market.

trading up. The converse of TRADING DOWN. The object may be to gain entry into an area of the market where higher quality prevails.

trade discount. *See* DISCOUNT, TRADE.

trade gap. The amount by which the value of visible imports exceeds the value of visible exports. (In this context, 'visibles' = goods and 'invisibles' = services, financial, technical and others).

trade, intra-Community trade. Trade conducted between members of the Community.

trade restraint of trade. *See* RESTRAINT OF TRADE.

trade mark. *See* BRAND NAME.

trade pack. The packaging normally provided by a supplier for the shipping of his goods. The purchaser must be aware of this if exportation is required. *See* TRADE, PACK EXPORT.

trade pack (export trade pack). The packaging normally provided by a supplier for shipment overseas. May need careful checking dependent upon the destination and storage at the final location.

223

training, 'distance learning',- ('open learning'). Terms coined to embrace other than 'face to face' training at an educational establishment or 'in house'. Suitable courses in purchasing and supply available from the Chartered Institute of Purchasing and Supply.

training, purchasing and supply, training in. Increasing complexities in the operations of purchasing and supply call for increased levels of training for all staff in this area. The Chartered Institute of Purchasing and Supply provide opportunities for, and advice on, training leading to qualifications based on the syllabuses of the Institute.

tramp vessel. (mar). One which carries cargo between any destinations, to no fixed schedule.

transactional relationship. A relationship between buyer and seller whereby the two parties do not get closely involved with each other, but simply exchange goods or services for payment.

transfer costs. *See* COSTS, TRANSFER COSTS.

transfer note. *See* MATERIALS TRANSFER NOTE.

Transfer of Undertakings (Protection of Employees) Regulations (TUPE). These public authority Regulations came into existence when the United Kingdom implemented the associated Community Directive. It applies in the event of a transfer of an undertaking, business or part of a business. TUPE has the effect of preserving the employment rights of individual employees and of transferring to the new employer the resonsibility and obligation to maintain these rights.

transferable credit. *See* CREDIT, DOCUMENTARY.

transit time. Time taken, actual or estimated for transit of goods from the time actually loaded on board to the time of arrival at destination. Purchaser must ascertain if time includes loading and unloading time.

transire. (ts). A permit granted by Customs for the removal of goods.

transit documentation (simplified). (EU). A system of transit documentation for intra-Community use. Procedures are: 1. movement certificates and 2. full 'T' FORM procedures.

transit shed. (ts). A place approved by the Commissioners at a seaport or airport for the deposit of imported goods which have not yet been reported to Customs, entered, or cleared from Customs charge.

transnational corporations (TNCs). (UN). Term for multinational corporations, usually understood to mean those private corporations with direct investments and production facilities abroad. It does not formally mean those companies whose overseas operations are confined exclusively to sales.

transparency. (EU). A fundamental principle of Community policy. It implies 'accessibility of information, responsiveness, realistic time scale for consultation and freedom from built-in bias'.

transportation. General term for carriage and distribution of supplies. It is a significant factor in the COSTS OF ACQUISITION and distribution.

transport bi-modal transport. The utilisation of more than one means of transport for shipments, e.g. use of ISO CONTAINERS on swap-bodies from road and rail for a transit.

transport capacity per ton-mile (or metric units per kilometre). The unit of costing transportation, viz. cost of operating the means of transport number of freight ton-miles transported.

Transport International per Chemin de Fer. (TIF). The international railways customs procedures similar to TIR for road haulage.

transport log book. A book in which are recorded the arrivals and departures of vehicles at an undertaking, giving date and time of arrival and departure, vehicle registration number, name of haulier and other details as required by the undertaking.

transport 'T form' procedure. (EU). Simplified Community procedure by a document which indicates to CUSTOMS Officers the status in the Community of the goods being transported. Provided the seals are unbroken the consignment can then proceed across frontiers without inspection.

transport, operating ratio. A ratio used in the transportation industry to assess the operating costs of the service. Operating costs are expressed as a percentage of receipts. The higher the percentage the lower the PROFITABILITY; over 100 percent indicates a loss.

transport payload. That position of a load which contributes to revenue for the enterprise.

travelling requisition. *See* REQUISITION, TRAVELLING.

treat, invitation to treat. A preliminary stage in any transactaion which may lead to a firm contract, e.g. a seller who sends a mail-shot, catalogue or price list, a quotation or estimate, or who places a price tag on goods is merely inviting the prospective purchaser to place an order, negotiate, or make an offer.

trend. The general tendency of data to move in a particular direction revealed by statistical analysis, e.g. a rising or a falling trend.

trend, forecasting of trend. If growth (or decay) is at a steady rate or constant then a forecast of

225

the trend may be calculated by EXPONENTIAL SMOOTH-ING.

trespass of goods. The unlawful interference with goods in the possession of another person, either by damaging them or by the mere moving of them.

tret. An allowance made for waste and evaporation on certain goods.

tribology. The science of interaction between moving surfaces which are in relative motion to one another, and the results of friction, lubrication and wear. An area for consideration when carrying out VALUE ENGINEERING.

trucks, straddle trucks. Lift trucks, (manual or powered) which handle loads between the points of support, i.e. between the wheels or rollers upon which the truck travels.

truss (a truss). Material formed into a loose unit for handling or transport, etc. without pressure, banding or other restraint. *See* BALE.

turning radius. (ts) (sh). The distance between the centre of turn of a vehicle such as a fork lift truck and the furthest point of the truck or other vehicle and its load. Similar calculations apply to all transport vehicles and also to their clearance above ground on slopes and curves.

turnover. CIMA. 'Amounts derived from the provision of goods and services falling within an enterprise's ordinary activities after deduction of trade discounts, value added tax and any other taxes based on the amounts so derived'. (Companies Act). This would normally be invoiced sales less returns and allowances.

turnover, stock turnover. *See* STOCK THROUGHPUT *and* STOCK TURNOVER.

two bin. *See* STOCK CONTROL, TWO BIN SYSTEM.

type approval. *See* QUALITY CONTROL, TYPE APPROVAL.

type tests. *See* QUALITY CONTROL, TYPE TESTS.

U

ullage. Customs term, 'what a vessel wants of being full', i.e. gap above the top level of the liquid or other contents.

ultra vires. Action, etc. which is beyond the legal power or authority of a body such as a corporation, etc. or a person such as a purchasing officer, or for example a sales agent.

unascertained goods. *See* GOODS, UNASCERTAINED GOODS.

uncoupling effect of stock. *See* STOCK, UNCOUPLING EFFECT OF STOCK.

undertaking. Any industrial or commerical ENTERPRISE. The latter is the preferred term.

undue influence. An improper exercise of 'power' possessed by one party to a contract over the mind of the other party. *See* NEGOTIATION.

unenforceable contracts. *See* CONTRACT, UNENFORCEABLE CONTRACT.

Unfair Contract Terms Act 1977. This Act restricts the ability of a party to contract in such a manner as to escape normal liability in a contract, for personal injury or damage to property. Under Section 5, the manufacturer cannot escape liability for negligence by the application of his own (so called) manufacturer's guarantees. Section 3 applies between a business and consumers, it also applies in a business situation if the contract contains standard terms and conditions by one party which are accepted by the other, regardless whether or not the second party is a consumer or in business.

Uniform Customs Practices. Standard rules for DOCUMENTARY LETTERS OF CREDIT developed by the INTERNATIONAL CHAMBER OF COMMERCE and adopted worldwide.

unit load. IM Checklist 35. A quantity of goods grouped together to form a single unit of dimensions and physical characteristics that optimise the costs of handling and transport throughout the distribution cycle applies particularly to the THROUGH TRANSIT CONCEPT. The Carriage of Goods by Sea Act 1971 which further defines packages or units recorded on bills of lading. Some relevant standards are: BS 5667 Unit loads, continuous handling equipment, safety requirements. BS 6884 Unit loads, plan dimensions. *See also* UNITISATION.

unit load device (ULD). Container or pallet designed to fit into the structure of an aircraft.

units of account. *See* ACCOUNT, UNITS OF.

unit of issue. BS 5191 (33029). The smallest measure of an item of stock that may be issued from a store. Normally it is the same as the stock-keeping unit.

United Nations Numbers. *See* COMMODITY NUMBERS.

units of measurement. *See* MEASUREMENT.

unitisation. The planning of suitable quantities of goods to form unit loads for transport and/or handling, and/or storage, and/ or use in process or at WORKCENTRES.

unliquidated damages. *See* DAMAGES, UNLIQUIDATED DAMAGES.

update. BS 4335. To modify an existing file or record so as to bring its contents up to date.

'upstream' management. Management of suppliers and supplies of materials and services, including, where appropriate, supplier's suppliers and so on.

usage (also off-take and sales). BS 5729. In the case of supplies the quantities actually used. May not be the same as DEMAND owing to rejects and other causes such as damage or loss. *See also* SERVICE RATIO.

usage rate, 'UR'. The *rate* of consumption of supplies e.g. stock, i.e. the quantity, or other measure, consumed (used) per unit time.

$$Ur = \frac{Qt}{T}$$

Where Ur is usage rate.
Qt is quantity in total time.
T is total time.

usaance (time or term) draft. SITPRO. A draft (BILL OF EXCHANGE) which is payable at a fixed or determinable future date.

utilisation factor, 'UF'. cf. **BS 3138.** Gives 'machine utilisation factor.' Ratio of: machine (or other plant and equipment running time) to: total machine or other plant and equipment available time.

$$Uf = \frac{Mrt}{Mat}$$

Where Uf is utilisation factor.
Mrt is machine running/operating time.
Mat is machine available time. Applies equally to fixed and mobile plant by suitable substitution.

utility, marginal utility. The amount of additional utility that can be gained by the addition of one unit of product. (CIMA).

V

valuable goods. *See* GOODS, VALU-ABLE GOODS.

valuation of stock. *See* STOCK, VALUATION OF.

value, Brussels definition of value. This specifies that Customs duty be taken on the value of the goods which corresponds to the value in open market in the country of destination. This may be defined as 'FOB Port of Shipment' or 'CIF landed' at port of arrival.

value. (Commercial definition). Intrinsic worth. It is determined by the lowest overall cost at which a satisfactory supply of goods or services can be reliably provided. *See also* ACCRETION.

value added. CIMA. The increase in realisable value resulting from an alteration in form, location or availability of a product or service, excluding the cost of purchased materials and services. *Note:* unlike conversion cost, 'value added' includes profit. In the context of purchasing and supply, value added (VA) is the increment in value which is added to an item by each process of manufacture (or handling).

$$VA = Ou - Iu$$

Where VA is value added.
Ou is price at output, sale or transfer.
Iu is input, materials and services used.

e.g. where Ou is £30 per unit and Iu is £15 per unit, then Va = £15 added value for that operation.
[Services used may include: advertising, fuel, power, communications, professional fees, etc.]

value added tax (VAT). IM. A multi-stage tax paid by each trader on the value which is added (*See* VALUE ADDED) to any goods or services. Thus tax liability is spread over every stage through which a product or service passes before it reaches the consumer. The tax at the final sale to the consumer represents the total collected.

value analysis. BS 3138 (21090). A systematic inter-disciplinary examination of design and other factors affecting the cost of a product or service in order to devise a means of achieving the specified purpose most economically at the required standard of quality and reliability. (In the case of plant an assessment is required of the LIFE-CYCLE and COSTS IN USE in relation to the purchase PRICE.) [der. 'The term 'value analysis' is used where an existing product is picked apart and examined.

value chain. The sequence of events through which a raw material is converted into a product for ultimate use or consumption. Value is added at various points in the sequence. *See* SUPPLY CHAIN.

229

value cost value. The cost of producing item.

value engineering. PD.6470 (6.2). A design activity involving the design of value into a product at the design stage. Supplies staff should be involved beause there are many points to which supplies and materials management may contribute. *See also* VALUE ANALYSIS.

value, esteem value. The subjective value given to an item by reason of its own prestige or other characteristic which makes it more desirable than others when compared with them.

value-in-use. The worth of an asset in terms of objectives which can be expressed in cash terms. In addition, where practicable, value should take account of subjective attributes such as social or environmental aspects which may only be evaluated by COST BENEFIT ANALYSIS, estimates or WEIGHTINGS.

value, face value. The value (price) stated or given in documents, price tags, etc. as distinct from other value measurements such as INTRINSIC VALUE, VALUE IN USE, etc. Where the face value is said to be a 'price reduction' the previous price from which the reduction was made should be shown. *See also* VALUE, MARKET VALUE, *etc.*

value for money. An attempt to maximise benefits from a purchase while minimising amount expended. *See also* COST BENEFIT.

value, gross present value. The present 'value' of the sum of the initial cost of a project or plant plus the interest foregone on the capital spent, during its expected LIFE-CYCLE. Estimates of maintenance and repair costs, etc. may also be estimated. *See also* VIABILITY.

value, intrinsic. The value contained in the substance from which an article is produced as distinct from its stated value or price tag. *See* VALUE, FACE VALUE.

value, market value. The sum that an asset would be sold for in a free, OPEN MARKET.

value, net present value. (NPV). A very important concept in purchasing and supply when giving consideration to a major purchase or project. The NPV of a purchase or project is the difference between the net present cost of the purchase or project and all the future revenues from the purchase or project discounted back to the present time. Various allowances may be needed, such as the value of the purchase or project at the end of its useful life, or in the case of nuclear equipment the possible costs of decommissioning.

value, residual value. Value of plant at the end of its useful life, and the value of an item which has served its purpose (e.g. recovered solvent) but retains some value.

value, use value. The value of the function performed or primary function.

value/volume ratio. The ratio of value of an item of supply in relation to its volume. Can be a useful measure and check on storage costs, and purchase price.

variable (a variable). BS 4778 (21.24). Term used in quality control to indicate a characteristic which needs to be measured, e.g. dimension, volume, etc. BS 4778 'A characteristic that is appraised in terms of values on a continuous scale'.

variable cost. *See* COST, VARIABLE.

variance. An expression of how ITEMS of a POPULATION vary from the MEAN of all the ITEMS in the POPULATION.

variance accounting. CIMA. (abb). A technique whereby planned activities of an enterprise are qualified in budgets, STANDARD COSTS, standard selling prices, and standard profit margins and the difference between these and the actual results are accounted for.

variance analysis. CIMA. An analysis of variances arising in a cost system and analysed into their constituent parts.

variation order. *See* ORDERS & CONTRACTS, VARIATION ORDER.

variety reduction. The process of reducing the number of types, sizes, grades, etc. of a product manufactured, purchased, or stocked. *See also* STANDARDIZATION.

vehicle scheduling. BIM Checklist 48. A plan whereby vehicles are allocated to specific tasks, generally on a timed basis and indicating the task on which each vehicle is deployed at a given time.

vendor. Strictly: a person who sells, particularly one who hawks his goods in public, but, term sometimes adopted in purchasing and supply for all who sell whether manufacturer or commercial undertakings, etc.

vendor appraisal. cf. **BS 4778 (11.11).** Assessment of a potential supplier's capability of controlling quality (delivery, quantity, price and all other factors to be embodied in a contract). Appraisal is carried out *before* placing orders.

vendor approved list. BS 4778 (11.12). List of approved suppliers. May also include a blacklist of non-approved suppliers with any comments kept under strict security.

vendor evaluation. ('Supplier evaluation'.) Assessment of a supplier's control of quality and other factors under consideration carried out prior to placing orders.

vendor rating. *See* SUPPLIER RATING.

very narrow aisle. A storehouse arrangement whereby specialised equipment operates in narrow gangways to maximise storage space.

viability. A viable idea, proposal, scheme, plan, etc. which is sound, workable and would be economic if translated into actuality. For a project, purchase or scheme to be viable the total of all outgoings through the life-cycle must not exceed present values at the time of purchase, etc. *See* NET PRESENT VALUE and CASH FLOW, DISCOUNTED CASH FLOW.

vice, inherent vice. Goods which by their nature are liable to deteriorate and/or cause damage to other goods with which they may come into contact are said to have 'inherent vice.' A carrier may not be liable for them if their nature makes them an exceptional risk unless this fact has been made known to him in advance.

Vienna Convention (1964). In 1964 two conventions were adopted on the international sale of goods and the formation of international sale contracts. Both Conventions were adopted by HMG/UK wef August 1972.

vocabulary, stores vocabulary. A list compiled of all the supplies contained under stock control in a storehouse and stockyard. The stores (or commodity) vocabulary should contain the unique name for each commodity with cross references from other names or nomenclatures, etc. *See* COMMODITY CATALOGUE and STORES CATALOGUE *and* CODING. *See* **BS 5729 Pt. 5 (0.4(b)).**

void. This term as applied to a contract refers to one that is 'destitute of all legal effect', and neither party can then enforce it.

voidable. When applied to a contract, it implies that although the contract is capable of being carried out it has some defect which would enable either party to stop its execution. *See also* ENFORCEABLE CONTRACTS.

volume cargo. Cargo which has low weight per unit volume and therefore occupies more cargo space than heavier goods.

von Thunen's belts. A series of concentric rings around a city determining the appropriate location for various kinds of agricultural activity, taking transportation costs into account. Can also apply to location of stores and storage distribution points.

vote head. An identification of finance allocated within a budget for specific tasks and against which all financial transactions are recorded for control purposes. *See also* SUB HEAD.

voucher. CIMA. A document serving as evidence for a claimed transaction which records for example a stores or financial transaction, and supports an accounting entry.

voyage charter. Under a voyage charter the charterer usually pays for an agreed rate per ton for a full and complete cargo. If the ship is not filled he pays for DEAD FREIGHT.

W

W.I.P. *See* WORK IN PROGRESS.

waiting time. BS 5191 (26010). The period of time for which an operator is available for production but is prevented from working by a shortage of material, or tooling, machine breakdown, etc. *See also* IDLE TIME and DOWN TIME.

warehouse. A place where goods (wares) are stored and on which storage charges will be imposed.

warehouse, automated warehouse. One in which the stacking, stowage and retrieval of supplies are effected by handling equipment programmed to transport, place and withdraw supplies automatically.

warehouse (or store) bonded warehouse. One in which dutiable goods are stored and upon which the warehouse (or stores) owner has entered into a bond with HM Customs. Goods are stored subject to the inspection and control of the Excise Officer until duties have been paid and the goods released.

warehouse stock. *See* STOCK, WAREHOUSE STOCK.

warranty, implied warranty. (law). A warranty which the purchaser may assume to apply to a contract without necessity for it to be written into the agreement. e.g. 'that the goods shall be suitable for use'.

warranty in contract. An agreement with reference to goods which are the subject of a contract of sale, but collateral to the main purpose of the contract, the breach of which gives rise to a claim for damages but not the repudiation of the contract. Sale of Goods Act 1979. *See also* CONTRACT, CONDITIONS OF CONTRACT.

warranty period. The period (usually 12 months) following completion of work (e.g. construction) or COMMISSIONING (e.g. of plant) in a contract. During this time the contractor is responsible for the repair and rectification of any defects in the work. Also referred to as the 'guarantee period'. *See also* RETENTION MONEY and MAINTENANCE PERIOD and TERMS AND CONDITIONS OF CONTRACT IPS.

Warsaw Convention (1929). The original convention, which still applies in modified form, controlling the carriage of goods by air.

wastage, damage and loss. Contingencies which must be allowed for in provisioning and which may occur at various stages of the SUPPLIES CYCLE, viz. in transit, loading and unloading, in stores and at issue from stores, etc. Avoidance of wastage, damage and loss is a matter for MATERIALS MANAGEMENT but allowances may be needed in purchasing and stock levels to allow for these.

waste. CIMA. 1. Discarded substances having no value, unreclaimable for SALVAGE or RECYCLING. 2. Rag, old clothing and similar materials provided for cleaning hands and machinery, etc. *See also* SCRAP and ARISINGS. BS 5832: Specification for compacated waste containers for lift-off vehicles. BS 5906: Code of practice for storage and on-site treatment of solid waste from buildings.

waste, controlled. *See* SUBSTANCES CONTROLLED.

waste, disposal of waste. Disposal of waste of CONTROLLED SUBSTANCES is covered by Section 33 of the Environmental Protection Act, 1990.

waste management. The control of the generation and disposal of waste to meet economic and environmental constraints.

wasting assets. *See* ASSETS, WASTING ASSETS.

waybill. A document by railways, airlines and other hauliers on which is recorded the list of goods and articles which are being carried on that particular journey from point to point.

waybill, air waybill. SITPRO. A form of waybill introduced by Warsaw Convention. It is used for air shipments instead of the normal BILL OF LADING used for sea transits. This is because the speed of transit shipment may have been completed before a normal bill of lading could be prepared. It is evidence of the contract between the shipper and the carrier. It serves as: 1. receipt of goods for shipment, 2. despath note listing any special instructions by the shipper, 3. invoice evidencing freight charges, 4. insurance – if insurance certificate – if insured through the airline, 5. document for import, export, and transit requirements by Customs, 6. delivery receipt.

waybill, sea waybill. SITPRO. A non-negotiable alternative to the bill of lading. It provides for delivery to a named consignee without presentation of the documents at destination. It thus helps to solve the problem caused by arrival of documents at the destination after the arrival of the goods. It is particularly useful when trading on open account or between multinational and associated companies or between long established trading partners. It can be used with documentary credits if the letter of credit specifically authorises its acceptance.

weight, dead weight. Heavy goods paying freight by weight.

weighting (W). A mathematical and statistical method for ascribing value to an item of data in proportion to its importance or 'weight' by the use of a WEIGHTING FACTOR. *See also* WEIGHTING, STATISTICAL WEIGHTING.

weighting factor (WF). BS 5191. A factor by which the results of statistical calculations can take account of the relative importance, frequency etc. of events and data in the range of data being analysed, etc.

weighting, statistical weighting. The technique of applying WEIGHTING FACTORS for presentation of statistical information. This weighting emphasises and reflects the importance of the various ITEMS in the data being studied, analysed or reported.

wharf. A bank or quay where vessels may tie up to be loaded or unloaded.

wharfage. The change made to a vessel for using a wharf.

wharfinger. The person in charge of a wharf. He acts as bailee for the goods and is under the same discipline as a warehouseman for this purpose.

'where-used-list' (prod). A list of all assemblies that use a particular part or assembly.

wholesaler. An enterprise which makes its profits through buying supplies in bulk at TRADE PRICES and sells and distributes them to retail, business and industrial enterprises on trade terms. Originally a wholesaler was so designed as a middleman who sold 'whole pieces' of materials and goods to retail customers via shop-keepers.

winding up, a business. The termination of trading by a business by its LIQUIDATION. 1. Compulsory liquidation as the result of a Court Order. 2. Voluntary liquidation by: (i) an ordinary resolution because it has achieved its objectives (ii) a special resolution for other reasons (iii) an extraordinary resolution if it cannot continue trading by reason of its liabilities.

WIP. *See* WORK IN PROGRESS.

without engagement. A phrase intended by a supplier as an EXCLUSION CLAUSE by which he may escape commitments implied in his offer or other document. [Should be resisted when negotiating any contract].

without prejudice. (law). A term used in correspondence or in making offers which renders such correspondence (or offers) incapable of being used as evidence and thus devoid of all legal force.

without recourse. A term used on bills of exchange, coupons, warrants etc when they are sold to a third party. The buyers have no recourse whatever upon the seller should the documents not be honoured when they are due.

works, clerk of. *See* CLERK OF WORKS.

work in progress (work in process). abb. **WIP. BS 5191 (23004).** Stock (or other supplies) upon which work has been performed or which has been made ready for work to be started, but which is not available to differentiate between 'shop' WIP and sub-contract WIP, etc. *See* CURRENT ASSETS.

work cycle. *See* PRODUCTION: WORK CYCLE.

work equipment. (HS). 'Any machine, apparatus, tool or installation used at work'.

work equipment directive (89/655EEC). This Directive implemented by the UK applies as does the FRAMEWORK DIRECTIVE and to all WORK EQUIPMENT (WE). The employer must ensure that all WE is suitable, properly adapted, can be used without risk to health and safety and is adequately maintained. Where likely hazards exist, access restricted to designated operatives. Where WE cannot be made totally safe risks must be minimised.

work measurement. BS 3138(10003). The application of techniques designed to establish the time for a qualified worker to carry out a specified task/job at a defined level of performance. *See also* BS 3375 Part 3 – GUIDE TO WORK MEASUREMENT and Part 4 GUIDE TO WORK PERFORMANCE CONTROL.

work measurement. BS 3375: Part 3. Guide to work measurement. Defines the objectives and establishes procedures for work measurement. Outlines the benefits to be gained by the use of work measurement in the field of operations management. It is aimed at senior managements, management services and practitioners and specialists in other disciplines. AMD 5478, March 1987.

BS 3375: Part 4. work performance. Guide to work performance control. Puts the terminology of **BS 3138** in the context of tasks being carried out by individuals or groups, either manually or in association with machines or plant. Deals with the means of control by indices based on achieved performance against standard performance, and with the remuneration of the individual according to the nature of the work and his performance in carrying it out.

workplace directive. (89/654EEC) to be implemented by a Regulation to require employers and others in control of workplaces to comply with health and safety requirements including welfare. These include: maintenance of equipment and devices, ventilation, temperature, lighting, cleanliness, space, workstations, falling objects, glazing, windows, seating, traffic routes, doors and gates, sanitary conveniences, drinking water, accommodation for clothing, washing facilities, eating and rest arrangements in facilities for non-smokers.

work requisition. BS 3811 (4129). A document requesting work to be carried out.

work specification. BS 3811 (4130). A document describing the way in which work is to be carried out. It may define the materials, tools, time, standards.

work station. BS 5191 (13005). the smallest set of resources or the purpose of planning and control that form a productive unit at a particular location.

work study. BS 3138 (11002). A management service based on those techniques (particularly METHOD STUDY and WORK MEASUREMENT) which are used in the examination of human work in all its contexts, and which lead to the systematic investigation of all the resources and factors which affect the efficiency and economy of the situation being reviewed, in order to affect improvement. See **BS 3138** for GLOSSARY OF TERMS USED IN WORK STUDY AND ORGANISATION AND METHOD. See also **BS 3375. BS 3138:** 1979 Glossary of terms used in work study and organization and methods (O & M), defining terms and symbols, with sections on organization study, method study, work measurement and work performance control. Diagram to illustrate the problem solving techniques used in work study. Examples of the construction of standard time for operator and machine controlled work. *See also* **BS 3375.**

works order. BS 3811 (4128). A written instruction detailing work to be carried out. (Note: BS 3811 depreciates the use of the word 'job card' for this).

works order. (prod). *See* ORDER, PRODUCTION.

writ. (law). A legal document by which the person named is summoned to attend a certain place at a time stated at a written instruction from a law court or other legal authority, or alternatively to perform some act (or to abstain from doing something) in accordance with the terms contained in the writ.

write down. Authorised financial adjustment to reduce the value of stock or plant as a result of obsolescence or/partial deterioration.

write off. (fin). Authorised financial adjustment to support the removal of an item of stock or plant from the financial accounts as a result of loss, damage or deterioration.

written communications. *See* COMMUNICATIONS, WRITTEN.

Z

'z' chart, *See* OGIVE.

zero defects. (prod). A production philosophy which reflects the fact that it is often less expensive to design and build quality into a product rather than attempt to ensure quality through inspection alone.

zoning. 1. A system of apportioning orders to spread the sources of supply. 2. In materials management the allocation of storage areas for location of stocks – may require indication on purchase orders to assist in off-loading and transit to storage point, particularly if computerised.

APPENDIX A

Checklist based on BS 3669. (Recommendations for the selection, formation and definition of technical terms).

1. '*A technical term* is an expression which is [or may be] deliberately restricted in its meaning and is applicable in a particular field'.
2a. 'Everyday words tend to be vague but rich in associations'.
  b. 'also, such words tend to change their meanings'.
3. 'Terms should provide precise definitions without irrelevant associations'.
4. 'New words are sometimes found for old meanings'. [A frequent trap for writers, examination setters, and lecturers].
5. 'Clear concepts are indispensable'. [A 'concept' is a mental construct or idea which may be used to define subjects or objects whether technical or not'].
6. 'Before a term can be adopted it must be clarified and the concept defined [See the 'bolt' example which follows].
7. The class or genus must be clear:
   [e.g. 'bolt'. A fixing device (= its class or genus) comprising a shaft (usually circular in cross section) having a head at one end and threaded at the other end to accommodate a nut.
   Physical dimensions then follow (length, diameter, thread, etc.)
   Technical characteristics (such as strength, suitability for a stated duty in a given environment) are given next, followed by:
   Application and use, (such as fixing components or members together)].
   [This discipline is vital for correct and meaningful coding and information technological applications].
8. Terminology:
   'If there are synonyms, select one as the preferred term'.
   'Seek and examine terms outside the field in a question'.
   'Distinguish between the characteristics which contribute to the concept to be defined'.
   'Well recognised abbrieviations may be used'.
   'Terms should be suited to the usage [and grammar] of the language. [See EU note which follows].
   'Words should be easy to pronounce'.
   'Ambiguity of pronunciation should be avoided'.
   'It is useful if words provide their own derivation'. [e.g. conveyor belt].
   'Roots from different languages should not, as a rule, be combined'.
   [but note, as trade expands in the European Union this stricture may become less valid, e.g. 'micro-printer', 'television', etc.].
   'A term should express a single concept and each concept should only be expressed by a single term'. [vital in commodity/stores coding, etc.].

9. Changes to existing terms and introduction of new terms should not be done without good reason, such as:

a) Existing usage is loose.

b) Existing terms logically inadmissable [e.g. 'flammable v inflamm-able, 'bought out' v 'bought in'].

d) Existing term does not conform to the system.

e) Usage has changed. [Perhaps term is inconsistent with equivalent concept elsewhere in the European Union].

APPENDIX B
ORGANISATIONS WITH ROLES OR RESPONSIBILITIES CONNECTED WITH PURCHASING AND SUPPLY

ASSOCIATION OF CERTIFICATION BODIES (ACB)
SECRETARY OF ACB
BRITISH STANDARDS INSTITUTE
2 PARK STREET
LONDON W1A 2BS

ASSOCIATION OF QUALITY MANAGEMENT CONSULTANTS
4 BEYNE ROAD
OLIVERS BATTERY
WINCHESTER
HAMPSHIRE
SO22 4JW

BRITISH BOARD OF AGREMENT
PO BOX 195
BUCKNALLS LANE
GARSTONE
WATFORD
HERTFORDSHIRE
WD2 7NG

BRITISH PRODUCTION AND INVENTORY CONTROL SOCIETY
UNIVERSITY OF WARWICK
SIR WILLIAM LYONS ROAD
COVENTRY
CV4 7EZ

British Quality Association (BQA). This body aims to promote better understanding of quality throughout industry and commerce and to assist improvement in quality practices.

BRITISH QUALITY ASSOCIATION
PO BOX 712
61 SOUTHWARK STREET
LONDON
SE1 1SB

BRITISH EXPORTERS ASSOCIATION
16 DARTMOUTH STREET
LONDON
SW1H 9BL

BRITISH INSURANCE ASSOCIATION
ALDERMARY HOUSE
10–15 QUEEN STREET
LONDON
EC4 1NT

BRITISH INSURANCE BROKERS ASSOCIATION
BIBI HOUSE
14 BEVIS MARKS
LONDON
EC3A 1NT

BRITISH INTERNATIONAL FREIGHT ASSOCIATION
REDFERN HOUSE
66 BROWELLS LANE
FELTHAM
MIDDLESEX
TW13 7EP

BRITISH STANDARDS INSTITUTE
2 PARK STREET
LONDON
W1A 2BS

British Standards Institution (BSI). The recognised body in the UK for the preparation and promulgation of national standards; it represents the UK in the *International Organisation for Standardisation (ISO)*, the *International Electrotechnical Commission (IEC)*, and the West European organisations concerned with harmonisation of standards.

BRITISH STANDARDS INSTITUTION (B.S.I.)
LINFORD WOOD
MILTON KEYNES
MK14 6LE

British Standards Society (BSS). A society of individuals concerned with the application of standards and interested in promoting the techniques and benefits of standardisation. It presents considered views to **BSI** on the practical application of standards and maintains contacts with similar organisations in other countries.

BRITISH STANDARDS SOCIETY
2 PARK STREET
LONDON
W1A 2BS

BUSINESS IN THE COMMUNITY
227a CITY ROAD
LONDON EC1V 1LX

CHAMBER OF SHIPPING
2–5 MINORIES HOUSE
LONDON
EC3N 1BJ

CHARTERED INSTITUTE OF MANAGEMENT ACCOUNTANTS
63 PORTLAND PLACE
LONDON
W1N 4AB

CHARTERED INSTITUTE OF MARKETING
MOOR HALL
COOKHAM
MAIDENHEAD
SL6 9QH

CHARTERED INSTITUTE OF PURCHASING AND SUPPLY
EASTON HOUSE
EASTON ON THE HILL
STAMFORD
LINCOLNSHIRE
PE9 3NZ

CHARTERED INSTITUTE OF TRANSPORT
80 PORTLAND PLACE
LONDON
W1N 4AB

CONFEDERATION OF BRITISH INDUSTRY
CENTRE POINT
103 NEW OXFORD STREET
LONDON
WC1A 1DU

DEPARTMENT OF TRADE AND INDUSTRY
BRIDGE PLACE
80–89 ECCLESTONE SQUARE
LONDON
FW1 1PT

DEUTSCHES INSTITUT FUR NORMING (DIN)
BURGRASSEN STRASSE 6
D-10787
BERLIN

EUROPEAN BUSINESS FOUNDATION
1 ST. MARY'S PLACE
LONDON
W5 5HA

EUROPEAN COMMISSION INFORMATION OFFICES
8 STOREYS GATE
LONDON
SW1P 3AT

WINDSOR HOUSE
9–15 BEDFORD STREET
BELFAST
BT2 7EG

4 CATHEDRAL ROAD
CARDIFF
CF1 9SG

7 ALVA STREET
EDINBURGH
EH2 4PH

FEDERATION OF SMALL BUSINESS
140 LOWER MARSH
WESTMINSTER BRIDGE
LONDON
SE1 7AE

FREIGHT TRANSPORT ASSOCIATION
HERMES HOUSE
ST. JOHN'S ROAD
TUNBRIDGE WELLS
KENT
TN4 9UZ

HM CUSTOMS AND EXCISE
CLEMENTS HOUSE
14–18 GRESHAM STREET
LONDON
EC2V 7BN

INSTITUTE OF CHARTERED SECRETARIES AND
ADMINISTRATORS
16 PARK CRESCENT
LONDON
W1N 4AH

INSTITUTE OF DIRECTORS
116 PALL MALL
LONDON
SW1Y 5ED

INSTITUTE OF DISTRIBUTION, SALES AND TECHNOLOGY
MANAGEMENT
4 BELVEDERE ROAD
BOURNEMOUTH
BH3 7LB

INSTITUTE OF ECONOMIC AFFAIRS
2 LORD NORTH STREET
LONDON
SW1P 3LB

INSTITUTE OF EXPORT
EXPORT HOUSE
64 CLIFFTON STREET
LONDON
EC2A 4HB

INSTITUTE OF FREIGHT FORWARDERS
9 PARADISE ROAD
RICHMOND
SURREY
TW9 1SA

INSTITUTE OF LINGUISTS
24a HIGHBURY GROVE
LONDON
N5 2EA

INSTITUTE OF LOGISTICS
DOUGLAS HOUSE
QUEENS SQUARE
CORBY
NORTHAMPTONSHIRE
NN17 1TT

INSTITUTE OF MANAGEMENT
MANAGEMENT HOUSE
COTTINGHAM ROAD
CORBY
NORTHAMPTONSHIRE
NN17 1TT
PHONE: 0536 204222

INSTITUTE OF MANUFACTURING
58 CLARENDON AVENUE
ROYAL LEAMINGTON SPA
WARWICKSHIRE
CV32 4SA

INSTITUTE OF PRACTITIONERS IN ADVERTISING
44 BELGRAVE SQUARE
LONDON
SW1X 8QS

INSTITUTE OF TRANSLATIONS AND INTERPRETING
318a FINCHLEY ROAD
LONDON
NW3 5HT

Institute of Quality Assurance. A professional body established to serve all those who are involved with QUALITY ASSURANCE. The IQA provides conferences, seminars, training courses etc.

INSTITUTE OF QUALITY ASSURANCE
10 GROSVENOR GARDENS
LONDON SW1W 0DQ

International Air Transport Association (IATA). An association aiming to provide safe, regular and economical air transport. Cooperates with International Air Transport Association.

26 CHEMIN DE JONVILLE
CH 1216
COINTRIN-GENEVA
SWITZERLAND

International Chamber of Commerce (ICC). The international Chamber of Commerce is a world business organisation set up in Paris in 1920 to exchange ideas on international commerce. It acts to promote the greater freedom of world trade, to harmonise and facilitate business and trade practices, and to represent the business community at international level. It

sets the rules for the Court of Arbitration which it administers. *See also*
INCOTERMS.

INTERNATIONAL CHAMBER OF COMMERCE
14–15 BELGRAVE SQUARE
LONDON SW1X 8PS

INTERNATIONAL CHAMBERS OF COMMERCE IN THE UK

BELGO-LUXEMBOURG CHAMBER OF COMMERCE IN GREAT
BRITAIN
6 JOHN STREET
LONDON
WC1N 2ES

FRENCH CHAMBER OF COMMERCE IN GREAT BRITAIN
2nd. FLOOR
KNIGHTSBRIDGE HOUSE
197 KNIGHTSBRIDGE
LONDON
SW7 1RB

GERMAN CHAMBER OF INDUSTRY AND COMMERCE IN THE
UK
16 BUCKINGHAM GATE
LONDON
SW1E 6LB

ITALIAN CHAMBER OF COMMERCE IN GREAT BRITAIN
WALMAR HOUSE
296 REGENT STREET
LONDON
W1R 6AE

NETHERLANDS-BRITISH CHAMBER OF COMMERCE
THE DUTCH HOUSE
307–308 HIGH HOLBORN
LONDON
VC1V 7LS

PORTUGUESE-UK CHAMBER OF COMMERCE
4th. FLOOR
22–25a SACKVILLE STREET
LONDON
W1X 1DE

SPANISH CHAMBER OF COMMERCE IN GREAT BRITAIN
5 CAVENDISH SQUARE
LONDON
W1M 0DP

International Civil Aviation Organisation (ICAO). Specialised agency of
the United Nations. Aims: safe and orderly growth of civil aviation:
development of airports and navigational aids: reduce wasteful competition:
ensure fair opportunities for traffic: avoidance of discrimination between
contracting nations.

INTERNATIONAL CIVIL AVIATION ORGANISATION
1000 SHERBROOKE ST. WEST
MONTREAL
QUEBEC, CANADA H3A 2R2

International Electronical Commission (IEC). Founded in 1906 the IEC
is the electrotechnical counterpart of ISO (*see below*). It publishes reports and
standards.

IEC CENTRAL OFFICE
CUSTOMER SERVICE CENTRE
3 RUE DE VAREMBE
1211 GENEVA 20
TEL. 41 22 7340150

International Labour Organisation (ILO). An agency of the United
Nations (set up in 1919) to promote justice in employment to all workers
world-wide. Concerns living standards, satisfactory conditions of work and
pay, through the creation of international labour standards. ILO reports
concerning safety at work, etc. ILO reports are embodied in UK and EEC
regulations, etc. These may affect purchasing and specifications of plant and
equipment.

INTERNATIONAL LABOUR ORGANISATION
4 ROUTE DES MORILLONS
1211
GENEVA, 22

**International Federation of Purchasing and Materials Management
(IFPMM)**
SECRETARIAT
ATTN. MR F.J. DE KRAKER
DIRECTOR GENERAL
PO BOX 289
1860 AGBERGEN
THE NETHERLANDS

International Maritime Organisation. IMO. The IMO aims to facilitate co-operation among governments on technical matters affecting shipping, particularly safety of life at sea. A specialised agency of the United Nations. HQ in London.

INTERNATIONAL MARITIME ORGANISTION
4 ALBERT EMBANKMENT
LONDON
SE1 7SR

International Organisation for Standardization (ISO). Founded in 1947 under the auspices of the United Nations produces international standards.

INTERNATIONAL STANDARDS ORGANISATION
RUE VAREMNE
POSTALE 56
CH-1211
GENEVA, 20

INTERNATIONAL PURCHASING AND SUPPLY EDUCATION AND RESEARCH ASSOCIATION
C/O CHARTERED INSTITUTE OF PURCHASING AND SUPPLY
EASTON HOUSE
EASTON ON THE HILL
STAMFORD
LINCS
PE9 3NZ

NATIONAL ACCREDITATION COUNCIL FOR CERTIFICATION BODIES (NACCB)
19 BUCKINGHAM GATE
LONDON
SW1E 6LB

NATIONAL MATERIALS HANDLING CENTRE
CRANFIELD INSTITUTE OF TECHNOLOGY
CRANIELD
BEDFORD
MK43 0AL

PARTNERSHIP SOURCING
THE CONFEDERATION OF BRITISH INDUSTRY
CENTRE POINT
103 NEW OXFORD STREET
LONDON
WC1A 1DU

RESOURCE
1–3 BIRDSCAGE WALK
LONDON
SW11 9JH
An independent organisation, jointly sponsored by UK government and BSI.
Aims: Technical co-operation in key overseas markets in fields of standards,
quality assurance, metrology, testing and the ways in which these practices
are applied to industrial and agricultural development in technological areas.

ROAD HAULAGE ASSOCIATION
ROADWAY HOUSE
35 MONUMENT HILL
WEYBRIDGE
SURREY
KT13 8RN

SIMPLER TRADE PROCEDURES BOARD (SITPRO)
29 GLASSHOUSE STREET
LONDON
W1R 5RG

SOCIETY OF AUTOMOTIVE-ELECTRICAL TECHNICIANS
PO BOX 62
SELSEY CHICHESTER
PO20 0JH

SUPPLY CHAIN DEVELOPMENT GROUP
CARDIFF BUSINESS SCHOOL
COLUM DRIVE
CARDIFF
CF1 3EU